FORUGH FARROKHZAD, POET OF MODERN IRAN

Dominic Parviz Brookshaw is Professor of Persian Literature and Iranian Culture at the University of Oxford, and Senior Research Fellow in Persian at Wadham College, Oxford. He has served on the editorial boards of both *Iranian Studies* and *Middle Eastern Literatures* and is a former member of both the Governing Council of the British Institute of Persian Studies and the Council of the Association for Iranian Studies. He has published widely on premodern Persian lyric poetry, women writers of the Qajar era, and twentieth-century Iranian poets. His most recent book, *Hafiz and His Contemporaries: Poetry, Performance, and Patronage in Fourteenth-century Iran* (I B Tauris, 2019), won the Saidi-Sirjani Book Award in 2020.

Nasrin Rahimieh is Howard Baskerville Professor of Humanities and holds appointments in Comparative Literature, European Languages and Studies, and Gender and Sexuality Studies. She served as Maseeh Chair and Director of the Samuel Jordan Center for Persian Studies and Culture from 2006 to 2014. Her teaching and research are focused on modern Persian literature, the literature of Iranian exile and diaspora, contemporary Iranian women's writing, and postrevolution Iranian cinema. Among her publications are *Iranian Culture: Representation and Identity* (2015), *Missing Persians: Discovering Voices in Iranian Cultural History* (2001), the English translation of the late Taghi Modarressi's last novel, *The Virgin of Solitude* (2008), and *Oriental Responses to the West* (1990).

T0281794

FORUGH FARROKHZAD, POET OF MODERN IRAN

ICONIC WOMAN AND FEMININE PIONEER OF NEW PERSIAN POETRY

EDITED BY

DOMINIC PARVIZ BROOKSHAW & NASRIN RAHIMIEH

Second Edition

I.B.TAURIS

LONDON • NEW YORK • OXFORD • NEW DELHI • SYDNEY

I.B. TAURIS
Bloomsbury Publishing Plc
50 Bedford Square, London, WC1B 3DP, UK
1385 Broadway, New York, NY 10018, USA
29 Earlsfort Terrace, Dublin 2, Ireland

BLOOMSBURY, I.B. TAURIS and the I.B. Tauris logo are trademarks of Bloomsbury
Publishing Plc

First published in Great Britain 2010
This edition published 2023

Cover design by Atefeh Zolghadr
Cover image: Forugh Farrokhzad © Pendar Yousefi

A catalogue record for this book is available from the British Library.

A catalog record for this book is available from the Library of Congress.

ISBN: PB: 978-0-7556-0067-0
       ePDF: 978-0-7556-0069-4
       eBook: 978-0-7556-0068-7

Typeset by RefineCatch Limited, Bungay, Suffolk
Printed and bound in Great Britain

To find out more about our authors and books visit www.bloomsbury.com
and sign up for our newsletters.

Contents

Acknowledgements

We would like to thank the Iran Heritage Foundation and the University of Manchester for their assistance in organizing the international conference 'Forugh Farrokhzād (1935–1967): 40-year anniversary conference' held at the University of Manchester on July 4–5, 2008, which served as the springboard for the current volume of essays. The generous support of the Iran Heritage Foundation made it possible for scholars from Canada, Germany, Great Britain, Iran, and the USA to attend the conference and to present new scholarship on Farrokhzād's poetry and cinema.

We would also like to thank the two anonymous peer reviewers selected by I.B. Tauris, who provided us with detailed and thought-provoking feedback.

Finally, we are also grateful to the contributors who traveled to the conference, engaged in debates and discussions, and developed their ideas further for inclusion in this edited volume.

Note on Transliteration

Any transliteration system will have its critics. We have endeavoured to standardize the transliteration across the essays in this volume as far as possible. We have adopted a very plain transliteration system for Persian based on pronunciation, rather than orthography: hence *s* not *th* and *z* not *dh*, etc. The long vowels are represented by *ā*, *i*, and *u*, and the short vowels by *a*, *e*, and *o*. The diphthongs are represented by *āy*, *ey* and *ow*.

Contributors

Wali Ahmadi, Associate Professor of Persian Literature, University of California, Berkeley.

Michael C. Beard, Chester Fritz Distinguished Professor Emeritus of English, University of North Dakota.

Dominic Parviz Brookshaw, Professor of Persian Literature and Iranian Culture, University of Oxford.

M. R. Ghanoonparvar, Professor Emeritus of Persian and Comparative Literature, University of Texas, Austin.

Maryam Ghorbankarimi, Lecturer in Film Practice, University of Lancaster.

Persis M. Karim, Neda Nobari Chair in Iranian Diaspora Studies, San Francisco State University.

Homa Katouzian, Roshan Institute Academic Visitor in Iranian Studies, St Antony's College, Oxford.

Nima Mina, Senior Lecturer in Persian and Iranian Studies, SOAS, University of London.

Marie Ostby, Assistant Professor of English, Connecticut College, New London.

Leila Rahimi Bahmany, Adjunct Lecturer in Persian Culture and Literature, Goethe-Universität, Frankfurt.

Nasrin Rahimieh, Howard Baskerville Professor of Humanities, University of California, Irvine.

Rivanne Sandler, Associate Professor Emerita of Women's Literature in Iran, University of Toronto.

Sirous Shamisa, Professor Emeritus of Persian Literature, Allameh Tabataba'i University, Tehran.

Marta Simidchieva, Adjunct Professor, York University, Toronto.

Kamran Talattof, Professor of Persian and Iranian Studies, University of Arizona.

Preface to the Second Edition

For generations of Iranian women, who since the 1979 revolution have seen their rights severely curtailed, their bodies strictly policed, and their protests brutally suppressed, Forugh Farrokhzad's person and poetry have remained a bright beacon of hope and a constant source of inspiration. There is no better proof of the timeliness of the publication of this second edition of our collection of essays on Farrokhzad than the protests calling for fundamental human rights now underway in Iran. These protests, that began as women-led demonstrations against Iran's mandatory *hijab* law, were sparked by the death of Zhina (Mahsa) Amini, a 22-year-old Kurdish Iranian woman from Saqqez. On 13 September 2022, Amini, while visiting Tehran, was arrested for a minor violation of the Islamic dress code by the dreaded *Gasht-e Ershād* (morality police) who then beat her so severely that she fell into a fatal coma and died three days later in hospital. Amini's tragic death rapidly galvanized women of all ethnicities and classes in villages, towns, and cities across Iran. In opposition to the state and its draconian, misogynistic laws, swathes of Iranian women – many of them in their teens and early twenties – took to the streets, removed their head scarves, and burnt them in public acts of defiance.

The astonishing degree of courage displayed by these women and girls in turn mobilized men and boys to march alongside them. Droves of predominately young protestors flooded major thoroughfares and squares chanting in unison: *Zan, Zendegi, Āzādi!* ('Woman, Life, Freedom!'); a slogan with roots in the Kurdish freedom movement. As a greater number of Iranians from all sectors of society joined the protests, so poets, filmmakers, actors, singers, musicians, athletes, academics, journalists, lawyers, human rights activists and many prominent dissidents spoke out. Together they lent their voices to those of ordinary citizens calling for equal rights for all regardless of gender, ethnicity and/or religion, and for an end to 43 years of the oppression, intimidation, and violence meted out by the state.

The protestors, who have now added *Marg bar diktātor!* ('Death to the Dictator!') and *Jomhuri-ye Eslāmi; nemi-khāym, nemi-khāym!* ('We don't want the Islamic Republic!') to their chants, are calling for the Supreme Leader (Ayatollah Khamenei) to go, and for the current theocratic system to be disbanded. As we write, the protestors' iron resolve shows no sign of waning and, though unarmed, they appear to no longer fear the state's brutality. Despite having deployed the Islamic Revolutionary Guard Corps, the Basij militia, armed riot police, plainclothes officers, and hired thugs, the government has so far not succeeded in silencing those propelling what is increasingly being seen as a revolution in the making. The lethal force used by Khamenei's henchmen has already left more than 250 protestors dead, including 23 children between the ages of 11 and 17. Many thousands of protestors who have been arrested, imprisoned, or sent to undisclosed facilities are now at risk of torture or worse. Armed police have stormed university campuses and dormitories to beat and detain students who have been vocal in their opposition to the government, and a number of high school pupils who have chanted anti-regime slogans have been attacked with deadly force on campus by security officers. As in previous uprisings, Iran's ethnic minorities have borne the brunt of the regime's rage with scores already killed in Baluch-majority Zahedan and Sanandaj, the capital of Iranian Kurdistan.

This current wave of mass protests in Iran resonates deeply with the subtle and enduring provocations Farrokhzad enacted in her poetry, cinema, and private life. More than half a century after her death, Farrokhzad's verses invite us to remember an earlier stage in the struggle of Iran's women for personal autonomy, freedom of choice in all aspects of life (from marriage, to career, to dress), and for a seat beside men at the decision table. Today, on the streets of Tehran, Rasht, Mashhad, Ardebil, Esfahan, Qom, and Bushehr, we see young Iranian women and men united in manifesting that same spirit of rebellion, rebirth, and belief in the possibility of a more equitable future that Farrokhzad embodied in her life and her writing.

Nasrin Rahimieh and Dominic Parviz Brookshaw
Irvine and Oxford, October 2022

Introduction to the First Edition

Dominic Parviz Brookshaw and
Nasrin Rahimieh

Forugh Farrokhzād (1935–1967) is one of the most renowned, revered, and controversial figures of modern Iranian literature and culture. Her life, tragically cut short in an automobile accident on February 14, 1967, at the age of 32, has come to represent more than that of an individual woman, poet, and filmmaker. Farrokhzād's bold and unconventional lifestyle and her poetic representations of women's subjectivity and sexuality have elevated her to the level of a cultural icon. In the words of the literary critic, Farzaneh Milani:

> She was a lonely woman, an intriguingly unyielding rebel; an adventuress of both body and mind; an iconoclast who asked (and sometimes answered) the wrong questions. Relentlessly, she trespassed boundaries and explored new domains. Zestfully, she demanded of life the gratification of her desires – intellectual, emotional, and sensual – troubling herself less and less about so-called moral proprieties.[1]

Seeking answers to Farrokhzād's uniqueness in her biography leads us to a life begun in Tehran in a middle class family of seven children, headed by an authoritarian father whose military career dominated his family life. Farrokhzād's relationship with her mother was also strained and difficult. The poet's education, after she completed the ninth grade, consisted of attending a girls' school where she was to learn sewing and painting. But this course of study did not last long. At the age of sixteen, Farrokhzād fell in love with and married a distant relative, Parviz Shāpur. The birth of a son, Kāmyār, a year later, did little to save the marriage which ended in divorce and Farrokhzād's loss of custody of her infant son. The break-up of the marriage, the separation from her son, and the return to her family home under the controlling and disapproving gaze of her father scarred Farrokhzād, culminating in a nervous breakdown and a period of hospitalization. She emerged from this crisis with renewed lust for life, and she immersed herself even more than before in writing poetry. Later, she also tried her hand at filmmaking through her work at the Golestān film studios, where she first began working as a secretary. The relationship that developed between her and Ebrāhim Golestān (a married man) has been the subject of much speculation and controversy, despite attempts by Golestān to deny the existence of anything but an innocent friendship.[2] Regardless of the nature of their relationship, it propelled Farrokhzād into the realm of cinema. This interest led her to travel to Europe (in particular to Italy, Germany, and England) to learn more about the art of filmmaking.

During her lifetime, Farrokhzād published four collections of poetry: *Asir* (Captive) 1955, *Divār* (The Wall) 1956, *'Esyān* (Rebellion) 1958, and *Tavallodi digar* (Another Birth) 1964. Her fifth collection, *Imān biāvarim beh āghā z-e fasl-e sard* (Let Us Believe in the Beginning of the Cold Season) was published posthumously in 1974. Farrokhzād is also known for her ground-breaking 1962 documentary, *Khāneh siyāh ast* (*The House is Black*), shot in a leper colony in north-western Iran. As this brief overview of Farrokhzād's biography and artistic works indicates, she had a very productive and varied artistic career. Farzaneh Milani sums up Farrokhzād's artistic output in the following way:

> The whole body of Farrokhzād's work ... resists the dominant cultural assumptions that framed her writing and its reception. It is a struggle against the institutions of both literature and society, an oasis of the conventionally forbidden – sexual, textual, and cultural. It disrupts social systems and hierarchies at their most intimate level. It reveals the pain and joy of transition from one cultural pattern to another. It personifies the pleasures of hybridization, of mingling the old and the new, but also of its pains and problems.[3]

If her poetry gave her an entreé into Tehran's literary scene of the time, it also became subjected to a voyeurism that insisted on conflating her poetry and her life; as Hillmann notes:

> Rumors about Forugh's life naturally increased as a result of the personal frankness of poems that were appearing in various newspapers and magazines, in particular the journal *Rowshanfekr*, which was then relatively

popular among Tehran literati. In several of these poems, Forugh voices a first-person recollection of a sexual encounter with a man presumably not the speaker's husband. In addition to the furor these poems created, several male literary figures even began asserting that they had had romantic relationships with Forugh.[4]

The impulse to read Farrokhzād's poetry biographically has continued to dominate the critical appreciation of her works. The interest in the poet's personal life is understandable in light of the pioneering nature of her writing and her independent lifestyle, but it is at odds with her own lack of interest in linking her biography and poetry. In a 1964 radio interview, in response to a question about her life, she distinguished between episodes in her personal life and what had become her life work:

> I really think talking about it is tiring and pointless. I mean it is a fact after all that everyone who comes into the world has a date of birth, lives in a city or village, studies at school, and experiences a handful of very ordinary and conventional events that occur when all is said and done for everyone, like falling into the courtyard pool as a child, or, for example, cheating at school, falling in love in one's youth, getting married, these sorts of things. But if the point to this question is the explanation of a handful of circumstances and issues relating to one's life work, which in my case is poetry, then I have to say that the time for such a review has not yet arrived, because I have just recently begun dealing with poetry in a serious way.[5]

The distinction between how she had lived her life and how her poetry was developing over the course of her life is crucial to understanding the transformation in Farrokhzād's poetry from her first collection to the last. Her own remarks in this interview point us away from a reductive reading of her poetry as a simple reflection of her life. On other occasions, she was even more dismissive of her earlier poetry, referring – as she does here – to a turning point in her writing.

While it is crucial to situate Farrokhzād's work against the backdrop of the social, political, and personal events that shaped her life, it is equally important to not subordinate her poetry and film to them. Like other Iranian women of her era, Farrokhzād would have been subject to conflicting views about women, with a strong traditional undercurrent of assumptions about women's place at home and an opposing current of modernity arguing for women's public presence. The contradictory strains shaping Iran's self-perception at the time carved out a space within which Farrokhzād's poetry could be published, and at the same time received and perceived through the lens of anxieties about rapidly changing gender relations. The need to read Farrokhzād's works against her biography is part and parcel of this collective apprehension about shifting boundaries that make it possible for a woman to speak about the corporeal and the sexual. This type of challenge to the cultural imperative of female chastity and modesty is not a rallying cry for women's equality. What we see in Farrokhzād's poetry are explorations into new modes of expression not subject to the law of male desire. To borrow from Hélène Cixous, we could say this writing lays bare the 'bond between woman's libidinal economy – her *jouissance*, the feminine Imaginary – and her way of self-constituting a subjectivity that splits apart without regret, and without this regretlessness being the equivalent of dying.'[6] It becomes a form of writing the body, an inscription of female subjectivity which acknowledges the force of multiple layers of repression at work:

> In a way feminine writing never stops reverberating from the wrench that the acquisition of speech, of speaking out loud, is for her – 'acquisition' that is experienced more as tearing away, dizzying flight and flinging oneself, diving. Listen to a woman speak in a gathering (if she is not painfully out of breath): she doesn't 'speak', she throws her trembling body into the air, she lets herself go, she flies, she goes completely into her voice, she vitally defends the 'logic' of her discourse with her body; her flesh speaks true. She exposes herself. Really she makes what she thinks materialize carnally, she conveys meaning with her body. She inscribes what she is saying because she does not deny unconscious drives the unmanageable part they play in speech.[7]

It is such moments of rupture that are captured in Farrokhzād's poetry as it moves toward a form of flight. Her pioneering spirit lies in this very working away from thematic and formal strictures to experimental expression, what Farzaneh Milani calls 'the voice of the Other in modern Persian literature'.[8] In this voice, as Milani points out, Farrokhzād grapples with the conflicting impulses and currents of her time:

> From the beginning of her career, Farrokhzad refused to evade her feelings. Her poetry reveals the problems of a modern Iranian woman with all her conflicts, painful oscillations, and contradictions. It enriches the world of Persian poetry with its depiction of the tension and frequent paralysis touching the lives of these women who seek self-expression and social options in a culture not entirely accustomed to them. It explores the vulnerability

of a woman who rejects unreflective conformity with the past and yet suffers from uncertainties about the future. Quite simply, it embraces the daily reality of the emergent Persian woman.[9]

In Milani's analysis we also discern the symbolic significance Farrokhzād acquired for a generation of Iranians who associated her with women's liberation from the confines of tradition. But even decades after her death, Iranians of a new generation, who did not know Farrokhzād in her lifetime, view her with reverence and admiration.

More than forty years after her death, as we celebrate her legacy and acknowledge her contribution to Persian poetry, it is befitting that we, Farrokhzād's readers and critics, also look for new ways of appreciating and understanding her works. The search for more complex readings of Farrokhzād's poetry and cinema informs the collection of essays included in this volume which originated in an international conference, organized in association with The Iran Heritage Foundation and held at the University of Manchester in July 2008 to mark the fortieth anniversary of Farrokhzād's death. Most of the essays here are based on presentations given at the conference, further developed and reworked in light of the exchanges that took place. The thirteen chapters in this collection represent the work of scholars from Canada, Germany, Great Britain, Iran, and the United States. The essays address various aspects of Farrokhzād's poetry and cinema, offering new insights into less-examined areas within her oeuvre. The contributors were encouraged to think beyond the boundaries of existing scholarship on Farrokhzād and to be less constrained by the biographical imperative. This decision is informed both by a desire to explore new avenues of research and the fact that Farzaneh Milani is completing a comprehensive biography of the poet. No collection of critical essays could rival the depth and the scope Milani will bring to bear on Farrokhzād's life, for that reason our focus has been on expanding the parameters of studies on Forugh Farrokhzād by allowing for multiple perspectives on her life, poetry, and film without insisting on a single, unified reading.

In their essays, Homa Katouzian and Marta Simidchieva analyse Farrokhzād's early poetry from a formal and thematic perspective, tracing shifts and developments from simple expressions of sexuality and sensuality, to more complex, poetic articulations of subjectivity. Dominic Parviz Brookshaw's contribution examines Farrokhzād's poetry in light of the classical canon of Persian poetry and demonstrates how her deployment of classical tropes and images engages with and transcends the traditional boundaries of Persian poetry.

Questions of the poetic and subjective self are taken up in the chapters by Rivanne Sandler and Leila Rahimi Bahmany, who complicate the equations of the poet and her poetic personae, offering up new ways of reading the speaker in Farrokhzād's poems.

Sirous Shamisa's study of Farrokhzād's apocalyptic writing delves into her prophetic vision of the impending disintegration of Iranian society. Shamisa's analysis situates Farrokhzād's poetry in the context of the intellectual movements of her time and her perception of their potential to serve as catalysts for change. Delving deeper into the associations between Farrokhzād's poetry and the social and political realities of her time, Kamran Talattof examines the limits of reading Farrokhzād's work as feminist poetry. Michael Beard delineates movement in Farrokhzād's poetry and illustrates the dynamic relationship between the represented and the real.

Farrokhzād's documentary film, *The House is Black*, is the subject of Nasrin Rahimieh's and Maryam Ghorbankarimi's essays. Their analyses highlight the film's technical innovation and its engagement with the metaphor of the nation as a site of affiliation and confinement.

M. R. Ghanoonparvar and Nima Mina address the issue of translation. Ghanoonparvar's essay offers a comparative study of some of the difficulties and potential pitfalls faced by English translators of Farrokhzād's poetry, and Nima Mina's reveals hitherto unexamined poetic translations by Farrokhzād from German into Persian.

Finally, Persis M. Karim takes us beyond Farrokhzād's immediate time and space and examines Farrokhzād's international appeal and the special position she occupies for Iranian diaspora writers.

Together the thirteen chapters in this volume present a re-evaluation of Farrokhzād's contribution to modern Persian literature and culture, and demonstrate how, even four decades after her untimely death, the field of Persian literary studies continues to grapple with the enigma that is the life, art, and legacy of Forugh Farrokhzād.

Chapter 1

Of the Sins of Forugh Farrokhzād

Homa Katouzian

'Sin' ('Gonāh') is probably the most well known poem of Forugh Farrokhzād, though it is not one of her best, even in comparison with most of the poems before the period of *Rebirth* (*Tavallodi digar*). Apparently a defiant declaration of feminist independence, a closer examination of that and some other early poems betrays a sense of guilt, bewilderment and remorse. It is in the later poems, and especially those of the period of her 'rebirth', that 'pleasure' gives way to acceptance, and 'sin', to real self-assertion and self-confidence. Nevertheless, analyzing her published letters, and especially the two long letters to her father, it will be argued that, in spite of the upward journey both in love and poetry, the poet's longing for deep fulfilment remained frustrated until the very end.

'Sin' is one of the earlier poems that openly describe a carnal engagement, though not the first one. Its enormous impact on readers and critics in and out of Iran is due to its apparently vocal, almost proud, defiance against the social conventions and the condemnation that the poet knew to be mandatory for committing such sins, especially if the 'sinner' was a married woman. Otherwise the artistic value of the poem is considerably lower than not only all the poems she was to publish after her *Rebirth* but most of the earlier poems as well. This is best appreciated when the poem is read in the Persian original, it being possible to camouflage, misinterpret, explain away or mystify the weaknesses of form and substance in English translation. It is a simple poem, describing a sexual experience in the form of connected doublets in six short stanzas, involving some repetition and employing commonplace or unlikely figures of speech and literary devices. The poem opens with its first doublet or stanza:

> I sinned a sin full of pleasure
> in an embrace that was warm and fiery.
> I sinned wrapped in arms
> that were hot, vengeful and made of iron.[1]

Describing something fiery as warm and then calling it hot is not very elegant. In fact, the word 'warm' is completely redundant and has been necessitated by the need to make up the metre in the Persian original, the metre being that of *fahlaviyāt: mafā'ilon, mafā'ilon, fa'ulon*, as in Bābā Tāher's doublets (*tarānehs*).[2] Other formal weaknesses may be shown in this short poem, especially if the Persian original is scrutinized: this is a short and defiant declaration of the commitment of a 'sin' which could well have been made in prose, its only poetical feature being versification by metre and rhyme which are made up by the use of any and all words and phrases such as, 'My heart impatiently trembled in my chest' (*delam dar sineh bi-tābāneh larzid*).

This is a relatively early poem, written long before *Another Birth*, but the poet was writing far more sophisticated poetry before and at the time of writing it. Take for example the poem 'The Kiss' ('Buseh'), which had been published in the earlier volume *(The) Captive (Asir)*, and ends with the stanza:

> A shadow leaned over a shadow
> In the secret hideout of the night
> A breath brushed over a cheek
> A kiss flamed up between two lips[3]

There can be many more examples – such as 'Shab va havas' ('Night and Desire'), 'Hasrat' ('Regret') and 'Mehmān' ('The Guest'), all of them from the collection *Captive* – to show that 'Sin' is a weaker poem than many that Farrokhzād had written before or about the same time.

In fact, it may be argued that the formal weaknesses of 'Sin' are not unrelated to the substance, where a sense of guilt and remorse is camouflaged by a brave gesture of defiance. The poetical voice, which is unmistakably that of the poet herself, confesses to what she herself describes as a sin; she ends the short poem by repeating the confession and remorsefully addressing God, saying:

> I sinned a sin full of pleasure
> beside a body, trembling and unconscious.
> O God I know not what I did
> in that dark, silent, secluded place[4]

The key words in the poem are sin and pleasure. The poem displays anger and defiance but it also reflects doubt and uncertainty. And it describes no more than a feverish physical experience resulting in pleasure. The confessor has committed a sin involving much pleasure, rather than giving herself up in a loving relationship resulting in a sense of liberation. This may be contrasted with an earlier poem which reads:

> He wants the wine of kiss from me.
> What shall I tell my hopeful heart?
> He is thinking of pleasure, unsuspecting
> that I want the pleasure which is eternal.
> I want sincere love from him
> so I could sacrifice myself.
> He wants a fiery body from me
> in which to burn up his anxiety.[5]

But the expression of guilt and remorse is familiar from other poems of this period. For example, in the poem 'Tramp' or 'Whore' ('Harjā'i'), the title of which alone confirms the society's judgement:

> You came late when I had lost control.
> You came late when I was drowned in sin,
> when by the whirlwind of wretchedness and infamy
> I had been extinguished and ruined like a candle.[6]

In the poem, 'Demon of the Night' ('Div-e shab'), the mother is singing a lullaby for her infant son, warning him of the ill intentions of the demon of night, who later comes to snatch the baby away and is defied and abused by the mother:

> Suddenly the silence broke;
> the demon of night shouted.

> Stop woman, I am not afraid of you;
> your lap is tainted by sin, by sin.
> I am a demon but you are worse than me
> being a mother, but tainted with the shame of sin.
> Take your baby's head off your lap!
> That is no place for the innocent babe to rest.

The mother accepts that judgment and says with a burning heart:

> I moan O Kāmi, Kāmi
> Take your head off my lap.[7]

Thus, it is clear that the statement issued in the poem 'Sin', although it is daring and rebellious, is the other side of the coin to such other poems as 'Tramp' and 'Demon of the Night'. Except that in 'Sin' the poet has had enough of the prevailing social judgements, which she herself also accepts and so loses patience and shouts: 'I sinned, a sin full of pleasure!' And it is precisely this sloganeering style of the poem that makes it look like a versified statement confessing to a sin. Whereas, as I shall try to show below, in her later poems, especially those written in the period of *Another Birth* (or *Rebirth*), sin and pleasure are replaced with profound love and self-assured submission to the beloved, although love itself is never quite realized and the search for it continues until the end of the poet's short life.

Before doing that, however, it is worth mentioning a poem whose significance has seldom been acknowledged in Persian or English studies of Farrokhzād's works. Made up of eleven stanzas, this longish poem – 'Dar barābar-e khodā' ('In the Presence of God') – is addressed to God, pleading with him to forgive her sins, and speaking of hating her own body:

> O God how can I tell you
> that I am tired of and disgusted with my body.
> Every night at the threshold of your splendour
> it looks as if I wish for another body.
>
> Give me a love that would make me
> just like the angels of your paradise.
> Give me a lover in whom to see
> an example of the purity of your nature . . .
>
> O God whose strong hand
> has founded the world of being

> Show your face and take from my heart
> the zest for the sin of selfishness . . .[8]

This hatred of her body completely disappeared in the latter part of her life and work and gave way to self-confidence, acceptance, sublime experience, as well as search for a love that was never realized, and in fact would have been very unlikely to be realized, as it was chasing after an illusion. A long letter by Farrokhzād to her father, published relatively recently, throws considerable light on herself and her poetry. It was written from Munich to Tehran on 2 January 1957, shortly before Farrokhzād turned twenty-two. It is strangely reminiscent of Kafka's famous piece, 'Letter to His Father', although Kafka's letter was dressed up as fiction and was never actually sent to a father from whom he was so alienated and of whom he had been so much afraid in his childhood.[9] Farrokhzād's letter also shows the great distance as well as conflict between her and her father, the extent to which she was frightened of him and felt humiliated by him, and how she had felt like a stranger in her paternal home. She says that if she wrote all that she wanted to say, it would fill a whole book and make her father unhappy, 'but I too cannot feel peace and contentment until I have told you all that is in my chest; and, being with you, try to be myself, rather than a being who neither laughs nor talks and can only sink into herself and stick to a corner.' She goes on to add:

> My greatest pain is that you never got to know me and never wanted to know me. I remember when I used to read philosophical books at home . . . You would judge me by saying that I was a stupid girl whose mind had been poisoned by reading journals. I would then fall into pieces inside myself, tears coming to my eyes for being so much a stranger at home, and sulk . . . And there are a thousand other cases like this . . ., every one of which will be enough to break the spirit of an individual.[10]

She goes on further to explain that many a time when she had committed an 'error' (*khatā*), she would have wanted to tell her father and seek guidance from him but that 'as ever' she had been afraid of him. Here she is referring to the time when she had been a girl living at home. Since then she had married, divorced with a little son and – after a short while when, due to a clash with her father, she had lived in a little rented room in a corner of town – she had been reconciled with him and returned home, only to face the same old regime. Thus, she wrote that even then, many a time when she had been trembling with remorse and regret for an 'error' which she had committed and wished to talk to her father and seek advice, 'I was as ever afraid and felt that I am a stranger to you'. And she goes on to add:

> Whenever I think of last year living at your house my heart sinks. I did everything, both good and bad things, secretly, just like thieves. Why did you lack respect for me, and why did you make me keep away from home, and just like a sleep-walker not to know where I am, what I do and whom I am talking to . . . And inevitably I used to commit errors, many errors.[11]

She points out bluntly that contrary to her father's belief she is not a 'street woman' (*zan-e khiyābāngard*), and now that she lives independently 'and no-one looks at me with hatred and contempt', she will take responsibility for her actions and would never forgive herself for making a mistake, although she does not blame herself, but 'others' instead, for her past mistakes.[12] She speaks of her intense suffering, feeling as if she is buried in a grave, and finally begs her father not to break his relationship with her again and love her as he does his other children. This shows that despite her sense of a new-found freedom, independence and personal responsibility, she is still deeply involved with her father and longs for his approval. She expresses regret that she cannot tell her father all that she wants to tell him, beginning with her childhood, because she is afraid that it might upset him. Yet she repeatedly says that she loves her father and wishes that he love her too, and even thanks him for the monthly allowance he was sending her from Tehran. But at the same time she does not tire of repeating how fearful and alienated she is.[13]

Whatever Freud, Jung, Adler and others might have done with material of this kind is a matter for speculation, though not very difficult to imagine. What is patently obvious is the strong sense of alienation that she feels from her father, while at the same time desperately longing for the gap between them to be closed and be turned into love and understanding. As will be noted below, it is this newly acquired sense of freedom, independence and responsibility that shortly results in her rebirth in life as well as poetry and closes the seasons of 'pleasurable sins', 'errors' and 'mistakes' combined with guilt, regret and self-reproach.

In an earlier letter to her father, also written from Germany, Farrokhzād declares that she has no worldly ambitions, that poetry is her god, and that if she loses the ability to write poetry she will commit suicide:

> Let others regard me as an unfortunate and wandering person, but I shall never complain about my lot . . . I sometimes wonder why God created me as I am, and brought to life in me this devil that is called poetry, so I would not be able to gain your approval.[14]

But writing poetry, not pursuing formal education and not seeking social success were some, not all, of the apparent causes of her father's strong disapproval of her. It was her entire mode of living and, as a part of it, her marriage and divorce and what he described as her 'being a street woman' that he didn't approve of.[15]

It is clear from her letters that she wishes to have, if not her father's love then at least his acceptance of her lifestyle. That is, although it is easy to observe her anger (both at this stage and previously) with her father – and it is explicit in some of the letters which she later wrote to her brother Fereydun from Tehran to Germany[16] – it is also evident that she wishes, perhaps even more strongly, that there had been a bond of love between her and her father from the beginning, and that at least such a bond may be established from now on. The love-and-hate syndrome is of course something almost commonplace.

Thus, we observe that since her childhood the poet has been longing for her father's love and that she had never found it by the time she wrote those letters to him; and not even later, when in 1959 we find her writing to her brother Fereydun from Tehran to Munich: 'It's only possible to say "Hello" to father'.[17] This was not a mere lack of kindness, which it is clear from the letters had existed between father and daughter, at least from time to time. On the contrary, it was a deep-seated problem which, in the case of the daughter, went back to the distant past, and its roots were to be found only in the depths of her unconscious. On the basis of this evidence, and more from all of her published letters, it is not difficult to imagine the motive for committing those 'sins' (as she calls them in her poems) and 'errors' (as she describes them in her letters to her father), a desperate search for the love of her father, each time ending with failure and remorse.

It is clear from Farrokhzād's life and works that she was constantly looking for a 'paradise lost' or at least not yet gained. And that the paradise that its seeker had in mind was a perfect object, which, by definition, was unattainable. Someone or something might suggest themselves from time to time as the perfect object and so would make the seeker stop looking for a while, but sooner or later this would come to an end, since they could not quench the seeker's thirst for that which was pure and flawless, allowing her to drown herself in it and bury her obsessions and 'sins' in a sea of absolute security and certainty, absolute and unqualified love. Hence, she was caught between God and the devil, faith and 'sin', unattainable love and the 'errors' she committed in her attempts to find it. Therefore, in her own words, she became 'lonely', and in the hope of combating loneliness, she sought asylum in her poetry, and turned it into a god. Although it did not quite replace the perfect object, it was nonetheless the most certain and secure substitute for it. She thus avers that 'poetry is my god'; and '[i]f I lose the ability to write poetry I will commit suicide'.[18]

Both Kafka and Hedāyat eventually became literature itself, not because there was nothing left that they wished to possess, but because in their desperate search for that unknown and unattainable object their body and soul turned into pure literature. In this sense, their literature was a product of the great suffering which they experienced, the only benefit of which for themselves was its use as a substitute for the lost paradise. However, precisely because it was not the perfect object itself but a mere substitute, it did not quite quench their thirst and in other ways even exacerbated their predicament. What we observe in Farrokhzād's life and work is not far removed from the experience of the two aforementioned writers.[19] In a letter to her brother Fereydun, written two years after the letters to her father, Farrokhzād wrote:

Here [in Tehran] I am very lonely. I work like a dog to compensate for loneliness. I've made a documentary film about the life of lepers, which has been successful . . . Such is life.

[But whatever you do] you are in any case lonely, and loneliness devours and breaks you. I look terribly aged and my hair has gone gray and I find the thought of the future suffocating . . .[20]

The letter dates to the beginnings of the latter part of her short life, that of *Rebirth* or *Another Birth*, both of herself and her poetry. As we shall see, from then on, there is no more talk of 'sin', 'error', remorse and regret. Yet the basic problem, the deep yearning for the unattainable love, the lost paradise, remains until the very end. For example, in a series of letters to Fereydun, written mostly in 1959, the first year of her 'rebirth', she writes that she is a:

[r]ootless person and it is only my loving (*dust dashtan-e man*) that sustains me, but what's the use . . . Oh my dear Feri I don't know why I am writing all this, but I am unhappy . . . unhappy, unhappy, and I am very lonely here.[21]

And in another letter she writes:

. . . I am very unfortunate, my dear Feri, and no-one knows. Even I myself don't want to know it. Because when I come face to face with it the only thing I can do is to throw myself out of the window . . . Oh, I'm writing rubbish.[22]

In a letter written a couple of years after the onset of her 'rebirth', which coincided with an apparently fulfilling and long-lasting relationship, she wrote to her partner: 'I feel as if I have lost my life'.[23] In another letter to him, she gives a poetical description of the acute thirst which she feels in the depths of her soul for the lost object:

I feel a confusing pressure under my skin . . . I want to drive a hole in everything and sink down as far as possible. I want to reach the depths of the earth. My love is there . . .[24]

In yet another letter to her partner she reflects the inner anxiety which is essentially a product of loneliness, insecurity and alienation by saying, 'I have always been like a closed door so that no-one would see and recognize my terrifying inner life'.[25] And in the next letter she writes: 'I don't know what it means to arrive, but it must be an end towards which the whole of my being moves';[26] to which she might have added, 'and I am afraid of never making it'. In the following letter it is almost as if it is Hedāyat, in his psycho-fictions and letters, who is judging 'a world where as far as one can see there is wall after wall after wall, a rationing of sunshine, and a famine of opportunity and fear, suffocation and abject existence'.[27] Finally she writes:

I am happy that I am no longer idealistic and dreamy. I am about to become thirty-two . . . But at least I am happy that I have found myself.[28]

And when she died she was just thirty-two. But the claim of not being dreamy anymore and having found herself, though it does reflect psychological development, refers only to the poet's consciousness, not what lurks beneath it in her unconscious. This may be discerned, for example, from one of her last poems 'Someone Who is Not Like Anyone Else' ('Kasi keh mesl-e hich kas nist'), written shortly before her death:

Why am I so little
that I get lost in the streets.
Why does father, who is not so little
and is not lost in the streets,
not do something, so that the person whom I have seen in my dream
brings forward the day of his coming.

And after she says that she has 'swept the stairs going up to the roof-top' and 'has washed the windowpanes', she asks, 'Why should father dream only when he is asleep?' It is at this point that she says:

Someone is coming.
Someone who is with us in his heart, with us in his breath, with us in his voice[29]

This is the one who does not look like anyone else, the unattainable hero who can only be seen in a dream. The poem ends with the words, 'I have had a dream . . .'

Two layers may be distinguished in this poem, the apparent layer, which prophesies the advent of a messiah or saviour, and the less obvious but a probably more real one, promising the coming of the poet's own messiah, the lost and longed-for hero, both of whom, incidentally, belong to the perfect time and space.

Nevertheless, the continuing development which was noted to have taken place at the level of consciousness is real and its signs may be seen in the very poems of *Another Birth* and after. The real rebirth is precisely in such developments, which take the substance of Farrokhzād's poetry to a different plane and significantly influence its formal qualities, the imagery, the metaphors and other literary devices. Otherwise, rebirth would not have happened just by using broken (sometimes called Nimā-esque) metres or, in the end, free verse.

To demonstrate the point, the poem 'Sin', written at twenty, may be compared and contrasted with one of the early poems of the *Rebirth* period, though not a very well known one, written at twenty-five and entitled 'In the Cold Streets of Night' ('Dar khiābān-hā-ye sard-e shab'), which opens with the following lines:

I am not remorseful.
I am thinking of this submission, this painful submission (*taslim*).

Contrast 'I am not remorseful' in this poem with 'I sinned', the opening line of 'Sin', since both poems are apparently telling a similar story, though in fact the stories are quite different. This time there is no defiant confession of a sin, nor is there any self-doubt, nor any regrets for what has happened. It is a submission, 'a painful submission', by a self-confident lover who has had the courage to take responsibility for her action, is not remorseful and does not address God in embarrassment. Her will is much stronger in surrendering herself here than committing that sin there. Therefore, there is no talk of pleasure but a self-sacrifice which is the very essence of her satisfaction:

I kissed the cross of my fate
on the hills of my killing ground.

This is an allusion to the Crucifixion, a metaphor for being willingly sacrificed. Incidentally, the much higher quality of form in this poem over 'Sin' is evident, especially in the Persian original, it being not so much because the equal quantitative metre has been abandoned for a broken metric structure, but especially because of what is being said in the new form.

The poet or poetical voice keeps repeating that she has no regrets, because she was quite sure of what she was doing, having taken responsibility for it and consciously kissed her own cross. Hence, there is no distinction between her and her lover and no mention of his 'hot, vengeful' and 'iron' arms, as there was in 'Sin':

> I am you, you
> and the one who loves
> and the one who suddenly finds
> a vague connection within herself
> with thousands of unknown, unfamiliar things.

Thus we observe that the 'pleasure' of that 'sin' has given way to this 'submission' of 'the one who loves' and to a vague connection with thousands of unfamiliar things. And, as noted above, if the issuing of the statement about that 'sin' and that 'pleasure', rather than showing real courage, was a smokescreen for covering the person's self-doubt, the description of the latter experience certainly reveals her uncompromising boldness and self-confidence:

> And I am the entire fervent passion of the earth
> that draws all the waters into herself
> to make all the plains bear fruit.[30]

This time the waters are sucked in, not for a passing pleasure but for impregnating the bond of love. Such is an example of that psychological-cum-literary development that apparently suddenly began to show itself with the onset of 'rebirth', resulting, among other things, in a spiritual union, in love rather than sin and pleasure. Thus the emergence of the roots of her erstwhile pleasure-seeking and 'sinfulness' in the shape of direct yearning for perfect and unconditional love, for which she is ready to be sacrificed. Yet, highly important though it was, all this change occurred, as noted, at the conscious level, while the fruitless search for the perfect hero, for the unfulfilled love of childhood which gave rise to the unattainable soul mate, remained until the very end. There is much evidence for this from the poems of the period of her 'rebirth'. Here I shall quote a few verses from the poem 'Let Us Have Faith in the Onset of the Cold Season' ('Īmān biāvarim beh āghāz-e fasl-e sard'), one of the last which she wrote, and which, together with a few others, was published posthumously:

> And this is me
> a lonely woman
> on the threshold of a cold season
> at the beginning of conceiving
> the contaminated existence of the earth
> and the simple and sad despair of the heavens
> and the helplessness of these granite hands . . .

That is how this long and fascinating poem opens, reflecting its author's thought processes. In it she repeats that she is cold, cold, cold, and she is naked, naked, naked, and goes on to say:

> And all my wounds are due to love
> to love, love, love . . .
> I told my mother: 'It's all over now'
> I said: 'It always happens before you think
> We must put our condolence letter in the newspaper.'
> Greetings, O strangeness of loneliness
> I surrender the room to you
> because it is always the dark clouds
> that are the prophets of new verses of purification.
> And in the martyrdom of a candle
> there lies a luminous secret
> that is known by that final and tallest flame . . .

That is how the voice of this poet, which, beginning with a relentless search for an unfulfilled love (the longing for which had been with her from childhood) sought asylum anywhere and in anything: from a prison to a wall, from a sin to a pleasure, from this demon to that god, finally, after untold and immeasurable sufferings, reached maturity in surrender and sacrifice. And yet, failing to realize that unattainable perfect object, at least in her own honest belief, she joined the order of the martyrs: 'And in the martyrdom of a candle / there lies a luminous secret /that is known by that final and tallest flame'.[31]

   This she discovered, when she had reached her tallest flame.

Chapter 2

Men and Women Together: Love, Marriage and Gender in Forugh Farrokhzād's *Asir*

Marta Simidchieva

Forugh Farrokhzād's poetry portrays candidly women's emotional responses to the men in their lives. For many of her readers, her self-described 'fearlessness'[1] in expressing her yearnings and desires signalled the arrival of the new woman, who boldly followed the dictates of her heart, casting aside traditional norms if they stifled her individuality. Marked by unprecedented 'emotional honesty' and 'brutal sincerity',[2] Farrokhzād's early verses caused a stir in a culture traditionally censorious of exposing the realm of the intimate to the public gaze, where rules of decorum and modesty demanded reticence of men, and silence and invisibility of women.[3] According to Farzaneh Milani, Farrokhzād's self-reflective poetry and her unwillingness to hide the sensual and emotional aspects of female individuality became emblematic of a new tradition of women's writings: a tradition of women who 'not only revealed themselves, but unveiled men' in their works.[4]

With this statement as a starting point, this study explores the construct of gender in *Asir* (*Captive*, 1955), Farrokhzād's first collection, paying particular attention to poems which divulge the *dramatis persona*'s sense of self vis-à-vis the significant other in her life: her husband, or lover. The argument rests on two assumptions: First, that the *dramatis persona* is a literary character distinct from the person of the author who created it, even in heavily autobiographical works. Secondly, that many of the poems in the collection are thematically connected, or comment on one another, so reading individual poems in the context of the whole enhances their understanding.

This study focuses on *Captive* because, as Michael Hillmann notes, the open expression of a woman's emotions and experiences in it had no precedent in the Persian literary tradition.[5] Its cultural impact is beyond doubt: this is the only one of Farrokhzād's collections which underwent multiple editions within the poet's own lifetime (in 1955, 1956 and 1963 respectively). And yet – overshadowed by her fourth collection, *Tavallodi digar* (*Another Birth* 1964) – the poetic breakthrough that is *Asir* is mentioned only in passing in most scholarly analyses of Farrokhzād's oeuvre. True, in her later years, Farrokhzād herself is on record stating that she regretted publishing her first three collections – *Captive*, *The Wall* (*Divār*, 1956), and *Rebellion* ('*Esyān*, 1958) – which she felt she had outgrown.[6] However, that statement, excerpted from Farrokhzād's interview with M. Āzād, should not be taken as her final verdict on the early poetry: shortly thereafter, she admits that she always likes her latest poem best, until that, too, loses its lustre, and appears simplistic and naive in her eyes.

Incidentally, the scholarly consensus concurs with Farrokhzād's own less than charitable evaluation of her early work. Critics distinguish two stages in her poetic development: before and after *Another Birth*, and they have focused almost exclusively on the second. Michael Hillmann's monograph, *A Lonely Woman*,[7] might be the only academic publication which dedicates a full chapter (entitled 'From Birth to Rebellion') to the early collections of Farrokhzād, but even there the emphasis is on the autobiographical aspects of the poetry: most of the citations are seen as poetic illustrations of her life story. Scholars of different generations and methodological orientations concur that, in her early works, Farrokhzād has not yet found herself as a person and is still in search of her own distinct style as a poet. Differences of opinion are more pronounced when it comes to the problem of gender and love in Farrokhzād's poetry. The brief assessments of the eminent Iranian scholars, Hamid Zarrinkub and Farzaneh Milani, sum up well the issues critics have raised with regard to the poetry of Farrokhzād's youth. For Zarrinkub, the poet's mature works are humanistic and universal, while her early poetry is individualistic and personal. Praising highly the unprecedented sincerity of her entire oeuvre, he singles out *Captive* for implicit criticism as the collection in which the boundary between person and *persona* is lost. In his view, the poet has poured into these verses her very being and her raw emotions, unmediated by artifice, and without regard for the mores and values of society. Love is the cornerstone of her life and her art, but when it fails her, disillusionment pushes her into an all-out rebellion against the established moral and religious norms – a nihilistic reaction he sees as typical of the lyrical poets of the age. In Zarrinkub's eyes, Farrokhzād abandons all moral restraints in open pursuit of sinful inclinations, but physical, superficial, self-centred love brings only grief to her. Unlike the rebellions of Khayyām and Hāfez, Farrokhzād's rebellion is lacking in philosophical depth, for it leads to the conclusion that the ultimate freedom of humanity is in the free expression of its instincts and sexual inclinations.[8] The feminist literary critic, Farzaneh Milani, also finds the early Farrokhzād confused and in search of her own identity. However, the category of gender in her analysis shows Farrokhzād's departures from the culturally acceptable patterns, which shocked Zarrinkub, in a different light. Milani praises Farrokhzād precisely for daring to integrate her undisguised female self in her verses, and for exploring female experiences shunned by traditional art. Her early poems convey the painful quest for self-realization of the modern Iranian woman, with all attendant conflicts, contradictions, and soul-searching. For the feminist scholar, the drawback of the early collections lies in the fact that while they bear witness to the crippling effects of the traditional sex role conditioning of men and women, they do not advocate change.[9]

There is little doubt that Farrokhzād's depiction of gender roles in *Captive* and her 'unpoetic bluntness'[10] when portraying passion and physical love are determining factors in the critical response to her early poetry, and perhaps even account for the relative neglect of her early collections by scholars. Public witness to naked desire – naked female desire in particular – still feels like a trespass, even in an age quite unfazed by the nakedness of the body in art. Yet the cultural and literary phenomenon that is Farrokhzād cannot be fully understood without the poems of *Captive* that so shocked, startled, and fascinated her contemporaries: with them emerged a new female literary voice, a new *dramatis persona,* in whose lyrical confessions, as Milani notes, '[feelings] are not rationalized, passions are not diluted, emotions are not flattened, details are not evaded, men are not absent.'[11] *Captive* is the first domicile of this *dramatis persona* in Farrokhzād's works, and the necessary starting point for charting her further evolvement.

The lover

The lover is the dominant male presence in the poems of *Captive* and the paramount transformative power in the female speaker's universe. The collection is framed by two poems, in which his figure looms larger than life. Tellingly, in both episodes the woman is alone with her dreams: the perfect lover is never with her in the flesh. In 'Shab o havas' ('Night and Desire'),[12] which opens the collection, the yearning of the *dramatis persona* for her absent mate transforms the sexual act into a cosmic encounter, as the forces of

nature find embodiment in the two rapt lovers of her imagination. Heeding the
urges emanating from her own body, she enshrouds herself in the phantom
presence of her lover. This is a paradigmatic encounter of the archetypal
woman and the archetypal man, cast as the *dramatis persona*'s initiation
into true womanhood. Predicated by the 'caressing hello of a kiss, of a glance,
of an embrace',[13] this rite of passage does not necessarily come with the first
sexual act. Rather, it arises from the first experience of ultimate oneness in the
union of two lovers, body and soul, in a moment 'overflowing with its own
completeness.'[14] In that instance of perfect harmony the woman and her
phantom-lover re-enact the act of creation in physical, scriptural, and
philosophical terms: the potent arms of the man 'coil tightly' (*pichad sakht*)
around the woman's very being, evoking the snake and Eve's temptation in
the biblical version of the Fall. The lovers' entwined bodies combine the four
elements of Aristotelian philosophy (wind, water, fire, and earth), which make
up the material world. Then, in the rapturous moment of oneness, the river,
that is, the woman, converges with the sea, that is, the man, and his passion
consumes her like a roaring fire. The intense metaphorical language of the
climax evokes the mystical state of *fanā'* in Persian mystical poetry, where the
drop joins the ocean, the moth is annihilated by the flame, and the lover's
'self' (*nafs*) is lost in the union with the divine Beloved:

> All over my neck and hair
> to wander the breeze of his breath
> to drink me, drink me up to the dregs,
> as this bitter river joins the sea that is him.
>
> Wild, hot, athirst and atremble
> like unruly, dancing flames
> to engulf me, to engulf me roaring,
> leaving nothing but dust of me in my bed.[15]

Beyond the moment of oneness, the allusions enter the domain of the mythical
and the archetypal, where the female principle is associated with Earth, and
the male – with Heaven: the woman, dust (*khākestar*) now, but perhaps just
as easily earth, seeks in her mate attributes of the sky:

> In the luminous sky of his eyes
> I would see the stars of supplication
> In the sparks of his kisses I'll seek
> the fiery pleasure of all temptation.[16]

In the four-fold repetition of the phrase 'I want him', which follows in the next stanza, we hear not only the 'shameless' assertion of female desire, but also the elemental, primal call of the female principle for the male. Their cosmic union has taken place beyond the bounds regulated by public mores and communal norms, hence the parity of the sexes, which mirrors the parity of the Yin and the Yang in the sexual act itself.[17]

At the other end of the spectrum in the gender relationships in *Captive* are the instances in which the *dramatis persona* looks at herself exclusively through the prism of paradigmatic patriarchal mores, which lay upon woman the entire responsibility for sexual misconduct. Thus, in 'Sho'leh-ye ramideh' ('Runaway Flame'),[18] she sees herself as a temptress and a sorceress, an 'instigator of riot and perpetrator of sin'; an errant woman, afflicted by [the dark passions of] the night, whose eyes call the man to a bed of sin. Her male partner, meanwhile, is free from any blame or responsibility. He is cast as a free agent, a 'runaway flame of the sun', whose nature it is to 'flood with light' expectant female eyes.[19] The woman clearly does not feel entitled to the same libertine licence, as the poem 'Harja'i' ('Tramp')[20] suggests. Here the traditional profile of the female as temptress is compounded by the portrait of the errant woman as a harlot: she is not only 'fickle, weak, and sinful',[21] harbouring a thousand carnal desires in her heart, but also drunken, boisterous, and wanton, shamelessly offering herself to a timid admirer. Warning her potential mate that her honour is stained from intimacies with others, the *dramatis persona* juxtaposes his innocence and her own iniquity in a paroxysm of adulation and remorse. The man's love for her is compared to moonlight unaware that it is shining over a 'slimy bog' (*lajan-zār*); or to rain, wasted on the barren 'stone-quarry' (*sang-lakh*) of her sinful heart.[22] The archetypal association of the male principle with the sky and the female with the earth is once again clearly visible in the imagery of this poem, but while the male lover retains his exalted status, here his female consort falls into her traditional role as Eve's daughter, the source of all temptation and sin, and the potential instrument of man's undoing. The *dramatis persona* reaches her nadir when she refers to herself as the embodiment of 'eternal darkness and depravity', terms associated with Jeh Div,[23] the concupiscent female demon from the Zoroastrian myth of creation, who seduces the first man, Kiumars, and brings him to his doom.

Between myth and parable, between the extremities of rapture and dejection, lie poems about mundane reality, and the cherished memories and routine despairs of the extramarital love affair. The female agency, to which the *dramatis persona* aspires in some of these poems, prefigures the 'episode' (Kamran Talattof's term) of feminist literature in Iran by more than two decades.[24]

Some of these works acknowledge unapologetically the powerful impulses of the flesh that drive men and women together, and assert woman's right to pursue actively both mutuality and fulfilment in love. Yet traditional gender roles and aspirations are not entirely abandoned. In 'Nā āshnā' ('Stranger'),[25] these two contradictory tendencies converge in a poetic study of the disparate expectations men and women have of a new relationship; and the conflicting impulses at the root of the complex, dynamic personality of the female partner. Built entirely on contradistinctions, the poem first visits the polarities of the female psyche. The *dramatis persona* celebrates exultantly yet another victory on the battlefield of the sexes, but at the first sight of triumph the female conqueror is transformed into a nurturer; a traditional role, albeit in a novel, erotic cast:

> Yet again, a heart fell at my feet.
> Yet again eyes stray not from my face.
> Yet again in the scrimmage of battle
> My love has bested a cold heart.
>
> Yet again from the fount of my lips
> Parched [lips] have quenched their thirst.
> Yet again, in the bed of my embrace
> A wayfarer has come to rest.[26]

In the next movement, the *dramatis persona* juxtaposes the expectations which women and men have of each other. Even though she has no designs on the man, the woman responds to his gaze tenderly (or perhaps coquettishly; *beh nāz*), just in case he turns out to be her romantic hero, ready to sacrifice all for the sake of love. The man, on the other hand, has very concrete expectations of the woman: he wants the intoxicating wine of her kisses and a fiery embrace in which to incinerate his turmoil. In their union he seeks the pleasures of the moment; she, the 'eternal pleasure' of a match in which his sincere love would give her cause to respond with total devotion. With their hopes and desires at odds, the partners cannot close the emotional chasm that divides them. She remains alien (*bigāneh*) to him, he a stranger (*nā āshnā*) to her.

The poem concludes on a classic note, with a lament of the forlorn lover, whose quest for a true soul mate remains unrequited:

> Woe to this heart, woe to this cup of hope (*jām-e omid*)
> It finally broke, and no one read its secret
> The hands of strangers played it like a *chang*
> But no one sang in unison with it.[27]

These four lines are remarkable not only for the oblique reference to the Sufi metaphor of the pure heart as the cup of Jamshid (*jām-e Jam*), but as a modern 'response' to Rumi's song of the reed flute, with which opens the *Masnavi*: 'All who loved [my song] saw their own longings in [it]/ no one sought the secrets of my soul.' This last stanza adds a whole new level of meaning to a poem ostensibly dedicated to the war of the sexes and to pure sensual delights. The implicit reference to Rumi's *Masnavi* draws attention to the connection between poetry and love, and, by doing so, introduces another juxtaposition of heavenly and earthly love as sources of creativity. In both texts, the lover (i.e. the *dramatis persona* of each poem) is identified as an instrument through which the song of love is played out, but their inspiration comes from different sources. The reed flute is animated by the fiery breath of the Divine Beloved. The *chang* (harp) sings when caressed by the hands of earthly lovers. Undoubtedly, such resorts to the Persian mystical tradition prompted Leonardo Alishan to see in Farrokhzād's poetry an expression of 'material mysticism', which – unlike the Sufis' heaven-centred spiritual orientation – is closely bound with the body and with the female Earth.[28] Whether or not one agrees with this formulation, it is clear that Farrokhzād sees her amatory verses in the context of the great Persian Sufi tradition of love poetry, in which earthly love ('*eshq-e majāzi*) is the gateway to true, divine love ('*eshq-e haqiqi*).

The marriage nexus

The abandon of the woman's love affairs in *Captive* and the depths of guilt and despair to which she sinks cannot be understood without the *dramatis persona*'s failed marital relationship which is their foil; a marriage which has become for her a cage, a silent prison.[29]

From the handful of poems in which we see the *dramatis persona* as a wife and a mother, only few address her husband directly. More often than not he is just a shadowy presence – her jailor, a haughty man, a selfish creature[30] – whose deeds and misdeeds remain unnamed. We seem to hear his voice only once, in 'Div-e shab' ('The Ogre'),[31] through the words of a terrifying monster who lurks around the dwelling of the errant woman, waiting to take away her son. But whether the reported speech in the poem conveys the words of the husband remains an open question, for the ogre's accusations that the woman's sin-stained skirts make her an unfit mother echo also the hectoring voice of her own conscience, burdened by internalized patriarchal norms, which prompts her to pull away from her own child in order to avoid contaminating him with her guilt.

But has the marriage of the *dramatis persona* always been a loveless prison? 'Yādi az gozashteh' ('Remembrance of Days Past'),[32] suggests that this was not the case. It is a love poem too, but it is hard to say at first glance whether the absent man, whom the *dramatis persona* calls to mind, is a lover or her husband. Memory takes her back to a city on the banks of a tumultuous river, amidst thickets of palms (presumably, a reference to Ahvāz, if one seeks parallels between the *dramatis persona* and Farrokhzād herself). The woman remembers the town fondly, for it welcomed the pair, and its nights were 'full of light.' On a more puzzling note, it is also the place where the heart of the woman is held 'captive' (*asir*) by a 'haughty man' (*mard-e por-ghorur*) – two signature phrases – used repeatedly in the collection to denote the *dramatis persona* and her husband, respectively.[33] Since the captive in this case is not the woman, but rather her heart, the verse could be an acknowledgement of her love for the man, rather than a complaint against the restrictions he places on her. Yet there is a hint of deliberate ambiguity here, especially in view of the emotional burden the two designations carry in the poem 'Captive', which precedes 'Remembrance of Days Past' in the collection.[34]

'Remembrance of Days Past' is unremarkable as a poem, for it draws on clichés from classical Persian literature to describe the lovers' tryst: the man '[steals] kisses from [the woman's] eyes and lips' on the beach under the palm trees, and the midnight stars observe the lovers' 'feast' (*bazm*) as the pair take their boat upon the heaving breast of the boundless sea.[35] The genteel reticence of this description and the tame romantic setting stand poles apart from the cosmic union of the elements in 'Night and Desire', a poem of rare intensity of feeling and originality of language.

Female agency has a more conventional hue here as well. As in 'Stranger', the *dramatis persona* boasts of her ability to spark yearning in her mate's 'wild and alien-coloured eyes',[36] but she is not intent on conquest. Instead, her feminine charm is employed as hallowed tradition prescribes: to tame her man, and to soften his heart through the magic of her affection. True to type, she is also a beguiling recipient of the man's caresses, rather than his partner in passion. The penultimate stanza of the poem offers a clue to the true nature of their relationship: the man is slumbering (*ghonudeh*) in the woman's lap trustingly, like a child; and the woman kisses lovingly his closed eyes in a maternal gesture. These scenes of shared affection, of tenderness and protectiveness are described in a language which the *dramatis persona* uses elsewhere with regard to her son,[37] but never to a lover. Her partner reciprocates her care and affection. When her skirt falls prey to the waves (lit. 'falls in the mouth of the waves'), it is the man who pulls it out of the water. The literal meaning of this verse is complemented by its idiomatic significance, which indicates loss of reputation or dignity.[38] This minor detail is the only clue to the marital status of the pair: when rumours savage the reputation of a woman, only her husband's defence can lay them to rest.

If 'Remembrance of Days Past' is a fond memory of shared tenderness between husband and wife, the sentiment is encountered rarely in the collection *Captive*.[39] Most poems paint the marital home of the *dramatis persona* as desolate, gloomy, and lonely – a ruined stopping-place, to which the woman returns with the chains of travel locked upon her feet;[40] or the unmarked grave, in which she takes refuge from the tumults and battles of life.[41] The estrangement that erodes the bond of affection between husband and wife, apparently, is not the result of mistreatment. The poem 'Vedā'' ('Farewell') suggests that the woman was quite content with her marital life, until she discovered what was lacking in it: the passionate mutuality of life-giving, all-consuming love, which makes the imperfect person complete – the type of love for which affection (*mahabbat*) and tenderness (*mehr*) are poor substitutes. 'God knows I was a happy bud/love came, and plucked me from the branch' laments the speaker her lost state of happy innocence and the anguish, pain, and shame that accompany the forbidden love which awakened the woman in her.

Yet even as new-found passion opens a chasm between husband and wife, the decision to leave does not come easily to the woman. Overwhelmed by a sense of guilt and despair, the *dramatis persona* tries time and again to hush up her crazy heart, to wash away the stain of love from her soul,[42] and to turn away from the valley of madness and sin into which love has enticed her.[43] Her struggle with her passions is driven by the reproaches of her own conscience, which forces her to flee from the arms of her lover to her husband's side, or '[from] the bed of loving union to the cold embrace of separation.'[44] The thought of the frightful emptiness which her absence will leave in her son's life, also keeps her captive in an increasingly loveless shambles (*virāneh*) of a marriage.[45] Yet, finally, she would choose to go away, even as her heart cries out at the thought of leaving her son behind. Surprisingly, perhaps, her resolve to break out of the marital cage is forged not by the anticipation of another love, but by the need to preserve her integrity as a poet.

Poetry and its perils

Judging by the tenor of the poetic monologues in *Captive*, poetry is indeed a major factor in the break-up of the *dramatis persona*'s marriage. At least three poems in the collection focus on the shame, which the addressee of the female speaker (in all probability her husband) experiences because of the frank poetry she writes, and on his attempts to make her stop revealing her raw naked emotions and amorous entanglements. In traditional, patriarchal societies, male honour rests on the chastity of the women of the house. Sexual indiscretion on the part of the woman brings public scorn on her entire family, and especially on her husband, who is seen as lacking in masculinity twice over – for his presumed inability to satisfy his wife's appetites, and for failing to keep her morals in check.[46] Composing poetry, which celebrates real or imaginary lovers' trysts and extramarital love affairs, would be no less damaging for a woman's reputation. Several poems in *Captive* indicate that the *dramatis persona* is under severe domestic pressure to desist baring her soul in verse. The poems "Esyān' ('Rebellion'), 'Bāzgasht' ('Return'), and 'Khāneh-ye matruk' ('The Abandoned House')[47] mark the highs and lows of the emotional roller coaster which she is riding as she struggles with the decision whether to preserve her integrity as a poet, or to sacrifice it at the altar of the family. It is worthy of note that the woman's first open revolt against the limitations imposed on her by marital life erupts not over a love affair, but over freedom of poetic expression.

The poem 'Rebellion'[48] is the most eloquent and forceful statement of the *dramatis persona*'s bid for preserving her integrity as a poet. It starts with her demand not to be silenced and to be set free from the limitations imposed on her. The poem is addressed, presumably, to her husband, for it alludes broadly to the poem 'Captive' and to the cage, which is emblematic of their marriage. She admits contemplating flight, for her poetic voice has been stifled. Repeating emphatically her demand for freedom of expression, she articulates her mission statement as a poet:

> Don't place the lock of silence on my lips
> For I must tell to all my [innermost] secret
> To all the people of the world I must make known
> The fiery cadences of my song.
>
> Open the cage, so I can spread my wings
> [soaring] in the bright sky of poetry
> If you allow me to take wing
> I'll become a rose in the rose-garden of poetry.[49]

The mission of the poet, as conceived by the *dramatis persona*, is akin to that of a prophet in Muslim tradition, for both have no choice but to spread the message they carry. The female speaker demands freedom not in order to fly to another man, but to soar on the wings of her poetic inspiration. However, poetry and the lover in *Captive* share a common denominator: both are envisaged as a 'bright sky',[50] as if poetry and love leave the same emotional imprint on the woman's soul, or impart the same sense of freedom and exuberance to a woman shackled by restrictions and limitations. Alluding to the classical metaphor of the nightingale and the rose in Persian poetry (where the nightingale stands for the lover/poet, while the rose represents the beloved/ object of the poet/lover's affection), the *dramatis persona* asks to be allowed to rise on the wings of inspiration [like a songbird], so that she can join the roses in the garden of poetry. The meaning of these verses is puzzling, for the poet envisages herself both as a nightingale and as a rose; both as the traditional subject of the poetic act and as its object. A clue to the interpretation of this unusual allusion can be found in Farrokhzād's afterword to the second edition of *Captive*, where she comments on the different standards of propriety to which poetry composed by men and women is held, and on her own efforts to break the barriers impeding women's literary self-expression. According to Farrokhzād, while men give free reign to their emotions and erotic experiences in verse without courting controversy, such openness is unthinkable for female poets. She views her own bold works as part of the effort to break down these barriers, so that everyone, men and women alike, could examine and articulate, without censure, the feelings which love and the beloved inspire in them. Farrokhzād believes female poets, too, should be allowed frank introspection and the freedom to examine and express the feelings which they find in their own hearts, without fear of censure.[51] In other words, they should have the unrestrained freedom to be both the object and the subject, or the nightingale and the rose, of their own song.

To attain such creative freedom as a poet, the *dramatis persona* of 'Rebellion' is ready to sacrifice her aspirations as a woman: she would endure stoically the bonds of a loveless marriage, surrendering to her husband, unconditionally, not only her body but also her suffering heart. Her only demand is that he would stop denigrating her art as shameful and sinful. This is the one condition on which she is not willing to compromise. If poetry is a sin, she would rather reside at the very bottom of hell than give away the 'eternal heaven', hidden in her heart.[52]

The poems in *Captive* occasionally reference one another, or draw on common threads, and might be ambiguous when considered in isolation, but gain in clarity as they are followed through in different contexts. Two such instances are evident in 'Rebellion'. The metaphor 'eternal heaven' of the heart echoes the expression 'eternal pleasure' in the poem 'Stranger', which the *dramatis persona* craves in contradistinction to the carnal pleasure her

male partner expects of her. In 'Rebellion', the eternal heaven of the heart
ensues from 'a book, solitude, a poem, and silence': all vehicles to the world
of dreams. These the female speaker juxtaposes with the houris and
the Kawsar river in paradise, which she readily leaves to her husband. Given
the constituent elements of the eternal heaven in the heart here, as well as the
eternal pleasure craved by the female speaker in 'Stranger', one might assume
both pertain to the reading and writing of poetry.

Perhaps the greatest surprise in the poem 'Rebellion' is contained in three
stanzas which cross-reference the theme of the lovers' cosmic union from
'Night and Desire'. Here, too, the cosmic forces (moon, sun, and breeze) are
summoned to a lover's tryst, but the passionate lovemaking in the silent night
is not an actual love encounter, but a projection of a young woman's unrequited
longings, as she lies in bed next to her slumbering husband:

> At night, as the moon dances sedately
> amidst the mute and silent sky,
> you are asleep, I—drunk with passion
> take moonlight's body into my embrace.
>
> A hundred kisses steals the breeze from me,
> a hundred kisses give I to the sun,
> and in the prison whose guardian are you
> a kiss did shake me to the core one night.
>
> Enough with talk of dignity, o man,
> for shame brings intoxicating pleasure.
> And the Creator will excuse this poet
> to whom He gave a crazy heart.[53]

As the last stanza suggests, these imaginary, fervent trysts are also the source
of the woman's poetic inspiration. It is hardly a coincidence that the
remonstrations of the *dramatis persona* with her silent addressee, over issues
of honour and reputation, centre not on a love affair, but on the erotic fantasies
which shape her verses.

The theme of poetry, the poet, and the perils of artistic sincerity are
addressed again in 'Return',[54] a conciliatory, tender letter to the speaker's
husband, whom she fondly addresses as 'essence of my hopes' and 'my distant
pillar [of strength]'.[55] A curious mixture of submission and resolve, this poem
apparently responds to the man's bitter complaints about the poem 'Captive',
for the woman pleads with him not to let the contents of her poetry upset
him, and is at pains to rework the images of the cage and the captive into a

more agreeable mode. Thus, she asks him to open the door of the cage yet again, but this time to let her in, for she has known happiness only behind the bars of that cage. In a very traditional strain, the chains that bind her to her husband are seen as a bar to temptation (*fetneh*) and guile (*farib*); an obstacle to 'the iron grip of variegated passions.'[56] The errant wife, willingly putting her husband in charge of her morals, seems to be gaining precedence over the poet in her. Yet although deeply remorseful about the hurt her poems are causing, the *dramatis persona* does not renounce her work, but pleads with her husband to accept it in all its outspokenness.

Apparently, among the multiple roles the *dramatis persona* is destined to play in life, that of the 'poet' is the only non-negotiable one. No other poem in *Captive* demonstrates the extent to which her calling determines her life choices than 'The Abandoned House',[57] which describes in heartbreaking detail the desolate state of a household from which the mother has departed. The picture before us is not drawn from nature, for the woman has not witnessed the scene she evokes. Rather, it is the emotional imprint left by the separation on her heart. Seared on her conscience is the image of a family's quiet, mundane despair and desolation: the child mourning his mother's absence; the husband – a broken, despondent shadow sitting next to the cold and empty bed; and the small scattered household items which spell neglect and the lack of a caring hand. In picturing the anguished household she has left behind, the *dramatis persona* does not spare herself any of the painful details. Yet, gripped by sadness, devastated by the pain she is inflicting on her son in particular, she nevertheless chooses the road to poetry, described as her friend and her lover.

Desire and the tempest of feelings, which an erotic encounter arouses in the poet's soul, is the well-spring of her creativity.[58] As 'Naqsh-e penhān' ('The Hidden Imprint')[59] suggests, the *dramatis persona* is well aware that her poetry is a function of love and resolutely seeks out a mate with whom to share tempestuous pleasure. In a striking role reversal of the traditional paradigm of sensual pursuits, the agency here is wholly the woman's: she is the bold one, the one who acts upon her desire, dismissing offhand the rumour mills busily shredding her reputation. She initiates the man in the secrets of love and of being and, perhaps not by chance, the sum of knowledge the female poet offers to lay open before him is envisaged as a book with no beginning and end, of which he has read no more than a page. This is a relationship between equals, in which each partner offers the precious gift that the other needs. The kisses of the man give life to the woman's 'dead lips', while she offers him 'a cup of the wine of being'.[60] One may wonder at the complete lack of inhibitions in the female speaker here, given the guilt and remorse which consume her in poems like 'Tramp'. It is fair to speculate that the difference arises from her decisive choice of the road leading to the 'calm embrace of poetry' in 'The Abandoned House'.[61] In her own eyes, she is no longer only a woman seeking pleasure, but also a poet seeking inspiration. Her strength and fortitude in the face of adversity, society's censure, and even the betrayal of a lover is rooted in the knowledge that not only the joys but also the pain of love fuel her poetry; or, as she exclaims in a complaint to an inconstant lover:

> My empty and silent loneliness
> you filled with memories, o man.
> My poetry is the flare of my feelings.
> You made of me a poetess, o man.[62]

Thus, the *dramatis persona*'s self-awareness as a poet is an essential factor in her self-perception as a woman, and – one may safely add – an important determinant in her relationships with the men in her life. If we seek the first shoots of gender awareness, female agency, and confident self-assertiveness in Farrokhzād's *Captive*, we are likely to find them in poems where the aspirations of the female *dramatis persona* as a woman are reinforced by her certainty in her mission as a poet. Mutuality and partnership between the sexes are also in evidence in the poet's mythopoeic works, where in the abandon of the act of love man and woman merge with the elemental forces of nature, beyond the realm regulated by social conventions.

The poems where men and women interact in a world dominated by conventional standards of manhood and womanhood are most numerous and most problematic for classification. They are riddled with contradictions, reflecting the flux of values and mores in a traditional society undergoing rapid modernization, as well as the *dramatis persona*'s struggle to find her own path amidst the conflicting demands on her as a mother, a wife, and a poet. The internalized patriarchal stereotypes, which at times dominate the female speaker's self perception, even as she defies society's notions of appropriate female behavior, are most problematic from a feminist point of view. On the other hand, readers unaccustomed to public confessionals, are taken aback by her readiness to give strangers access to her innermost thoughts, wants, and desires, and attribute the speaker's frankness to young Farrokhzād's unchecked obsession with physical love. However, as some of Farrokhzād's poems and her comments on the second edition of *Captive* suggest, her delving into the realm of the intimate is neither uncontrolled, nor lacking in a broader objective. For her, poetic integrity rests on the refusal on the part of poets to disguise their feelings and to censure their thoughts. She is convinced that the poetic mission demands courage to weather collective opprobrium and assert the right of the individual to self-realization. Her 'unpoetic bluntness' in portraying the trials and tribulations of the female self, which shocked and enthralled her contemporaries, was meant also to shake and shatter the barriers which traditional norms of public propriety erected before female artists.

With all its undeniable shortcomings, *Captive* captures the spirit of a dynamic age, where established norms clashed with rising aspirations, while gendered rules of engagement were being rewritten amidst confusion, uncertainty, and turmoil. Troubled and troubling, Farrokhzād's first collection unquestionably broke new ground and sowed the seeds of women's self-expression and agency in poetry, in love, and in life. *Captive* and Farrokhzād's early poetry, in general, merit closer consideration.

Places of Confinement, Liberation, and Decay: The Home and the Garden in the Poetry of Forugh Farrokhzād

Dominic Parviz Brookshaw

This essay explores the spatial dynamics of Forugh Farrokhzād's poetry, in particular in relation to the 'home' and the 'garden'. The 'home' (or perhaps more specifically the 'house') is depicted in much of Farrokhzād's poetry as a place of confinement, silence, and boredom. In her early poetry, Farrokhzād's garden is a locus characterized by hope and life; a setting shielded from much of the negativity that surrounds the speaker. In some of her later poems, though, and specifically in her much celebrated 'Delam barā-ye bāghcheh mi-suzad' ('I Feel Sorry for the Garden'), the garden itself becomes a source of negativity: it is characterized by putridity, death, and suppressed feelings of anger and frustration. This essay examines the varied ways in which Farrokhzād evokes the 'home' and the 'garden' in her poems, how her understanding of these spaces and their associations change with time, and the extent to which the poet's vision of these settings is in harmony and/or conflict with that found in classical Persian poetry. Although a good number of Farrokhzād's poems bear a strongly autobiographical tone, it is perhaps worth signaling that in this study I am not reading her poetry biographically, but rather socio-culturally. Elements of the poet's life naturally enter into my discussion, but my aim is to uncover different dynamics in her work.[1]

The home

There is no real precedent in pre-modern Persian poetry for the descriptions of the home or the domestic environment as found in the poetry of Farrokhzād. There is one main reason for the lack of this precedent: pre-modern Persian poetry is almost exclusively non-confessional in terms of its tone, voice and content; and, therefore, there is almost no description of the private space, of the home or home life of an individual to be found in pre-modern Persian poetry.

Another reason for this paucity of descriptions of the home in medieval Persian poetry is that so little poetry written by women has survived from the pre-modern period. One can hypothesize that if more poetry penned by women had survived from pre-twentieth-century Iran, more references to life within the home would be available to us, since the domestic space was dominated by women in the pre-modern Iranian cultural context.[2] Indeed, the extent to which the domestic space is described in Farrokhzād's poetry and the detail of this description are, I would argue, clear indicators of a female poetic voice.[3]

The four walls of the homes described in Farrokhzād's poetry act as veils which obscure the outside world. In her verse, these walls are often penetrated by windows which provide some possibility of interaction with or, at the very least, observation of the outside world. These windows, however, more often than not are obscured in part or totally by shutters (sing. *daricheh*)[4] and curtains (sing. *pardeh*), which restrict the gaze of both the speaker and the reader, and thereby diminish the liberating impact of the windows. It should be noted, however, that the home or house in Farrokhzād's poetry is not an exclusively or uniformly negative space. For example, the bed described in her much discussed poem 'Gonāh' ('Sin'), which contains a frank and essentially unabashed description of a sexual encounter with a man, is located within a home, presumably either that of the speaker or her lover.[5] For the most part, though, the home is used by Farrokhzād as a desolate backdrop for some of her bleakest depictions of women and their place in mid-twentieth-century Iranian society.

In Farrokhzād's poetry, the walls of the house, on the other hand, perform the opposite function to the walls of the garden. Those of the house keep life and love out, whereas those of the garden keep love in and protect it from the destructive forces of a hostile outside world. Descriptions of the domestic environment – whether familial or marital – abound in Farrokhzād's poetry. Here I will limit my discussion to those poems in which the home looms largest.

The first poem discussed here comes from Farrokhzād's fourth collection, *Tavallodi digar* (*Another Birth*, 1964), and is entitled 'Jom'eh' ('Friday').[6] 'Friday' is a bleak poem in which the stifling and desiccated atmosphere of the family home is described in stark terms. In the first seven lines of the poem, Friday (the day of rest in Iran) is described in concise, staccato phrases in which the poet uses adjectives synonymous with muteness, mourning and loss to sketch a desolate picture. In Farrokhzād's poem, Friday is a day filled with nothing more than futile thoughts and spells of protracted boredom, punctuated only by yawning. Friday is a day on which nothing happens, a day devoid of anticipation. It is a day for resignation:

جمعهٔ ساکت

جمعهٔ متروک

جمعهٔ چون کوچه های کهنه، غم انگیز

جمعهٔ اندیشه های تنبلِ بیمار

جمعهٔ خمیازه های موذی کِشدار

جمعهٔ بی انتظار

جمعهٔ تسلیم

Silent Friday
Abandoned Friday
Friday, a day as sad as old alleyways
Friday, a day of languid, ill thoughts
A Friday of annoying, lengthy yawns
A Friday without expectation
A Friday of submission[7]

The repetition of the word *jom'eh* ('Friday') at the start of each of the first seven lines of the poem reinforces the sense of monotony felt by those stuck at home with no hope of escape on the weekend. For the speaker, these dreary Fridays seem to stretch for a whole seven days; the weekend seems as long as the week itself, and not in a good way. This poem is a reflection of the dead time when offices and schools are closed and the streets are quiet. The first seven lines of the poem are balanced by the following six lines, which all begin with the word *khāneh* ('house' or 'home'). The two sections reinforce the connection in the reader's mind between Friday's stifling boredom and the family home: one main reason why Fridays are so unpleasant in the speaker's eyes is that they are spent confined to this stale, suffocating environment. The house on Friday is described as a disheartening void. It is a space which lacks light, where the sun is something to be imagined, rather than experienced. It is a place filled only with isolation, where the mind of the captive is racked by false predictions and uncertainties. Friday's house is a house peopled only by furniture and other inanimate objects, one of which is presumably the speaker:

خانهٔ خالی
خانهٔ دلگیر
خانهٔ دربسته بر هجوم جوانی
خانهٔ تاریکی و تصوّر خورشید
خانهٔ تنهایی و تفأل و تردید
خانهٔ پرده، کتاب، گنجه، تصاویر

Empty house
Depressing house
A house whose doors are shut against the onslaught of youth
A house of darkness, where the sun must be imagined
A house of loneliness, divination and doubt
A house of curtains, books, cupboards and pictures

Perhaps most significantly, the walls of this house try to confine and control the urges of the young; they stand in the way of all that is natural. Hillmann sees a culturally specific context in this poem. He reads 'Friday' as Farrokhzād's attempt to convey the reality of the life of a female adolescent as experienced in the Iran of her day.[8] There is no definitive indication in the poem as to the gender of the speaker, though. I think 'Friday', therefore, should be read more generally as a comment on anxieties surrounding adolescent sexuality in Iran in the 1950s and 1960s.[9] The speaker's bland weekend is peppered only with idle daydreams. Confined within the family home, the speaker is sealed off from any possibility of experimentation – sexual or otherwise – that the outside world might offer.[10]

As a child and a teenager, Farrokhzād witnessed radical changes in the position of women in her society first-hand.[11] It would be a mistake to think, however, that prevalent attitudes towards women and their role in society changed overnight: the middle class Tehrani milieu in which Farrokhzād grew up in the 1940s and 1950s remained overwhelmingly conservative and patriarchal, especially in terms of its attitudes towards the moral education of girls. As Rahimieh has noted:

If Iran's pre-revolutionary obsession with modernization succeeded in displacing the religious discourse on women's sexuality, it did not erase its secular traces to which women were subjected.[12]

In the final stanza, the poem moves away from describing the generic, dull Friday house as the speaker turns the focus on her/himself, reflecting on how life has passed slowly by during these silent and abandoned Fridays, like an 'unknown and alien stream' flowing through a series of 'empty, depressing' houses.

A similarly bleak description of a house is found in one of Farrokhzād's earlier poems, 'Deyr' ('Monastery'), from her third collection, 'Esyān (Rebellion, 1958), which the poet wrote during her stay in Munich in 1957.[13] The religious overtone of this space (as suggested by the title) has abstemiousness, chastity, and barrenness at its core. In 'Monastery', the house represents loneliness, isolation and death; it is seated like a 'grave in a cloud formed from the dust of trees.' This ghostly house is filled with 'silent and dark' corners, from which emanate hundreds of 'mute and mysterious' greetings. This ominous atmosphere is emphasized in the fifth stanza where the 'heart of darkness' is described as beating in a small, sad room, where the night 'creeps like a black snake upon the thin, multi-coloured curtains.' The subsequent description of the wall clock as 'devoid of any strike or sound' and of the faded photographs in old frames, which display 'laughable, mortal faces', remind the reader of houses described in a number of Farrokhzād's later poems. The image of the mirror as a large eye which sits quietly 'engrossed in observation' is an unsettling one: even within the secluded home environment, one is not free from the prying gaze of others.

The next poem I wish to discuss comes from the same collection as 'Friday' and is entitled 'Arusak-e kuki' ('The Wind-Up Doll').[14] The house in 'The Wind-Up Doll' is reminiscent of the house depicted in 'Friday', although here the house described is that of a married couple. In this poem, Farrokhzād describes the stifling atmosphere of the marital home in which the stay-at-home wife, hidden from the prying gaze of strangers, enjoys an existence not dissimilar to that of a mechanical, wind-up doll, packed away to protect it from being damaged, but which dutifully squeaks in delight when handled by its owner. The faded patterns on the rug, the cracks in the wall, and the heavy curtains all serve to conjure up an oppressive and suffocating atmosphere which is at once both static and stale:

میتوان ساعات طولانی

با نگاهی چون نگاه مردگان، ثابت

خیره شد در دود یک سیگار

خیره شد در شکل یک فنجان

در گلی بی رنگ بر قالی

در خطی موهوم، بر دیوار

One can, for hours on end
With the fixed look like that of the dead,
Stare into the smoke of a cigarette
Stare at the shape of a coffee cup
At a colourless flower on the rug
At an imaginary line on the wall

In this poem, Farrokhzād attacks what she sees as the passive role that patriarchal Iranian society traditionally dictates for women; a life confined to the home in which the sole objective of a woman's existence is to please and serve her husband and to maintain a veneer of beauty, compliance, and contentment. Since the life of such a woman is conventionally confined to the house, a description of the domestic environment is therefore central to the poem.[15]

There is no respite from the atmosphere of the empty, marital home. Even a peek through the window to the outside world brings little relief from the crippling boredom. Drawing back the curtains with 'stiff' hands, the woman's lifeless gaze fixes upon a no less muted scene: the heavy rain which pours down in the street outside has forced a child holding his kite to seek shelter under a porch. The child's fun has been cut short, and the one source of movement and noise – a 'dilapidated cart' – quits the empty square at great haste, presumably to escape its depressive atmosphere.

In the next stanza, Farrokhzād turns her attention to the passivity of the sexual role of the wife in this kind of marriage:

میتوان فریاد زد
با صدایی سخت کاذب، سخت بیگانه
‹‹دوست میدارم››

One can cry out
With a voice both terribly fake and alien
'I love'.

In the next few lines, the marital home is presented as the setting for the 'pollution' of the innocence of love – possibly a reference to the taking of the woman's virginity on the wedding night. This 'pollution', Farrokhzād says, can take place in the bed of a drunk (*yek mast*), a madman (*yek divāneh*) or a tramp (*yek velgard*). I believe these three characters – the drunk, the madman, and the tramp – symbolize the varied personae of the abusive husband.

The poet then returns briefly to the theme of boredom embarked upon at the beginning of the poem by alluding to solving mind-numbing crossword puzzles – a reminder of the humdrum existence of the middle class wife. What follows is a tirade against what she sees as the futility and outmoded nature of religious practices popular among more conservative strata of Iranian Shi'i society. Farrokhzād ridicules the common practice of visiting a small shrine or *imāmzādeh* – which she describes in irreverent terms as an 'unknown grave' – where one can pray before a 'cold tomb', or else 'rot' in the chambers of some mosque like an 'old prayer-chanter' (a man paid by less literate pilgrims to recite visitation prayers [sing. *ziārat-nāmeh*] on their behalf). This is one of Farrokhzād's most damning indictments of traditional Iranian religiosity and, as we shall see, is echoed in her description of the Mother in her posthumously published masterpiece, 'Delam barā-ye bāghcheh mi-suzad'. By including an attack on traditional religiosity in a poem critiquing the role prescribed to the middle class wife in patriarchal Iranian society, Farrokhzād intends her readers to draw a direct connection between the sublimation of women's desires and aspirations, and religion.

Following this brief interlude, Farrokhzād turns her attention back to the marital home and its function as a place in which the wife can conceal not only physical objects, but also feelings and emotions. The dutiful wife, out of 'shame' and her sense of propriety, can 'hide away the beauty of a moment', like one hides away 'silly' snapshots at the bottom of a chest. She can plaster the walls with pictures to cover their 'fissures', just as one might try to cover up the cracks in an unhappy marriage by concealing (but not repairing) them.

Ultimately – as spelled out in the last stanza – the speaker says her society dictates a perfect wife should be like a 'wind-up doll', who views the world through two expressionless eyes. This Iranian Stepford Wife should be cosseted like a precious, delicate toy, stored away from the outside world.[16] Like a wind-up doll, she should be ready to perform her duties on demand:

میتوان همچون عروسک های کوکی بود
با دو چشم شیشه ای دنیای خود را دید
میتوان در جعبه ای ماهوت
با تنی انباشته از کاه
سالها در لابلای تور و پولک خفت
میتوان با هر فشار هرزهٔ دستی
بی سبب فریاد کرد و گفت
«آه، من بسیار خوشبختم»

One can be like one of those wind-up dolls
And observe one's world through glass eyes
One can sleep for years, in a cloth-lined box
With a body stuffed with straw,

Wrapped in lace and sequins.
One can, with the squeeze of every vulgar hand
Without any reason cry out:
'Oh, how fortunate I am!'

An earlier poem which stands as a poetic antecedent to both 'Friday' and 'The Wind-Up Doll', in terms of its depiction of the marital home and the middle class Iranian wife, is 'Khāneh-ye matruk' ('The Abandoned House'),[17] from Farrokhzād's first collection, *Asir*.[18] Farrokhzād's first three collections, *Asir* (*Captive*, 1955), *Divār* (*The Wall*, 1956) and *'Esyān* (*Rebellion*, 1958),[19] were dismissed by Farrokhzād herself as 'juvenile'. Certainly they do not share the maturity – whether emotional or literary – of her last two collections, but as Milani has noted, even at this early stage, it is clear from Farrokhzād's poetry that she intended to portray the life of a modern Iranian woman – a life she had first-hand experience of – not a life created, or imagined by others.[20] The poet wrote 'The Abandoned House' in Tehran, in the spring of 1955, having returned to the capital after her divorce from Parviz Shāpur, and after having lost custody of her son Kāmi to her ex-husband's family.[21] In this poem, Farrokhzād appears to describe her former home. The house is distant from her physically, but yet not emotionally. She imagines her child crying bitterly, searching for her in vain in the bed she once shared with her husband, which she says is now both 'empty' and 'cold'. In describing the interior of the recently abandoned house, the poet focuses on the image of the floral design on the rug, something which pops up again in 'The Wind- Up Doll'. This culture-specific reference to a Persian rug reinforces the fact that, on one level, Farrokhzād is talking about her own personal experience and that of other Iranian divorcees of the time, many of whom lost custody of their children.[22] The poet imagines a house no longer well cared for: the window has been left open, the curtain hangs precariously from the door frame, and the water in the vase has dried up. The hungry cat and the expiring candle only serve to add to the feeling of neglect. The repetition of the first stanza of the poem as the penultimate stanza reinforces the message expressed at the beginning of the poem: the former family home is now a desolate wasteland:

دانم اکنون کز آن خانهٔ دور
شادی زندگی پر گرفته
دانم اکنون که طفلی به زاری
ماتم از هجر مادر گرفته

I know now that life's joy
Has flown from that distant house
I know now that a child cries bitterly,
Mourning his mother's departure.

Before moving on to a discussion of the garden as depicted by Farrokhzād, it is worth pointing out that not all representations of the family home found in her poetry are negative ones. The poem, 'Ān ruz-hā' ('Those Days'),[23] which opens her fourth collection, contains a number of positive references to a family home. In 'Those Days', the speaker depicts a home synonymous with warmth and comfort. Much of this poem can be read as a positive reflection by Farrokhzād on the home she and her six siblings grew up in, and a nostalgic longing for it. It is from behind the window of her warm room that the speaker stares outside at a wintry scene on those 'silent, snowy' days, when the family gathered around the 'sleep-inducing' heat of the brazier. However, the fact that seven – that is, more than half – of the stanzas of this poem start with the phrase, 'those days are gone' (ān ruz-hā raftand), reinforces an uncomfortable reality: that time in her life has long passed and these comforting childhood memories which console her sit in stark contrast to her present predicament.[24]

The garden

Unlike descriptions of the domestic environment, there is a strong precedent for the description of gardens (sing. bāgh) in pre-modern Persian poetry. Gardens depicted in pre-modern Persian poetry that do not carry a primarily or exclusively mystical significance can be divided into three main categories:

(i)   Royal and aristocratic walled gardens. Descriptions of these are found predominantly in panegyric odes or qasidehs;[25]

(ii) Privately-owned pleasure gardens and spring meadows which are frequently described as venues for convivial parties (majāles), during which wine and sweetmeats were consumed to the accompaniment of music. At these parties the beauty of the wine-servers and other slave-attendants would be lauded in verse, and the departure or aloofness of the unobtainable beloved lamented;[26]

(iii) Gardens and garden pavilions which served as safe meeting places for lovers in Persian romances, such as Gorgāni's Vis o Rāmin or Khvāju Kermāni's Homāy o Homāyun.[27]

The pre-modern garden descriptions which seem to have influenced Farrokhzād the most are those found in short lyrics on love (ghazals) and romance epics. Farrokhzād's garden is, accordingly, often the setting for the celebration of and indulgence in pleasure, in particular, sexual pleasure. Garden descriptions which draw heavily in terms of vocabulary (but less so in terms of imagery) on pre-modern Persian poetry are common in Farrokhzād's earlier collections, which contain poems of a consciously neoclassical style. Farrokhzād's early poetry is closer to pre-modern Persian poetry in terms of form and diction, but, from the very start, her subject matter is modern in that it deals with contemporary issues. Here I will highlight a handful of examples from the poet's third collection, *'Esyān*:

In 'Bolur-e ro'yā' ('Crystal Vision')[28] (another poem written in Munich), the poet skilfully remoulds classical Persian paradisiacal garden imagery and its archaic diction after her own taste:

گویی فرشتگان خدا در کنار ما
با دستهای کوچکشان چنگ می زدند
در عطر عود و نالۀ اشپند و ابر دود
محراب را ز پاکی خود رنگ می زدند

It was as though the angels of God, by our side
Played harps with their little hands
And in the perfume of the aloes, the lament of the wild rue, and the cloud
of smoke
Painted the prayer niche with their purity

Another poem in the collection, 'Jonun' ('Madness'),[29] reads as a modern take on the *taghazzol* or amorous prelude of the medieval Persian panegyric ode (*qasideh*). 'Madness' opens with a stanza describing the imminent arrival of spring and its rejuvenating breeze, which banishes all memory and trace of winter. This metaphor is commonly employed in medieval Persian panegyrics to celebrate the accession of a new, just king, or else in the short lyric where the arrival or return of the beloved is likened to the coming of Nowruz, the Iranian spring festival, after a harsh winter of separation.[30]

In 'Zendegi' ('Life'),[31] the reader encounters stanzas such as the following one, which would not seem out of place in a poem by one of the masters of medieval Persian love poetry:

با هزاران جوانه می خواند
بوتۀ نسترن سرود ترا
هر نسیمی که می وزد در باغ
می رساند به او درود ترا

Accompanied by a myriad of buds,
The sweetbrier bush sings your song
Every breeze which wafts in the garden
Delivers to him your greeting.

This drawing on the garden and nature imagery found in pre-modern Persian poetry is not confined to Farrokhzād's first three collections, and in her fourth collection, *Tavallodi digar*, we encounter a poem whose subtle blend of neo-classical Persian garden description and the poet's own audacious avant-garde take on female sexuality in a modern Iranian context, testify to her poetic maturity. This poem, entitled 'Fath-e bāgh' ('Conquering the Garden'),[32] opens with the ominous image of a crow flying over the heads of two lovers. The crow is a stock character in pre-modern Persian poetry, used to symbolize the malicious gossipmonger:[33]

و صدایش همچون نیزۀ کوتاهی، پهنای افق را پیمود
خبر ما را با خود خواهد برد به شهر

And the crow's voice, like a short spear, travelled the breadth
of the horizon:
'He will carry our news with him to the city.'

The fear is that the crow will disclose the lovers' secret union to the inhabitants of the town, thereby jeopardising it. Here, there are echoes of the *shohreh- ye shahr* found in the medieval Persian *ghazal*; the poet-lover who becomes famous for the extent of his unwavering, wholehearted devotion to his beloved, as the fourteenth-century Persian poet Hāfez says:[34]

منم که شهرۀ شهرم به عشق ورزیدن

I'm the talk of the town for my love-making

With this fame comes the threat of infamy on the part of the lover; the fear that the disclosure of his crazed love will cause him to suffer rebuke and ridicule at the hands of the city's inhabitants, who represent the outside world. In 'Conquering the Garden', the crow is described flying a considerable distance from the garden to the town. This location of the idealized garden beyond the city walls, surrounded by untamed nature, is one found typically in medieval Persian poetry, where the lovers seek the security of a private walled garden, beyond the city limits, for their liaisons. The garden envisaged in 'Conquering the Garden' is set apart from the focus of everyday life. This clear demarcation between the idyllic garden and the tainted city is important in Farrokhzād's conceptualization of the space depicted in this poem; in 'Conquering the Garden' the lovers are in a state of semi-willful exile from the town.[35] Farrokhzād's garden idyll is unadulterated by society's controlling normative attitudes. It is a secure enclave in which the lovers shield themselves against an unfavourable exterior environment.[36]

It is significant that the speaker informs us that she and her lover first spied the garden from a, 'cold, grim-faced window'.[37] The lovers gazed on the garden from the confines of a dreary house – an environment both controlled and controlling, and one diametrically opposed to the atmosphere they encounter upon entering the garden.

The reference to the plucking of the apple in this stanza immediately calls to mind the description of the Fall found in the Torah.[38] Interestingly, the woman and her lover *together* pluck the fruit; they are *equally* responsible for their actions.[39] As Milani notes, in this poem the male and the female protagonists act as individuals on an even footing:

> Gone is the age-old antagonism between man and woman. Gone with it, too, is mistrust. Here, union, rather than separation is celebrated ... Spontaneity is not feared. Intimacy is experienced rather than idealized. To show desire and seek gratification are no longer solely man's prerogatives. The woman can also experience and express both.[40]

In this garden there is no gender imbalance: here woman and man are equal partners in love. Perhaps it is this new-found equality and sharing of responsibility that causes them to lose their fear of guilt or sin? Fear is what everyone else (all those who have not entered the garden) feels – a fear which prevents onlookers from acting with the same abandon as the lovers:

همه ميترسند
همه ميترسند، اما من و تو
به چراغ و آب و آينه پيوستيم
و نترسيديم

Everyone is afraid,
Everyone is afraid, but you and I
Have joined with the lamp, the water and the mirror,
And we did not fear

Here Farrokhzād has succeeded masterfully in adding her own twist to this age-old tale of the origins of human existence and human love.[41] Her idealized lovers are not bound by a traditional marriage recorded in a tatty, old register;[42] theirs is a union voiced by her 'joyful locks' and sealed with the 'burnt poppies' of his kisses. Theirs is a true and complete physical union and intimacy (*samimiyat*). As Milani explains, 'Conquering the Garden' is not a tale of unrequited, frustrated desire as found in the Persian *ghazal*:[43]

> Intimacy is experienced rather than sought or idealized. Love is not determined by motives of security, power or possessions. Pleasure is reciprocated in kind, and sexuality is not turned into a bargaining table. There is no exchange of sexual favors for economic support, loyalty or matrimony. Companionship, sexual gratification, and devotion are freely sought and freely given by both partners.[44]

The uninhibited sexual encounter the lovers experience in the garden is juxtaposed with the awkward fumbling between man and wife within the four walls of the traditional marital home:

سخن از پچ پچ ترسانی در ظلمت نیست
سخن از روزیست و پنجره های باز

It's not about fearful chattering in the dark
It's about daylight, and open windows

The contrast between the freshness of this garden and the stale odour of the marital home as described in 'The Wind-Up Doll' and 'The Abandoned House' is undeniable.[45] In this garden utopia, in which the speaker and her mate become one with nature, the lovers are – like Adam and Eve before them – devoid of all contact with other humans, and so they turn to the animals (hares and eagles) and even invertebrates (oysters) for advice on what they should do.[46]

As the poem develops, the description of the garden takes on a more mystical tone, reminiscent of ecstatic medieval Persian love poems, such as those of the thirteenth-century Persian mystic Rumi (d.1273). The speaker announces that she and her lover have found their way to the 'cold and silent dreams' of the mythical Simorgh birds; that they have found the 'truth', the 'ultimate reality' (*haqiqat*) – the goal of the mystic's quest – in this garden. They have attained 'eternal existence' (*baqā*), a state conventionally sought by the Sufi through union with the Divine. Here Farrokhzād has raised sexual, earthly union to the highest level.[47]

In the penultimate stanza, the speaker addresses her lover beseeching him to leave the safety of the garden and to 'come to the meadow, come to the vast meadow' and to call after her, like the 'gazelle calls after his mate'.[48] The meadow (*chaman-zār*) is beyond the confines and constraints of the urban setting and, because of this, it – like the garden – represents liberation from societal norms. For all its positivity and celebration of human love, 'Conquering the Garden' ends with the ominous image of curtains, which Farrokhzād uses to convey a sense of oppression and suffocation. The curtains are described here as 'over-flowing' with a 'hidden spite' (*boghzi penhāni*);[49] a reference to those in society who are jealous of what true, liberated lovers experience and who seek to destroy their Eden.

But Farrokhzād's most profound and lasting description of a garden is that found in a poem published posthumously in 1974, 'Delam barā-ye bāghcheh mi-suzad' ('I Feel Sorry for the Garden').[50] The garden depicted in this poem is located in an urban setting, at the centre of a family home, and at the heart of the family itself. The garden is the family's emotional nucleus. In this poem, the poet is not concerned with the *bāgh* or large, walled garden as described in 'Conquering the Garden', but rather with the *bāghcheh* or *hayāt*: the small courtyard garden found at the centre of traditional Iranian homes, such as the one Farrokhzād grew up in, located in an old neighbourhood of south Tehran.[51]

In 'I Feel Sorry for the Garden', it is through the various family members' interaction with the courtyard garden that their individual ills, as well as their collective misery, are revealed to the reader. In this sense, the garden acts as a mirror to what is a troubled and disintegrating nuclear family – a family under siege from the onslaught of modernity and the antagonism of mistrustful neighbours; a family which bears the scars of the indifference of its individual members towards one another, as well as those of their own personal despair. In this poem, the garden has none of the idyllic qualities possessed by the *bāgh* in 'Conquering the Garden'.[52]

In 'I Feel Sorry for the Garden', the garden acts as the repository of the collective memory of the family. Since this garden stands at the very heart of the house, all the members of the family cannot help but interact with it, even if their interaction takes the form of withdrawal or rejection. In this poem the garden's sick state reflects the ill health of the family as a unit.[53] For Hillmann, the speaker in this poem 'points to the individual self-centredness, superficiality and phoniness' of the middle class of her day.[54] One of the reasons for the garden's degeneration – and, by analogy, that of the family – is that it has been neglected, in particular by the Father who has withdrawn into his own world, into an emotional as well as a professional 'retirement'. The Father has become physically and emotionally detached from both the garden and from the rest of his family. The reader imagines the Father seated in a dimly lit room located off the courtyard. In that dark seclusion, the Father's only sources of company are two books: Ferdowsi's eleventh-century voluminous epic poem the *Shāhnāmeh,* and the *Nāsekh ol-tavārikh*, a history of the life of the Prophet Muhammad and the Imams. By associating these two works with the Father, Farrokhzād is suggesting that both tomes are backward-looking and out-of-touch with the reality of modern Iran. Farrokhzād's implicit critique of Ferdowsi's *Shāhnāmeh* (the Iranian national epic) is striking, given the importance attached to the poem by the Pahlavist ideologues, who drew heavily upon the myths recounted in it to mould a collective national pride in Iran's pre-Islamic past, a project which culminated in Mohammad Rezā Shāh Pahlavi's extravagant celebration of 2,500 years of Persian monarchy held at the ancient Persian city of Persepolis in 1971.[55] It is worth remembering that 'I Feel Sorry for the Garden' was written some time around 1965, a good five years or so before the Shah's celebrations at Persepolis, and so Farrokhzād's critique of the glorification of Iran's pre-Islamic past here strikes the reader as somewhat prophetic.[56]

The Father's affections have been diverted from his family to his reading material of choice. His negativity towards the garden and towards his family, which here stands for the Iranian nation as a whole, could be understood as a critique of Mohammad-Rezā Shāh Pahlavi himself:

و در اتاقش، از صبح تا غروب

یا شاهنامه می خواند

یا ناسخ التواریخ

پدر به مادر می گوید:

«لعنت به هر چه ماهی و هر چه مرغ

وقتی که من بمیرم دیگر

چه فرق می کند که باغچه باشد

یا باغچه نباشد

بر ای من حقوق تقاعد کافی ست»

And in his room, from dawn till dusk
he reads either the *Shāhnāmeh*
or *Nāsekh ol-tavārikh*
Father says to Mother:
'Damn all the fish and all the birds!
When I die,
what difference will it make if there is a garden or not?
My pension is enough for me!'

The Father has disengaged from the garden and his family, and he is content to allow both the garden and the family to go to pot. He believes his time to be over and he is now content to lose himself in the past and prepare himself for his imminent demise. The Father stands, in a more general sense, for the low-ranking civil servant who has buried his head in the sand and who does not want to rock the status quo of the second Pahlavi period.

From the Father, the speaker turns her attention to the Mother, who is trying in vain to keep the garden (and the family) alive by resorting to what are portrayed as the outmoded tools of religious piety and ritual prayer. The Mother believes some sin or blasphemy has led to the garden's demise, and does not want to accept the simple fact that neglect and a lack of love have caused the decay she sees before her; a decay she is powerless to stem. The Mother represents those more traditionally minded elements of the Iranian lower middle class who, in the late 1960s and 1970s, saw Twelver Shi'ism as the only force powerful enough to hold their disintegrating society together. The depiction of the devout mother in this poem reminds the reader of the religiosity of the people of south Tehran as described in the poem, 'Kasi keh mesl-e hich-kas nist' ('Someone Who is Like No one Else'), from the same collection.[57]

It is the Brother who is next in line for scrutiny. The Brother is more self-absorbed than the Mother, but perhaps less detached than the Father in that he is aware of the garden's decay. He is described as being 'addicted to philosophy', and he believes that the garden's cure lies ultimately in its destruction. The Brother is too caught up in his own turmoil to care about the garden, which he calls a 'graveyard'. He represents a lost generation, those youth who have turned their backs on the history and religion revered by their parents, and who seek solace in pop philosophy and alcohol, and who are fundamentally disillusioned and dangerously detached from the people around them.

From the Brother the speaker moves to the Sister, who is criticized for having abandoned the family – and, by extension, the garden – when she left home after marriage. The Sister moved to one of the new suburbs, perhaps to an apartment in a high-rise block. The Sister represents a newly affluent generation that has embraced an alien, consumerist attitude to life. The Sister's new home is described as an inauthentic and altogether artificial space:

او خانه اش در آن سوی شهر است
او در میان خانۀ مصنوعیش
با ماهیان قرمز مصنوعیش
و در پناه عشق همسر مصنوعیش
و زیر شاخه های درختان سیب مصنوعی
آوازهای مصنوعی می خواند
و بچه های طبیعی می سازد

Her house is on the other side of town
She, in her artificial home
With her artificial goldfish
Sheltered by the love of her artificial husband
And under the branches of artificial apple trees
Sings artificial songs
And makes natural babies

Most significantly in terms of the garden, it was the Sister who tended it. She was a friend to the garden, and sought solace and refuge there from the Mother's beatings. She was the one who kept the garden alive and who cared for the goldfish in the pool. Now that she has left and has turned her back on where she comes from, the garden is dying. The Sister stands for the 'westoxicated' (*gharbzadeh*), modern Iranian who has – consciously or unwit- tingly – severed her ties with her past, thereby becoming worryingly rootless in Farrokhzād's eyes.[58] The Sister epitomizes the artificiality and superficiality of the 1960s, when many urban Iranians appeared to disregard their 'Iranianness', preferring instead to adopt Western modes of behaviour.[59] Even more disturbing is the fact that in the whole poem, the only reference to growth is in relation to the Sister's reproductive fertility and her endless stream of children: Farrokhzād implies that future generations of Iranians, having been born from such mothers, will be even more rootless.

In the last few stanzas of the poem, Farrokhzād broadens the scope of her vision beyond that of the nuclear family to comment more generally on contemporary Iranian society as a whole.[60] She depicts the neighbouring gardens planted with mortar and machine guns; a hellish, prophetic vision of the impending strife of the period surrounding the 1978–1979 Revolution. In her apocalyptic premonitions, neighbours have emptied the tiled pools in their gardens to hide secret stashes of ammunition, and their children – future martyrs of the revolutionary struggle and the eight-year war with Iraq – carry hand grenades in their school bags.

Conclusion

By the early 1960s, Farrokhzād had fully embraced modernist Persian poetry and was producing work of increasing significance, both in terms of its impact on the Iranian literary scene, and in terms of the socio-political critique she expressed through it. Although still concerned with the struggle of the individual woman for autonomy and the right to define her own life trajectory, towards the end of her short life Farrokhzād was primarily concerned with broader, human issues which affected all members of her society, and with the life of the Iranian nation as a whole.[61]

By the mid-1960s, Farrokhzād had succeeded in harnessing her energies to produce poetry with a broad, human perspective that transgressed that of the individual woman; a perspective that went beyond gender itself.[62] Farrokhzād's last poems are arguably more universal in their message than the poetry of the other four leading poets of twentieth-century Iran (Nimā Yushij, Mehdi Akhavan-Sāles, Ahmad Shāmlu and Sohrāb Sepehri).

In Farrokhzād's earlier work, descriptions of the house and the garden are focused on the extent to which those environments assist or else hinder the individual in her quest for romantic and sexual fulfilment. Poems such as 'Friday', 'The Abandoned House', 'The Wind-Up Doll' and even 'Conquering the Garden' have the individual and her desires as their focus.[63] In her posthumously published 'I Feel Sorry for the Garden', however, the poet subtly diverts her gaze (and that of the reader) away from the individual, towards the entirety of Iranian society, with strikingly lucid insight. Before her death, it is true to say, Farrokhzād was concerned more with social issues than those of gender. The last seven lines of 'I Feel Sorry for the Garden' seem to sum up how the poet felt at this stage in her life: the garden of the nation was rapidly losing the rejuvenating powers Farrokhzād believed it once to have possessed, and she was becoming increasingly isolated, clinging onto a faint, but ultimately unrealistic hope in its possible salvation:

و فکر می کنم که باغچه را می شود به بیمارستان برد
من فکر می کنم...
من فکر می کنم...
من فکر می کنم...
و قلب باغچه در زیر آفتاب ورم کرده است
و ذهن باغچه دارد آرام آرام
از خاطرات سبز تهی می شود.

And I think the garden can be taken to hospital
I think . . .
I think . . .
I think . . .
And the garden's heart has swollen in the heat of the sun
And the garden's mind, little by little
Is becoming emptied of all green memories

Chapter 4

Forugh Farrokhzād's Romance with Her Muse

Rivanne Sandler

This study suggests that Forugh Farrokhzād's poetry of love may be read as an intimate dialogue with a muse. And further, that the muse is not an external agent, but rather the poet herself, the source of her creativity.[1] I am encouraged in a reading of Farrokhzād's poems as a 'courtship' of the muse by a study of nineteenth-century English women poets who concentrated on 'the craft of poetry' as a means of documenting themselves. They used their poetry to speak about the personal aspects of their lives. Poetry was their outlet for the expression of the 'self'.[2] Farrokhzād too, used poetry to articulate her personality. It is striking that she expresses an impetus for her art, which is similar to the women poets referred to above:

> Artistic endeavour is a kind of searching, to leave a legacy, leave something behind of 'self' . . . I don't seek anything in my poetry, except to find my undiscovered self.[3]

Although the idea of a muse as a companion in the poetic enterprise of self-expression stems from the example of nineteenth-century English women poets, the origin of my argument lies in Farrokhzād's own words. In an interview, Farrokhzād spoke about her experience of love as unlike the norm: '. . . the emotion that existed within me was different; *it shaped me and will complete me.*' [emphasis is mine][4]

This study begins with four lines from Farrokhzād's poem 'Panjereh' ('Window') from the posthumous volume *Imān biāvarim beh āghāz-e fasl-e sard* (*Let's Believe in the Coming of the Cold Season*),[5] which are quintessentially expressive of Farrokhzād's poetic impulse:

> When my life was nothing more
> Than the ticking of the clock on the wall
> I knew I must I must I must
> Love insanely

Any reader of Farrokhzād's body of work will appreciate that love is an absorbing theme for this poet. But the lines cited above place love against a backdrop of ticking clocks, which is a somewhat unusual context for this sublime emotion. Farrokhzād expands on her notion of a love that shapes and completes her:

> Today people measure love by the ticking of clocks. They document it, and keep a record of it, in order to make love respectable. They write laws for it, put a price on it and set its boundaries, ranging from loyalty to betrayal. But the emotion that existed within me was different; it shaped me and will complete me.[6]

In the poem 'Āsheqāneh' ('Lovingly') from the 1963 collection, *Tavallodi digar* (*Another Birth*),[7] Farrokhzād expresses ardent love, unfettered by social expectations. In the final lines of 'Āsheqāneh', she gives a distinctive role in the creation of a poem to a presence identified only as 'you':

> Oh you who mixed poetry's melody in me
> And made my poems so fervent
> You kindled such a feverish love in me
> You made certain my poems would smoulder

The poem is an ode to 'you' and to poetry inspired by love. However, what is striking in this passionate poem is the sense of 'you' as gender-less. 'You' is clearly the inspiration and the impetus for poetry. But the character that kindles 'feverish love', and inspires ardent poetry, is neither male nor female. If we do not automatically presume a male identity, 'you' is a neutral presence. In the poetic lines that opened this study ('I knew I must, I must, I must love insanely'), love is a remedy, but for what is not readily apparent.

Let us turn to the thrice repeated 'I must, I must, I must'. Farrokhzād has expressed a view of herself as 'obstinate and stubborn'.[8] But when she states,

'I must' in her poetry, Farrokhzād seems to be speaking from the perspective of a poet. Although her poems are, to Farrokhzād's mind, a response to a natural force within her, creativity is a difficult process. Her poetic creations are born of turmoil and conflict; they are the product of her determination and defiance. Farrokhzād speaks poetically about the strength of purpose that is crucial to the creative process:

> Why should I stop
> The four elements alone command me
> And the local government of the blind has no business
> In drafting my heart's constitution[9]

Farrokhzād uses the word 'must' in another poem in which she answers 'the friend's' question, 'Is it day or night?' with the gloomy words 'the evening never ends.' The poetic speaker hears 'far away voices from some strange dry plain/ wandering uncertain, and at loose ends.' She is resolved to give these rootless voices a home in her poetry. 'I must speak, I must', she says (*sokhani bāyad goft/ sokhani bāyad goft*).[10] This determination is obvious in Farrokhzād's verse generally. At the same time, many of Farrokhzād's poems are tinged with disappointment and a sense of failure. In the poem 'Panjereh', which opened this study, Farrokhzād protests society's compulsion to suppress spontaneity and to suffocate the rashness of love that is young at heart and free from guilt. She tries to resist the compulsion to curb the reckless love that is the inspiration for her poetry:

> They were blindfolding the childlike eyes of my love
> With the black handkerchief of the law
> And blood gushed
> From the pounding temples of my desire

Thus far, this argument has illustrated that love is a compelling poetic motivation for Farrokhzād. Most important, Farrokhzād has an idiosyncratic view of the act of loving as a defiant and bold assertion of herself against conservatism. The source of inspiration is her unique personality, liberated from social expectations:

I feel such a sense of loneliness. I feel that I will burst from being so choked up . . . Until you have reached your free self, comfortable and separate from all sorts of agreeable personalities, you won't amount to anything.[11]

Farrokhzād began her exploration of the creative life from the start of her career. From early on, she identified poetry as the central element of her life; or as she puts it, the love of her life. In a line from a poem which appears in her first collection of poems, *Asir (Captive)*, published in 1955, when the poet was twenty years old, Farrokhzād states unambiguously that poetry is her mate, her beloved:

> My friend is poetry and my sweetheart is poetry (*yār-e man she'r o deldār-e man she'r*).[12]

The beloved of the poem 'Ma'shuq-e man' ('The One I Love')[13] is no doubt a portrait of manliness and even of an ideal male lover. Readers may be tempted to supply a name for the beloved from the details of the poet's life. But if we examine the beloved in the context of the statements made by the poet about poetry, the beloved emerges convincingly as a manifestation of the poet's 'friend' and 'sweetheart', i.e., her poetry.

In an interview, Farrokhzād spoke about the artist's wish to defy extinction, by leaving a legacy of herself in her art:

> I think that artists have a kind of unconscious need to confront and resist extinction. Artistic endeavour is a kind of searching, to leave a legacy, leave something behind of 'self' and negate the meaning of death.[14]

At the beginning of 'Ma'shuq-e man', the beloved emerges as strong and dynamic, eliciting a profound and intense response from the poetic speaker. We meet a beloved with self-assurance and confidence, a force to be reckoned with:

> My beloved
> stands exposed, without shame
> looming powerfully
> like death

The beloved is quixotic, unmanageable and unreliable. Nevertheless, the poetic speaker is determined to pursue and to confine the beloved on paper:

> Unstable, slanting lines
> follow
> disobedient limbs
> in an unwavering design (*tarh*)

In the next lines, the poem characterizes the beloved as an inheritor of 'forgotten generations', which is reminiscent of Farrokhzād's comment about how poetry provides a link to the past and into the future:

> Poetry for me is like a window that opens up by itself whenever I turn to it. I sit there, I look, I sing, I shout, I cry, I mix with the images of the trees, and I know that on the other side of the window there is a space, and someone hears – someone who could exist two hundred years from now or three hundred years ago – it makes no difference, it is a means for communicating with being, with existence in its full meaning.[15]

The poem continues with the portrayal of the beloved as:

> Fiercely free
> Like a robust instinct
> Deep within an uninhabited island

In 1965, Farrokhzād was a participant in private and informal conversations with fellow poets Ahmad Shāmlu and Mehdi Akhavān-Sāles. In one of their talks together, Akhavān-Sāles spoke about the importance of metre:

> Obviously we cannot ignore the Persian poetical heritage of a thousand and some years with all those voluminous *divān*s . . . just because we have composed a few poems which may or may not have meter . . . if we do so the outside world will not respect our views.[16]

Farrokhzād's views on metre and on poetry generally are different from the views of her colleagues. She tends to play down the importance of form, which she views as 'a technical matter'. Form does not convey the personality of the poet; or, in Farrokhzād's words, form does not bear 'the poet's personal stamp'. She spoke positively about the contribution of Nimā Yushij (1895–1959) to the modern canon; but her admiration for him does not rest primarily on his innovation in form.[17] She focuses instead on the fact that only Nimā was, 'brave enough to deviate from, and confront tradition in an age when poetry meant something totally different'.[18] Nimā's example encouraged the spontaneity and free imagination that Farrokhzād values; she gives an example of a poet (without giving a name) who was inspired and 'wrote it down, and that is that.'[19]

Farrokhzād's colleagues were always respectful. But they were not at all bashful about expressing strongly held opinions on poetry. Their views are often at odds with those of Farrokhzād. Farrokhzād was by turns outspoken and modest in setting forth her opinions on poetry. For example, she claims unfamiliarity with 'the technical rules of classical poetry'.[20] But she made use of the classical *do-beyti* form early in her career. Reading through the conversations between the poets, it is clear that Farrokhzād appreciates a different kind of poetry, a personal view of poetry which she asserts to be 'natural'. To her mind, a 'natural' style of poetry is less contrived:

> Basically I am a simple person, and the poem comes to me naturally, I mean it comes to me through simple and ordinary words, just as I am speaking now. There is no complexity in it, i.e. it contains no . . . strange words. The form [of a poem] . . . follows a normal word order, i.e. subject, predicate . . . I have not tried to change the order to make the words conform to a particular meter. They have their own meter, the simplicity of their original form.[21]

Farrokhzād observes the rules of metre. But her use of metre mimics conversation.[22] Since a poem comes as naturally to her as conversation, 'this simplicity is reflected in the poem'.[23] In stressing the natural over the formal, Farrokhzād seems to be highlighting the intuitive nature of her poetry; and even perhaps, its inherent femininity. The poet Simin Behbahāni, born almost a decade earlier than Farrokhzād, defines her poetry as 'conversations with the heart'.[24] Her difficulty as a young poet, of finding a poetic language to adequately express her emotions does bear a comparison to Farrokhzād's poetic challenge.

Farrokhzād concedes that poetry needs shaping:

> A thought needs formulation . . . I believe in limitations . . . I believe that a work takes shape within limits and then comes into existence . . . one needs to work within a form . . . I believe in a container.[25]

But the type of poetry she preferred was unembellished; or as she puts it, 'unaffected':

> Since a poem comes so naturally, as naturally as my conversation, this simplicity is reflected in the poem.[26]

Elizabeth Barrett Browning has written of her struggle to find a poetic language that would serve as 'a marker of a personal encounter with the world.'[27] Farrokhzād too, sought the appropriate language for self-expression. She chose a straightforward, uncomplicated style which she terms 'conversational'.

Farrokhzād was prepared to use words that were not yet established as a language of poetry.[28]

The similarity between the beloved of 'Ma'shuq-e man' and Farrokhzād's prototype of poetry is striking. The beloved that emerges from the adjectives, metaphors and allusions of this poem is the epitome of simplicity. The beloved possesses 'the invariably clear intent of nature'. Furthermore, the beloved is like the wild lover Majnun, who (like Farrokhzād) loves recklessly, and insanely. The beloved:

> Wipes away
> The street's dust . . .
> With fragments of Majnun's tent

In a line from an early poem 'Ramideh' ('Disillusioned'),[29] Farrokhzād implores: 'Oh Lord, put an end to all this madness.' Although one commentator understands these words to address Farrokhzād's personal and artistic difficulties,[30] Farrokhzād does not appear to want to end the madness. Rather, she wishes to capture and preserve it in her art:

> I believe that every emotion should be articulated without condition and limitation, as you cannot place restraint on art. If you did, this would rob art of its essence.[31]

In the concluding lines of 'Ma'shuq-e man', the poem's descriptive language gives the impression of a beloved who is Farrokhzād's muse, her companion in the creation of the poetry to which she aspires:

> A man (*mardi*) in centuries past
> A memorial to the nobility of beauty
> . . .
> Speaking out with insolence and sentiment
> Loving genuinely
> Every atom of life . . .
> My beloved
> Is a simple human being (*ensān*)
> . . .
> Whom I
> Conceal
> In the forbidden land of marvels
> Like a final vestige of a depleted creed
> In the enfolding crucible of my breasts

Selected lines from a few of Farrokhzād's other poems will serve to further illustrate how poetry is, for Farrokhzād, a search for her muse, and ultimately herself. In 'Shab o havas' ('Night and Desire'),[32] composed in Ahvāz in 1953, when the poet was eighteen, the poetic speaker is submerged in memories of love. By turns patient and impatient, the poet waits for the night to end, anticipating the beloved's return. But the night is endless. The language of the last lines suggests that both the elusive flying creature (literally *parandeh*; the caged bird, is a classical poetic allusion to the captive human heart) and the poet's restless heart are despondent [emphasis is mine]:

> Perhaps *it* is sobbing
> On the roof of a wandering star

While the source of the poetic speaker's agitation is vague in 'Shab o havas', Farrokhzād can be direct in laying blame, if she so wishes. The circumstances of her broken heart are spelled out in 'Yādi az gozashteh' ('A Recollection of the Past').[33] Farrokhzād was no more than seventeen and living in Ahvāz, when she directly attributes her unhappiness to a person:

> There is a city near a river, and my heart
> Captive in the grasp of an arrogant man

In another early poem, 'Sho'leh-ye ramideh' ('The Dispirited Flame'),[34] once again we meet an inhibiting presence [emphasis is mine]:

> I shut both my burning eyes
> So as not to see *its* eyes
> So that the flame of *its* disturbed glance
> Won't scar my pounding heart

This poem may be read as a personal meditation on the muse's failure to cooperate:

> Through the long darkness
> The moon burning in the window
> In the night, her own solitary heart
> Bursting in her golden sob[35]

The moon, creativity's assistant, offers encouragement to the poet to blend, 'the scent of her silent kiss/with sounds of delight.' The poetic speaker tries madly (*divāneh-vār*) to pour 'love and desire/into the curls of that enchantress.' But the end of the poem's story is despair:

> I set fire to the harvest of your hope
> With a torch of regret and defeat
> Oh sinning, rebellious heart
> How to relieve this disquieting turmoil

These lines remind us of the poet's determination and will power. These qualities are necessary handmaidens in the work of creativity; but not always available, or dependable. 'Sho'leh-ye ramideh'[36] closes with a sense of failure. The weary 'bird of the heart' has failed in its effort to tell its tale of grief and sadness. On the same theme, the poem 'Anduh' ('Grief')[37] begins with a picture of the river Kārun snaking like the windswept ringlets of a young woman along the exposed shoreline. We are immediately in another world, where the light of day has faded to night, and the river's throbbing heart is calm in the moist darkness. The poetic speaker stares at the river's moonlit shore, off in the distance, and is transported by the enchantment of night:

> The distant vision of your grasp draws near, your scent wafts in
> The water glimmers with hope

But then everything is covered in darkness. The promise of love is unfulfilled:

> My wretched heart, so hopeful, so eager
> Broken in your grip, became a captive of love
> You left these parts to go your own way
> Oh crushed twig of my desire

Farrokhzād was thirty when she expressed disappointment in herself for not being more productive. She feels that she has not said everything she wants to say. She calls herself lazy; and puts the blame on her inability to maintain an optimistic outlook:

My work falls short of saying everything I want to say. I am lazy, quite lazy. I tend to veer away from an optimistic frame of mind and let myself flounder in negativity; this cannot help but affect my poetry. When I look at the number of poems in *Tavallodi digar*, I regret that four years of my life produced so little. I don't take out a scale and weigh my poetry. But I would have expected, and do expect more from myself. When I go to bed at night, I ask myself what I did that day. I could have been more productive and developed more quickly.[38]

At first reading, we wonder if the poet was not unduly harsh on herself for her lack of productivity. But she concludes her comments by saying that she wanted 'to live and experience new things.'[39] In the course of her conversations with her colleagues, Farrokhzād spoke about the life of the artist:

If one has become a poet . . . has discovered her own world, has an insight into the fundamental elements of life, and has discovered what she thinks about life, then any subject can become a poem. She can write anything on the page and turn it into a poem . . . Everything is poetry. The first step is to become a poet. . . . The poet is a creature who . . . how can I put it . . . is someone who understands her own weaknesses, and is able to look at herself from a distance. She has found a perspective on her own problems and the questions of life and attained a certain awareness, that is, she has become a philosopher.[40]

She is accepting of human frailty. She highlights the artist's need to be self-aware and to understand life as it is. Farrokhzād sets high standards for herself. She could not always count on herself to produce. She is not always the poet she wishes to be. ''Arusak-e kuki' ('The Wind-up Doll'),[41] which is usually read as the portrait of a frivolous female, serves this study as a portrait of the 'anti-muse'. Farrokhzād's mechanical doll is her creative nemesis, because she moves at the whim of others and says what others wish to hear.[42] Throughout her career, Farrokhzād jousted with several black knights to express her thoughts sincerely; to write the straightforward, ardent, personal (and womanly) poetry she values. She worked in a culture of poetic expectations of metre and form that apparently did not suit her poetic needs. She wrote outside the circle of acceptable subject matter for a woman. She challenged her own self-doubts, because poetry was her way of saying 'I am here':

A poet [is the kind of person who] establishes her existence by writing poetry. Poetry says this was my life. Poetry gives meaning to existence (*she'r beh budan-ash o hasti-ash ma'nā mi-dahad*).[43]

Farrokhzād regards the age of thirty as a good time of life. But in her mind, her poetry is 'much younger' (*javān-tar*).[44] The poet continually searches for revitalization. Her 'hands and lips' desire the solace of creativity. In the poem, 'Bād mārā khvāhad bord', the sounds of the night and of trees swaying in the breeze offer hope of transport out of the darkness. The moon, under optimum conditions a friend to creativity, in this poem is 'red and troubled' and does not offer comfort. The possibility of limitless vistas offered by the window in this poem permits 'the unknown' to stare at 'you and me through the window.'[45]

The poet asks 'the embodiment of green (literally: green from head to foot)' to 'brand my hands with the burning memory of your green hands.' It is only when the poet's tools of trade (literally 'hands and lips') adequately meet the artistic challenge, only then will the wind carry 'us' to the realm of the unusual. This poem suggests a love relationship. But the extent of the personal frustration suggests a loss of even greater proportion. The page beckons. But the poet is unable to step over the boundaries of her despair, to write.

The long poem, 'Let's Believe in the Beginning of the Cold Season', in the volume which opened this analysis and was published after Farrokhzād's death, covers moments of happiness and sadness in the poet's life. Commentators have viewed Farrokhzād's later poems as more crafted examples of her poetic genius.[46] But this poem seems to carry on the dialogue which began in her early poetry. This final poem is a coming to terms with a new season in the poet's creative life:

> I am this
> Woman
> . . .
> On the threshold of a cold season
> Beginning to understand a life diminished by time

There is a tone of mourning throughout this poem, especially for the passage of time. The poet asks herself whether artistic creativity outlives the end of the natural biological cycle. The language of this poem has many allusions to the conclusion of the female capacity to create. The poet seems to question an aging muse:[47]

> Will the ringing doorbell lead me to hope once again for the voice (sedā)[48]
> I am cold and I know
> that of the wild poppy's fantasies of red
> a few drops of blood

will be all that remains[49]
Oh friend, most unique of friends (*Ey yār, ey yegāneh-tarin yār*)
What if the wine is several years' old[50]
How kind you were oh friend, Oh most intimate of friends
How kind you were when you . . . carried me through the oppressive
darkness to the pasture of love[51]

The shimmering, beckoning stars of so many of Farrokhzād's poems are, in
this poem, fashioned out of cardboard. Green hands, the vibrant hands of
creation which enliven other poems, are in this poem withered or as
cumbersome as concrete. The candle's flame is viewed through 'the
unblemished memory of the window.'[52]

Love is no longer an intimate friend. Love is a raw sore: 'All my wounds
are from love / from love, love, love'[53]:

Will I comb my curls again in the wind
Will I ever again plant pansies in the flowerbox
Will I place geraniums against the sky beyond the window
Will I dance again on goblets
Will the doorbell's ring lead me to hope for the voice (*sedā*) again[54]

Do black clouds really expect the sunlight's generosity[55]

What is silence, what, what, oh most intimate of friends
Except unspoken words[56]

And finally, a reaffirmation of the life of the artist:

I remain forever, by speaking, but [only] the language of sparrows
The language of life are sentences flowing from the celebration of nature
The language of sparrows, by which I mean the spring, a leaf, spring
The language of sparrows, by which I mean the breeze, a fragrance, a
gentle wind
The language of sparrows dies in the factory[57]

In the final lines of the poem, the candle slowly burns down but is confident
that it will not fade away completely:

In the dying candle
There is a bright secret that

Only the last of the burnt-out candle knows best

. . .

Next year . . . there will be blossoming oh friend, oh dearest of friends
Let us believe in the beginning of the cold season[58]

It seems the journey of discovering the self would never end as long as
Farrokhzād asks herself:

Who is this person with the crown of love on her head?[59]

Conclusion

We expect an artist to construct a persona for public consumption, if only in
the interest of self-preservation. Forugh Farrokhzād's many interviews attest
to her interest in documenting herself. But an astute and shrewd observer of
life, she knew how to utilize this medium. She is adept at presenting herself
as she wished to be seen; and making excuses for herself, according to the
demands of the occasion. In the following comments, Farrokhzād confirms
the poetic identity she established for herself by distancing herself from other
poets:

> Being a poet is being human. I know some people whose day-to-day actions
> have no relation to their poems, I mean they are only poets when they are
> writing poetry. And then it is finished. And once again they transform into
> a greedy, hungry, oppressive, narrow-minded miserable needy person. So I
> don't believe in what they have to say. I value the reality of life and when
> these gentlemen make fists with their hands and protest and scream at the
> top of their lungs – I mean in their poetry or writings – I am disgusted and
> I don't believe they are being truthful. I think, please don't let it be me that
> they are protesting . . .[60]

Farrokhzād took every opportunity to assert her poetry as an honest, a sincere
and 'natural' expression of herself. As one example of many:

> Nothing is important in life because nothing is true and everlasting . . . It is
> only our work that remains, and this work is the essence of ourselves.[61]

Her oft-repeated assertion of the 'genuineness' of her poetry supports a reading of her poems as self-revealing and spoken without guile (that is, over and above the obfuscation of poetic language). Her relationship with poetry, her dearly loved friend, underpins this study's idea of the muse as her companion in the creative process. The relationship, which Farrokhzād herself suggests, is the basis for reading her poems as segments in a documentary about her creative journey.

In her conversations with her colleagues, Farrokhzād stresses the importance of content over form. Rather than spend time speaking about the look of a poem, she preferred to dwell on 'what's in a poem.'[62]

'Form is a requirement of all art . . . but the content is what makes a poem into a work of art.'[63]

When she was pressed by her colleagues to say what sort of content she considers worthy of poetic expression, she declined to be specific: 'I'm not going to specify any particular subject.'[64] She concedes that poetry needs shaping:

> A thought needs formulation . . . I believe in limitations . . . I believe that a work takes shape within limits and then comes into existence . . . one needs to work within a form . . . I believe in a container.[65]

But content makes a poem personal. The language of a poem also contributes to its personality. Like Elizabeth Barrett Browning, whose efforts to find a poetic language to serve as 'a marker of a personal encounter with the world'[66] began the argument of this study, Farrokhzād too searched for a poetic language that was pertinent to herself:

> For me, the word is supreme. It is the language of a poem that determines the form and the rhythm of the poem, not the other way round.[67]

Farrokhzād was a believer in the creative potential of conversations. She tells her colleagues that a 'face-to-face exchange of ideas and beliefs . . . contributes to our growth . . .'[68] This study has explored Farrokhzād's relationship with her muse. In an environment that was not always (if ever) conducive to her creativity, the muse mirrors her 'self', her poetic aspiration.[69]

This study actually had its beginning many years ago at an academic conference. A Farrokhzād specialist repeatedly used the adjective 'sincere' to characterize Farrokhzād's poetry. There is no question about the genuineness and authenticity of Farrokhzād's poetry. How then to account for a long-standing uncertainty about Farrokhzād's beloved. The love poems seem to me to be descriptions of generic and habitual situations and circumstances which are real enough. But the beloved does not emerge, at least to me, as a fully developed component of the moment. This study was my attempt to 'find' Farrokhzād's beloved. By looking at the object of the poet's desire through the prism of the muse/self relationship, both the poet's beloved and the poet herself have come to life.

Chapter 5

Bewildered Mirror: Mirror, Self and World in the Poems of Forugh Farrokhzād

Leila Rahimi Bahmany

Mirror imagery plays a crucial role in the poetry of Forugh Farrokhzād. The poet's use of mirror imagery is not limited to the recurrent, traditional, or even clichéd images and symbolism found in classical Persian literature. Farrokhzād manages to move beyond the traditional and establish herself as a feminine, modern and anti-transcendentalist poet. Through the mirror, Farrokhzād expresses her desires, fears, anxieties, doubts and many other feelings. Her psychology of mirroring undergoes radical transformations indicative of her personal and poetic development. An overview of mirror imagery in the entirety of her work shows her feminine history of disturbed ego formation and at the same time her artistic development. This is because almost any psychological stance of a woman can arguably be interpreted in reference to her relationship with her reflection in the mirror.[1]

The mirror changed its meaning and function in Farrokhzād's poetry markedly at different stages in her life. The titles of her poetry collections reveal much about Farrokhzād's personal life: the first and second volumes are entitled *Captive*, and *The Wall*, respectively, while the third and fourth collections, published during psychologically turbulent phases of her life, are entitled *Rebellion* and *Rebirth*. It could be argued that there is a trend to be detected in Farrokhzād's choice of titles, which seem to reflect how she felt at a given stage in her life. It would be spurious (if not impossible) to draw absolute, clear-cut lines of demarcation between these phases, though, since she oscillated back and forth at psychologically critical times.

For Farrokhzād, the mirror was a powerful tool for negation, creation, rejection and, ultimately, for the realization and presentation of her 'self' in these different phases. Like many other modern female writers and poets, Farrokhzād demonstrates her heavy reliance on the mirror and mirroring when defining her true self and also for relating her subjectivity to the world around her.[2]

In this essay, I study only some of the most illuminating samples of mirror imagery in the poems of Forough Farrokhzād. Whether Farrokhzād was consciously engineering her mirror imageries or unconsciously resorting to them is inconsequential to this study.

Captive to the male gaze

In the quest for her true self, Farrokhzād initially starts out as a captive of the male gaze. In this initial phase, she has internalized the male-defined concept of woman as a mere object, whose totality can be presented within the frames of a mirror. She is a woman seeking a man's desire. Early in her poetic life, she is completely dependent on men for the realization of her self and for her position in the world. In this regard, her specular image gains an overwhelming significance. For her the mirror functions as a replacement for an absent lover and his gaze. She uses the mirror primarily as an instrument to verify how she appears to men. For a woman who has no other self outside its confines, the mirror can determine her destiny in society, since everyone (including the woman herself) relies on that specular image for the definition and evaluation of her identity.

This usage of mirror represents Farrokhzād's initial stage of feminine imitation and internalization of patriarchal gender definitions, as well as the masculine conceptualization of a woman as pure object. Accordingly, the mirror is considered a tool for self-creation, whose end is to gratify the male's desire and his gaze. Although Farrokhzād finds this reliance on men and the male definition of her feminine identity far from desirable, she is still unconscious of this structuring and, instead of rejecting this conceptualization, she rejects the mirror, her image and thereby her very self through the act of breaking the mirror:

تا دو چشمش به رخم حیران نیست

به چکار آیدم این زیبایی

بشکن این آینه را ای مادر

حاصلم چیست ز خودآرایی

As long as his eyes are not amazed by my face,
What use is this beauty to me?
O Mother, break this mirror
What do I gain by adorning myself?[3]

In this poem Farrokhzād expresses her melancholic longing after her beloved and his gaze; the beloved who has deserted her without even sending a letter. In her misery, the poetic persona – who is Farrokhzād herself – obsessively seeks the reason for this desertion. In her frustration she asks herself the pathetic question: Why has he stopped watching her? This shows the importance of the male gaze to her and her reliance on it for her happiness. By posing the rhetorical question as to the futility of a mirror in a context where the male gaze is absent, Farrokhzād intends to emphasize the certainty of the fact and its acknowledgement on the part of her readers. To rephrase it in the terminology of speech act theory, the 'illocutionary force' of the rhetorical question is not to inquire after information but to assert the information already acknowledged.

The mirror is as a tool for her to observe how she would appear to him. Now that the mirror has turned into something useless without his gaze, she wishes it to be broken. In a context where a woman is defined only through the reflected image, that is to say, a context which equates a woman with her specular image, wishing to break a mirror can also be interpreted as self-destructive behavior. Asking her mother to be the agent of breaking the mirror is significant. The mother is invoked here as the perpetuator of this tradition by serving her as a model and by teaching her how she should think and how she should behave.

In her poem 'Ārezu' ('The Wish'), Farrokhzād employs the image of the mirror of the heart to express her wish for her beloved's presence and physical intimacy with him. Mirror imagery has been recurrently used in both non-mystical and mystical classical Persian literature. In non-mystical usage of this metaphor, the sincerity of the mirror in reflecting an exact image has been drawn upon to liken the heart to a mirror. In Islamic mystical thought, it is believed that the pure heart can reflect the divine light of God. Through self-indulgence, however, this mirror gathers rust, hampering its ability to reflect the divine light. The perfect, spotless polish of this mirror is maintained only when the seeker succeeds in attaining the state of absolute self-annihilation and self-effacement.[4]

In this poem, instead of being lit by the divine light, Farrokhzād wishes her heart to be lighted by the light of an earthly love:

كاش چون آينه روشن مى شد
دلم از نقش تو و خنده تو
صبحگاهان به تنم مى لغزيد
گرمى دست نوازنده تو

I wish that my heart
would, like a mirror, be lit by
your image and your smile
That each morning the warmth of your caressing hand
would touch my body[5]

In the simile she employs, the image of her beloved and his laughter function like daylight upon the otherwise darkened mirror of her heart. Sincerity, self-less receptiveness and brilliancy are considered qualities common to both the mirror and her heart. The mirror is meant to reflect the external world, but here Farrokhzād uses her poetic imagination to have the mirror depict her interiority, the internal world into which she interjects her beloved. In this poem (as in many others), Farrokhzād is concerned with her bodily existence and transforms the notion of a divine mirror of the heart to that of a mundane mirror; that of spiritual love, to a this-worldly love. Farrokhzād often comes across in her poetry as anti-transcendentalist; she accepts her physicality and tends to reject the transcendentalism so much adored in classical Persian literature. Indeed, in some of her poems Farrokhzād glorifies what is down-to-earth.[6]

The stranger in the mirror

The metaphorical image of the mirror of the heart originated in ancient Neoplatonic thought, and the twofold division of macrocosm and microcosm, where one reflects the other. According to this tradition (which was subsequently developed by Muslim mystics), the whole of creation, in particular human beings, are mirrors in which God sees himself. God, who is beautiful and loves beauty, has brought creation into being in order to reflect his own beauty. Creation was necessary for God's beauty to be revealed and reflected, and man is considered potentially the most perfect being mirroring this beauty.[7]

Farrokhzād depicts man as a mirror of God in her poem 'Bandegi' ('Servitude'). However, the poet uses this poem to convey a rebellious, one might even say blasphemous meaning. 'Servitude' is a long poem of some four hundred lines, filled with Qur'anic allusions; it is an apostrophe to God. In this poem, the speaker complains to God and questions his grace. Like the mirror of the mystics, she is transformed into a mirror devoid of any agency, subjectivity or distinctive identity of its own. The speaker is utterly passive, having no will to act, nor any control over her fate. To her, man is created and doomed to life and death for no other reason than to be 'the manifestation of your [God's] power'.[8] But in contrast to the mystics, this passivity and lack of will for the speaker is not a source of absolute peace and consolation. Sometimes she sees reflected in this mirror God's 'power', sometimes his 'injustice' and sometimes his 'self-worshiping eyes'. To Farrokhzād, God has created her as a mirror out of solipsism, out of sheer narcissism, just to see himself in her:

خویش را آیینه ای دیدم تهی از خویش
هر زمان نقشی در آن افتد به دست تو
گاه نقش قدرتت، گه نقش بیدادت
گاه نقش دیدگان خودپرست تو

I saw myself a mirror devoid of my self
At any moment an image falls upon it by your hand
Sometimes the image of your power, sometimes your injustice
And sometimes the image of your self-worshiping eyes[9]

Farrokhzād goes on to enumerate many other proofs of God's vanity. Servitude here has a twofold significance. Not only has God created her as a passive servant, but he is also himself subservient to his own name and his own glory, by virtue of having created the world to function as a passive mirror:

تو چه هستی؟ بنده نام و جلال خویش
دیده در آیینه دنیا جمال خویش
هردم این آیینه را گردانده تا بهتر
بنگری در جلوه های بی زوال خویش

What are you? A slave to your own name and majesty
He has seen in the mirror of the world the reflection of his own beauty
At every moment you turn this mirror around
to better gaze upon your immortal manifestations[10]

For Farrokhzād, God is continually busy changing his creation, as if playing at having different perspectives of himself reflected in it. Again, this change of mirrors has its origin in the mystical belief that all creation and its particles function as countless mirrors, all reflecting different aspects of one unity.[11]

It is widely believed in Iranian culture that women turn to the mirror merely out of solipsistic self-love and pure vanity, but Farrokhzād uses the mirror in her later poetry to convey her painful experiences of anxiety, pain, shock and terror. Like many other modern female writers, she expresses through her use of mirror imagery the problematics of her female subjectivity, her identity crisis, and the lack of a secure, stable, and acknowledged subjectivity. At times of psycho-emotional crisis, when Farrokhzād finds no other proof of her subjectivity or true identity within society, she turns to the mirror for answers. Farrokhzād does so in the hope that the mirror will relieve her of painful inner conflicts and give her an existential proof of her being and its essential quality.[12]

For Farrokhzād, confrontation with the mirror image raises doubt and a sense of bewilderment in the essence of her being – a bewilderment that she attributes to the mirror. La Belle observes, 'when a woman feels a disunity between herself and the image in the mirror, it is often a sign of revolt or the beginning of a psychological disorientation', whereas for a man, 'the split is normative'.[13] At times when Farrokhzād turns to the mirror in her existential angst, she is shockingly confronted with something unknown, unnamed – something monstrous. As she says in her poem, 'Sedā'i dar shab' ('A Sound at Night'):

جستم از جا و در آیینه گیج

بر خود افکندم با شوق نگاه

آه، لرزید لبانم از عشق

تار شد چهره آیینه ز آه

شاید او وهمی را می نگریست

I jumped up, and in the bewildered mirror
cast a look at myself with eagerness
Ah, my lips trembled with love
The mirror's face darkened from my sigh
Maybe she (*u*) was looking at an illusion?[14]

The whole atmosphere evoked in this poem is one of extreme loneliness; the speaker longs for companionship. The mirror is personified, and the speaker's bewilderment is projected onto it. Here the subject and the object (the poet and her mirror image) change places, and there is a shift in mood parallel to this shift in perspective, from one of enthusiasm and hope, to one of disillusionment and melancholy. The mirror for the speaker becomes the agent, a powerful tool capable of changing her feelings. Here, as in some other poems, Farrokhzād conveys her inability to recognize and acknowledge her image, partly through the grammar of the poem. Despite the use of the first person singular pronoun *man* ('I') throughout the poem, Farrokhzād, at this point, adopts the third person pronoun *u* ('she' or 'he') to indicate the exteriority of her female self-conception and her self-detachment.[15] Farrokhzād lacks a sense of 'self-continuity' because she is not sure if her existence extends beyond her own experience. The mirror is obfuscated by her sigh. It is her inner darkness that dims this external apparatus. The interjection *āh* ('Ah') and the mirror are frequently paired in classical Persian literature. The ancient mirrors were actually made of polished steel, iron or some metal amalgam. Given mirrors were traditionally made of metal, sighing onto them caused mirrors to rust, and they darkened with the humidity.[16]

Through her constant oscillation between the mirror and the window, Farrokhzād demonstrates her consciousness of the mirror's complex reciprocity with one's self-image, identity and worldview. The 'alienated', 'frozen' and 'reversed' image in the mirror (to draw upon Lacan's terminology) serves to bridge the gap between the subject and the world. The function of the mirror stage, inaugurated by the child's initial self-recognition of her mirror image, is to establish a relation between the two dialectical worlds. In Freudian terminology (which Lacan turns to), these two worlds are known as the *Innenwelt*, the imaginary interior space that the 'I' occupies, and the *Umwelt*, the external physical world, in which the living human subject is situated. Lacan holds that this initial recognition and identification of the image in the mirror, which is an introduction to a process of later identifications, is essentially a 'misrecognition'. Lacan emphasizes the essential role of the mirror image or 'virtual complex' in the development of the human psyche and the individual's entrance into social and linguistic identity.[17]

In her poetry, Farrokhzād is in constant fluctuation between the world inside and the world outside. The blurring of the distinction between these two worlds (normally represented by the mirror or an opening such as a window) reveals this interaction in her poetry. For instance, in the poem 'Didār dar shab' ('Meeting at Night'), all through the night the speaker is involved in a desperate dialogue with an 'astonished face' (supposedly her interior self), which she spies through a shutter, a window or a crack:[18]

و چهرهٔ شگفت
از آنسوی دریچه به من گفت
«حق با کسی است که می بیند
من مثل حس گمشدگی وحشت آورم
اما خدای من
آیا چگونه میشود از من ترسید؟»

And the astonished face
from the other side of the shutter said:
'Whoever sees is right
I am terrifying like the feeling of being lost
But, my God,
How is it possible to be afraid of me?'[19]

Seeing this 'astonished face' through a shutter fills the speaker with an overwhelming sense of horror. It is the sense of being lost – the realization of the
fragmented and detached self – that fuels her panic. In her horror, the speaker
asks another rhetorical and ambiguous question: 'How is it possible to be
afraid of me?' Are others afraid of her, or is it she who is afraid of herself? At
this point, again, Farrokhzād opts for the gender-free third person singular *u*
('s/he'), despite having adopted the first person *man* ('I') elsewhere in the
poem. This hints at the disparity between the self and self-image, and also
between the self and body, which makes the speaker (and by extension
Farrokhzād) feel so lost and terrified.

This omnipresent stranger, this unknown alienated 'I', declares herself to
be dead: 'Believe me/ I am not alive' (*bāvar konid/man zendeh nistam*). La
Belle asserts: 'To exist in multiplicity is, in a sense, not to exist at all because
self-conception requires some conviction in the singularity of one's being.'[20]
Further on in the same poem we read:

حق با شماست
من هیچگاه پس از مرگم
جرئت نکرده ام در آئینه بنگرم
و آنقدر مرده ام
که هیچ چیز مرگ مرا دیگر
ثابت نمیکند

You're right
I have never dared to look
in the mirror after my death
And I am so dead,
that nothing proves
my death anymore.[21]

Farrokhzād not only considers her real self dead, she extends this lifelessness
to the world outside and to others. Later in the same poem, she depicts people
as corpses, calling them 'pale statues' (*mujassameh-hā-ye parideh-rang*).
The speaker shivers, 'splits', 'disintegrates' and extends her begging hands

forwards through the cracks. Fantasies of corporeal disintegration, decomposition and dismemberment, which we find expressed in this poem (and some others), bear similarities to fantasies manifested in the dreams of depressive and neurotic people. According to Lacan, before the identification of the self in the mirror, the child conceives of himself as a *corps morcelé,* as an 'aggregate' in a 'fragmented body image', or 'a body in bits and pieces.' With the identification and internalization of his mirror image, the child can, for the first time, conceive an image of his body in its *gestalt*; a totality, a whole body. But at times of crisis the disturbed subject regresses to the previous infantile state.

In a letter to her ex-husband, Parviz Shāpur, Farrokhzād expresses her feelings towards herself and her body thus:

Today I was watching myself in the mirror. Now, gradually *I fear my face.* Am I the same Forugh? Am I the same Forugh who used to stand in front of the mirror from morning till night and make herself into a hundred faces and was contented with it? Are these sick eyes, this broken and gaunt face and these untimely lines beneath eyes and on the forehead mine? . . . My dear Parviz it is not easy to persist. Like a termite, desperation is turning my soul into dust . . . I don't know where I will end up with these *sick nerves* . . . If I don't leave here I will go insane . . . Sometimes it is as if *I collapse into myself.* While walking in the street, I feel as if *my body turns into dust and collapses from my sides* . . . no longer can I deceive myself. My soul is burning in the hell of distress and I am gazing into its ashes with desperation. . . . [Italics mine][22]

Here Farrokhzād overtly talks about the fundamental changes in her relationship with her mirror image. The fragmentation of the self is often translated into the fragmentation of her whole world, where she is unable to find any logical relationship among the exterior realities. As revealed in many of her poems, Farrokhzād sees a continual process of disintegration and degeneration working its way in any outside or inside phenomenon.[23]

The saviour in the mirror

After passing through the tumultuous developmental stages of the non-recognition of her image; the consequences of constant social non-recognition; uncertainty over the reality of her self or of her image; fragmented multiple self; fragmented body image indicative of a split personality; a highly disturbed and alienated self; and rejection of the mirror, Farrokhzād finally reaches the stage of acknowledging the power of the mirror to construct a unified female identity, and as a tool for self-realization. Rising above the disturbing division between her self and her image, the poet aims at a more promising unity. With this fusion of multiplicity into a unity, there emerges a sense of rebirth.

In this process of rebirth, the mirror turns into a primary tool for self-realization. It becomes a means of empowerment, rather than something that terrifies or disheartens. Now the mirror is a liberated and liberating tool. The mirror has finally liberated itself from its culturally infused associations, and it liberates others by becoming a means for self-awareness. From her fourth collection – *Tavallodi digar* (*Rebirth*) – onward, Farrokhzād becomes a 'new woman'[24] by constructing herself, through visual and mental reflection, as an independent female will. The development of profound self-involvement, and consciousness of the corporeal being are at the very heart of the feminist call, a call that appeals for the heroic act of reconstituting the psychology of the mirror experience within the boundaries of a self-conception closely associated with a woman's reflected image.

The poem, 'Imān biāvarim beh āghāz-e fasl-e sard' ('Let Us Believe in the Beginning of the Cold Season'), starts with the words, 'And this is me' *(va in man-am)*, in which Farrokhzād presents herself from a first person point of view.[25] The poem can be read as an open declaration of her maturation, of her attaining unto an understanding of the world, an understanding of the 'earth's contaminated existence', and of her self; of her 'impotence' as 'a lonely woman' at the beginning of a cold season. The mirrors are holding mourning ceremonies, since she is approaching old age and death. She has lost her illusions by experiencing life, and now those experiences have turned pale with the passage of time; these experiences are now things of the past. Through the use of a mirror, Farrokhzād objectifies herself and her despair, and through this objectification she gains knowledge over both her despair and her true self:

چرا نگاه نکردم؟
...
و آنکسی که نیمه ی من بود، به درون نطفه ی من باز گشته بود
و من در آینه میدیدمش،
که مثل آینه پاکیزه بود و روشن بود

Why didn't I look?
...
And the one who was my half had returned within my seed
I was looking at her/him in the mirror:
clean, clear, and bright as the mirror[26]

In patriarchal cultures, women are robbed of their independent identity and their authentic voice. Patriarchal cultures socialize women to be self-effacing. Women are forced to present an image that has been dictated to them, acting as obedient daughters and wives, as sacrificial mothers, and if they insist on having any voice at all, that voice must echo those already well-established patriarchal voices. In such cultures, women rely on their specular image to affirm their presence, their existence and their identity. Spencer remarks that within those cultures where 'the male gaze is perceived as an agent of objectification and nullification of feminine identity, [. . .] it seems natural to turn to a feminine gaze for affirmation.'[27] This is why women's activity in gazing and contemplating their mirror image becomes more 'an act of self-exploration and discovery', rather than 'an act of self-expression.'[28] The female gaze at one's specular image can lay the foundation for constructing one's agency and also for developing one's authentic voice.

In 'Panjareh' ('Window'), Farrokhzād maintains that a single window (and nothing more) is sufficient for her as an opening to understanding and awareness:

یک پنجره برای من کافیست
یک پنجره به لحظه ی آگاهی و نگاه و سکوت
...
از آینه بپرس
نام نجات دهنده ات را
آیا زمین که زیر پای تو می لرزد
تنهاتر از تو نیست؟

One window is enough for me,
a window to the moment of awareness, seeing, and silence

. . .

Ask the mirror
the name of your savior
Isn't the ground that trembles under your feet
lonelier than you?[29]

Here the mirror has reversed its function for Farrokhzād, from her initial conceptualization of it. The mirror is not a tool of captivation. On the contrary, it is a means of liberation. It is now a vehicle of the truth, though not in the mystical sense. It has become a vehicle for self-reflection. The poet oscillates between the window and the mirror as the means whereby to gain 'awareness' (āgāhi). The mirror helps in the formation of self, and therefore the concept of the saviour as the 'other' is categorically rejected. This is also emphasized by the final rhetorical question in the poem about the loneliness of the earth. It is a direct appeal to the reader in general, but is of particular poignancy for women.

Farrokhzād, in her earlier poetry, was not oblivious to the temporal dimension of the mirror. After all, the mirror registers multiple changes in what appears before it with the passage of time. Here the issue is not that of identification or ego formation, nor that of the narcissistic gaze, but rather that of reidentification. The individual is reassured that she closely resembles the person who last glanced at herself in the mirror. She traces in her mirror the painful advance of old age, of physical degeneration. When she turns to the mirror and is confronted with her mother's image instead of her own, it signifies the ability of the mirror to map the passage of time and the onset of old age. It also gives a sense of destiny, which is usually an unhappy one; the implication is that the young woman is doomed to the same destiny as that of her mother and grandmother before her. In other words, the viewer is set to perpetuate the same tradition of self-effacement.

In her poem 'Beh āftāb salāmi do-bāreh khvāham dād' ('I Shall Salute the Sun Once Again'), Farrokhzād draws upon the temporality of the mirror to show that she has attained a certain peace with her self and her world. Although she is alarmed at the approach of old age and death, she seems to have peacefully accepted it, even to the point of saluting it. After her 'pangs of growing' and passing through 'seasons of drought'; after greeting the 'stream' running through her, the 'clouds' which are her 'lengthy thoughts', the 'painful growth of aspens' and 'the flock of crows', the speaker salutes her mother:

به مادرم که در آئینه زندگی می کرد

و شکل پیری من بود

و به زمین، که شهوت تکرار من، درون ملتهبش را

از تخمه های سبز می انباشت ـ سلامی، دوباره خواهم داد

shall salute my mother
who lived in the mirror
and was the image of my old age
and the earth, whose lust to repeat me
crammed its burning inside with green seeds[30]

Self-mirroring

Apart from the mirror, for Farrokhzād, the only other alternative means to prove and sustain her existence is her writing. This is because, for any such artistic production, there must be subjectivity. Thus, through a sustained act of creation and re-creation, the poet is able to reassure herself of her continual existence. For her, texts perform similar psychological functions to mirrors. They remain the two semiotic modes – the catoptric and the linguistic – for her consciousness and objectification of self. By objectifying herself either in the glass or on a piece of paper, Farrokhzād gains self-knowledge; she relies heavily on reflection – specular or mental – for her sense of being. As La Belle explains, 'Texts and mirrors can perform similar psychological functions for women, particularly during periods in their lives when objectification and consciousness of self becomes necessary'.[31]

Farrokhzād herself has articulated that poetry is an opening to her 'existence'; something through which she can justify her being, and discover her self:

> Poetry is a means for communicating with being and existence in their general sense. The advantage of it is that when one composes a poem one can claim 'I exist' or 'I existed.' Otherwise, how can one claim one's own being? I do not search for anything in my poems. Rather, I discover 'myself' in my own poems.[32]

Self-realization for Farrokhzād is closely related to her self-narration. Non-productivity for the poet equates with non-existence. This is also because, as Cixous explains in 'The Laugh of the Medusa', her manifesto on feminine writing, women write from the imaginary, from where the 'unconscious is speaking':

> To write. An act which will not only 'realize' the de-censored relation of woman to her sexuality, to her womanly being, giving her access to her native strength; it will give her back her goods, her pleasures, her organs, her immense bodily territories which have been kept under seal; it will tear her away from the super-egoized structure in which she has always occupied the place reserved for the guilty (guilty of everything, guilty at every turn: for having desires, for not having any, for being rigid, for being 'too hot'; for not being both at once; for being too motherly and not enough; for having children and for not having any; for nursing and for not nursing . . .) – tear her away by means of this research, this job of analysis and illumination, this emancipation of the marvelous text of her self that she must urgently learn to speak.[33]

For Farrokhzād, producing an artistic work, especially one of a highly personal and subjective nature, becomes like seeing one's reflection in the mirror, an existential necessity. In her poetry, she expresses her fears, anxieties, desires, pleasures and her experiences. These objectified feelings on the paper become a source of knowledge for her. Put very simply: Farrokhzād mirrors herself through her writing.

Despite the rich body of mirror imagery in classical Persian literature, Forugh Farrokhzād proves that her grasp of the mirror phenomenon (and its functions) was not confined to the model of her literary forefathers or foremothers. Farrokhzād's use of mirror imagery remains mainly feminine in that she depends on it for the realization and definition of her true self and also for that of her worldview. In her developmental journey, she portrays her diverse and even contradictory personal experiences by means of the mirror. In her earliest poetry, the mirror serves as a tool by which she prepares herself for the male gaze. Farrokhzād relies on this male gaze and the male desire that drives it for a happy consciousness of her existence. Her painful growth out of this stage is exposed by her problematic relationship with her mirror and mirroring. Ultimately, Farrokhzād comes to realize the constructive nature of the mirror at a stage where she is peacefully embracing her bygone 'pale experiences' and approaching old age and death. For Farrokhzād, poetry is also a mirror on which she depends as much for her self-discovery as for relating that self to her world. Poetry, like her mirrors, remains a site of subject formation.

Chapter 6

Personal Rebellion and Social Revolt in the Works of Forugh Farrokhzād: Challenging the Assumptions

Kamran Talattof

By making connections between Forugh Farrokhzād's aesthetic efforts and her narrative of life and by detailing the ways her approach to personal and social issues changed as she espoused different philosophies, this essay challenges a number of common assumptions about her work and her notion of the self and gender. It will question the accuracy of the long-standing division of Farrokhzād's poetry into two distinct categories: unrefined personal poetry presented in her early works – *Asir* (The Captive, 1955); *Divār* (The Wall, 1956); and *'Esyān* (Rebellion, 1958) – and 'valuable' social poetry presented in her last two works – *Tavallodi digar* (*Another Birth*, 1963) and *Imān biāvarim beh āghāz-e fasl-e sard* (*Let Us Believe in the Beginning of the Cold Season,* 1973).[1] Furthermore, this analysis rejects the notion that Farrokhzād's thematic and stylistic shifts were the result of her acquaintance with renowned author and filmmaker, Ebrāhim Golestān, as has been asserted repeatedly over the years.[2] In addition, the essay disputes the notion that Farrokhzād's poetry represented a feminist discourse, as expressed by a number of critics in recent years.[3] Finally, the article questions another repeated notion that Farrokhzād faced extraordinary obstacles, criticism and suffering in her poetic career because she was a woman.[4] These inquiries will point to the patriarchal or one-dimensional thinking that influences the construction of a woman's life story.

Many aspects of the early life of Farrokhzād, to the extent that we know them, are ordinary. Things changed drastically when, at the age of sixteen, she fell in love with Parviz Shāpur (1924–1999), an author and a distant relative, who lived in an adjacent house. She convinced her family to let her marry him a year later, at age seventeen. These events and her relationship with her husband had the first significant effect on her poetic annunciations, which until then had no specific direction. Then she dedicated most of her poetry to the expression of love and relationship issues and her disenchantment with domestic life. But, as we will see, other occurrences such as taking art classes, her divorce, travelling to Europe, the publication of her books, dating other men (including Golestān) and her cinematic experiences, all in one way or another influenced her thoughts and writings.[5]

Her poetry, letters and short stories, all represent the impression of life and mostly undesirable encounters through the eyes of a young, intelligent and emotional woman whose feelings are constantly hurt because she never feels fulfilled in her love relationships. As human beings, we all create narratives as we walk, run or dream. We construct narratives to explain life to others or to ourselves. On Bakhtin's notion of narrative, Kinser writes:

> Any *narrative*, oral or written, allies its author with other 'participants' in the discourse such that anything narrated is communicated simultaneously on two levels, that of the author and that of the person speaking at any given point in the narrative.[6]

Farrokhzād's narrative is consistent in the sense that it reflects many changes and spontaneities in the narrator's situation and in her own life and psyche. In different times, however, she allies and communicates with different audiences.

Her letters to Shāpur help us understand Farrokhzād's autobiographical poetic evolution.[7] The letters tell of preparation for marriage, family issues, love and suffering due to separation from her love and later from their child, especially during her time abroad. The young woman behind these letters seems to be an idealist, an aspiring, still hopeful person seeking happiness in joining the man she loves. The letters show that, like many middle class women of her time, Farrokhzād had to manoeuvre between strong family traditions regarding marriage and her desire to be a free woman in charge of her own destiny. She also seems to have had a great facility for decision making; she even guides her controlling fiancé in solving problems. The letters illustrate how much she loves Shāpur even after their divorce. They also reveal Farrokhzād's increasing interest in artistic activities and her growth as a poet and writer.

Farrokhzād and Shāpur apparently separated because of some vicissitudes in their relationship, which were the result of their different views on life and lifestyle; their different ambitions. After separation, she returned to Tehran to her father's house for a brief time, where she faced his displeasure.[8] Yet, according to her letters, she missed her husband terribly when she was away from him. During this time, she published her poem 'Gonāh' ('Sin') in *Roshanfekr*. For the most part, it is a confessional poetic expression because she seems to be still in love with her husband despite the 'sinful' experience portrayed in the poem. Soon thereafter, during those eventful years, she published her first collection of poetry, *Asir*, which evoked Shāpur's disapproval, and their relationship worsened.[9] At this point, she went through a nervous breakdown and ended up briefly in the Rezā'i Psychiatric Hospital.

The influence of Farrokhzād's life experiences on her poetry is evident in *Asir*, which breaks the traditional boundaries between women's real lives and poetry. Its poems portray a warm soul and inspire passion. The speaker or, if I may say, the protagonist in all 44 pieces seems to have an inquisitive character with a certain desire, expectation or need that remains unfulfilled. Nevertheless, the mood in the poems changes constantly; it is sometimes happy, sometimes sad, and at other times hopeless, remorseful and nostalgic. One poem reads:

> You are the clear blue bright sky
> I am a captive bird, cornered in this cage
> I think constantly of an opportunity
> To fly away from this silent prison . . .
> To start anew my life with you.[10]

If read autobiographically, the 'cage' could be understood as a reference to the place she wishes to leave – her room in her father's house – in pursuit of her beloved. By using the word 'fly', she insinuates that there is distance between her and her beloved, a man – not an abstract, mystic notion as in classical poetry. Her letters written around this time support this interpretation. However, even before she gets the chance to fly away, she has started reciting her poem, which conveys not only a sense of hope for the future, but a longing to escape a disordered life. Other poems, or even specific lines that represent the gist of the whole collection, indicate this struggle of a young soul dealing with her desires and feelings of guilt.

Farrokhzād's *Asir* reflects the emotional dissatisfaction of a young woman who constantly faces contrasts between the realities of life and her passionate understanding of love and relationships. The man in the poem, the subject of her passion, also plays an important role in setting the mood and reflecting the emotional status of the speaker who sometimes even seems to yearn for death. She loves him, but she is not sure if her love is reciprocated. She admires him, but she is not certain he admires her. When she is with him, she is happy. When he is away, she is sad. Yet, sometimes she feels stressed upon rejoining him. Writing instinctively about this specificity, this changing emotional status caused by simultaneous internal and external factors, distinguishes Farrokhzād from other poets who have written about love.

Her missives after her divorce and before the publication of *Divār* shed light on her state of mind. In the first series of letters, she seems to be tired and unconfident. She refers to her room as a prison, yet she says she is certain she will not find tranquillity anywhere else.[11] She wishes to have someone in her life on whom she can rely, or a religion from which she can draw strength. She asks Shāpur for help. She refers to the past as holding good memories and calls to mind her son who provides inspiration for many of her poems and short stories.

In 1956, two years after she officially separated from her husband, aged twenty-two, Farrokhzād went on a trip to Italy and then Germany, for a total of fourteen months, to escape a situation in which she 'could not laugh anymore.'[12] It might not be a coincidence that, as she explored other worlds and enjoyed a new-found freedom, the 25 poems in her next collection, *Divār*, revisit the themes of her previous book in bolder language and with a renewed sense of liberty.

The poem 'Gonāh' was probably written after an encounter with her lover, referring to their intimacy as a sin. 'I sinned, / I sinned with great pleasure / I sinned in his warm and fiery arms . . . / Then, next to a trembling, senseless body / I wondered, "What did I do, O' God / in that dark, silent secluded place?"'[13] It was an audacious and avant-garde literary act for a woman to publish such personal enunciations. Beyond this significance, its publication also illustrates the struggle of an artistically ambitious woman against the cultural limitations that deny the right to explore and express intimate emotions and thoughts, the very self. But, generally, the poems in *Divār* indicate that many of the internal conflicts underpinning the first book continued to weigh on the author's mind.

After *Divār*, Farrokhzād published a number of short stories in *Ferdowsi* magazine, toward the end of 1957. They, too, display Farrokhzād's thoughts and aspirations, her master narrative on life, with motifs taken from daily experiences presented in recurring structures. They narrate some of the doubts and deep contradictory feelings of individuals struggling in their relationships within middle class cultural environments. The first one, entitled 'Bi-tafāvot' ('Indifferent'), depicts a woman's encounter with an intellectual, well-read man who seems to avoid reciprocating her feelings. He makes her guess what he is thinking and all of this bothers her so that she begins to doubt herself and her very existence.[14] The story resembles so many of the themes of her poems.

Farrokhzād said she was feeling choked in Iran before taking her first trip to Europe.[15] This trip, she said, gave her back her health and sanity. The poems in *'Esyān* reflect the poet's attitudes about women and society. Within the collection's seventeen poems, Farrokhzād ponders the relationship between personal agonies and social quandaries. Therefore, her personal rebellion gains a social colouring if not a discursive character; the beginning of a collective voice on behalf of a collective revolt, transcending the earlier boundaries of her personal experiences. Also, the poems in this book are significantly longer than the ones in her first two collections, suggesting a departure from the poignant snapshot depiction of personal and emotional moments that could have only been felt and enunciated by the younger, more sensitive, and embittered Farrokhzād. In *'Esyān*, the contradictions are not limited to Farrokhzād's own perception of individuality but are revealed to permeate the social fabric of societies, philosophy, religious beliefs, and identity. She writes, 'If I were God, I'd summon the angels one night / to boil the essence of eternal life in Hell's cauldron.'[16] Or 'If I were God / How would the flame of this rebellion / burn my entire existence?'[17] The personal narrative also gains a social aspect by engaging an audience concerned with the larger questions of identity, theology, free will and destiny, all subject to debate among intellectuals in the late 1950s and 1960s. The thematic and structural changes Farrokhzād displays in this collection point to two central questions in this essay; one related to the poet's aesthetic shift and the other related to the factors that helped her achieve such a shift. A number of these poems were in fact composed in Rome and Munich. Soon after these poems, she abandoned the use of the *chahārpāreh*, a contemporary version of the classical Persian quatrain. We will return to both of these issues.

Farrokhzād travelled to Europe on several occasions (in 1956, 1960 and 1964). There she came into contact with Europeans and expatriate Iranians, learned new languages, and translated German poetry into Persian with her older brother. It seems the more she travelled, the more her horizons and narrative broadened. I believe through these experiences, she not only became inspired by, but also familiar with, the dominant literary discourse of her day. She understood the exigencies of the ideological representation of the committed literary movement that had broader social significance than the mere prosodic differences, say, between Yushij and Tavallali. (As for the prosody, she had already established her own style using long lines, soft rhythms, unconventional assonance, unprecedented use of plural nouns, and lyrical compositions, allowing smooth reading as in classical poetry.) Even though it was difficult to talk about her meetings with leftist activists in Germany, her travelogue reveals the issues that preoccupied Farrokhzād's mind during this period and which appeared soon afterward in her poetry.[18] In an introductory note, she explains her motivation for taking the trip. She says, there was nothing in her soul except 'darkness, absolute confusion'; there was nothing to satisfy her curiosity or her 'thirst for exploration.' She says that she could not cope with the pressures of life because she 'had no power left in her.'[19] By all indications, Europe restored her energy, allowed her to look back at Iran and see it, its society and her life there in different, innovative ways.

The piece entitled 'She'ri barā-ye to' ('A Poem for You'), illustrates some of Farrokhzād's new preoccupations. She talks about her child in the poem and expresses worries about the socio-political situation and her hopes for the future, a topic that would again find a wider appeal. The poem reads:

> This is the last lullaby I sing
> by your cradle
> My dear sweetheart,
> Our town
> Has long become Satan's nest
> The day will come when
> Your rueful eyes will
> Glide over this pained song;
> Searching for me in my words,
> you will say inwardly:
> '*she* was my mother.'[20]

Elsewhere, she writes, 'More than anything and above anything, I love my art and my son and my wish for him is that he becomes a poet or a writer when he grows up.'[21] Such enunciation is not a mere result of the author's maturity; it is part of the broadening of her narrative of life, which soon included much more than lovers, and her individual struggle, both domestic and emotional.

In 1958, not long after the publication of '*Esyān*, Farrokhzād found a secretarial position at the Golestān Film Studio managed by Ebrāhim Golestān. At this point, she was already well known and respected in the literary community. During the time she worked there, she accomplished much, and continued to enjoy success as a poet. In 1963, she published her fourth collection, *Tavallodi digar*, which she dedicated to Golestān. Critics perceived this collection as a radical shift in her poetry. The first poem in this collection, 'Ān ruz-hā' ('Those Days'), portrays a woman who has given up on love, or at least on personal, carnal love, and is now lonely. 'Those days are gone / those fine days . . . / And the girl who colored her cheeks / with geranium petals, ah . . . / is now a lonesome woman.'[22] This portrayal is certainly different, but the changes in her ideas and poetry during this time, I argue, should not be surprising because she had proven she was capable of improving, rather quickly, her skills in any area into which she ventured. In fact, this and other poems in the new collection resemble her earlier works and show that the poetic change and philosophical approach to life are neither sudden nor the miraculous result of finding a mentor in Golestān. The changes are rather the natural flourishing of a sensitive mind and demonstrate her long-fought battle to be a respected part of the literary community, which at the time was highly influenced by idealistic revolutionary discourse.

Furthermore, distinguishing a shift in Farrokhzād's poetic narrative is also relevant, when speaking about her style of writing and her portrayal of socio-political issues. However, *Tavallodi digar* as a whole might not represent such a shift; I believe that the single poem 'Dar ghorubi abadi' ('In an Eternal Sunset') is the pivotal piece in the collection, in which she displays poetic, representational, and discursive shifts. If you will, this is where 'another birth' actually occurs. Even with its use of natural elements, the poem has a strong social message that is still very personal. It reads, 'I think of something to be said in poems . . . / I think of the myth of bread . . . / I wish to surrender to an outburst . . . / I wish to say / No, no, no / Let us move, / Let us say something.'[23] In this collection, love, playful games, and old alleyways belong to the past. Even though there is a sense of nostalgia about them, they are not the focus of the poems; the narrator does not crave them. Instead, there is an immense sense of urgency for a revolt – albeit through words and poetry. The poetic rebellion indeed echoed the poetic discourse of the committed literary movement that sought above anything else social change, a move away from the 'silent' status quo to a ruling structure attuned to the needs of the masses.[24]

The poem 'Āyeh-hā-ye zamini' ('Earthly Verses'), one of the longest poems in *Tavallodi digar*, offers a new, unconventional set of expressions and metaphors to convey meanings that go beyond individual preoccupations with nature or the things which belong to an ordinary lifestyle.[25] It is about elements that may appear contradictory on the surface, such as pacifism, intellectuals, prisons, escape, blood – all of which allude to ominous social upheaval. The larger intellectual discursive field of the time explains these metaphors; all poets used them, some beautifully and others not so creatively. The explanation of her adherence to certain types of metaphors with specific meanings is that, in society, the revolutionaries were clamouring for the use of force against a powerful regime. Sympathetic prominent poets and authors echoed social unrest with explosive words. To accompany them, Farrokhzād upheld the discourse in her own way.

Eventually, in her posthumously published collection, a poem reads, 'After that / We went to the streets / And shouted: "Long live" / And: "Death to."'[26] The speaker is no longer excluded from life's grimness. She pays heed not only to those who ignore the flowers but also to those who are making a noise outside. In another poem in the same collection, 'Delam barā-ye bāghcheh mi-suzad' ('I Feel Sorry for the Garden'), words such as 'explosion' and 'bomb' make it an unprecedented example of Farrokhzād's take on the social events of the time, and in particular the rise of a militant leftist discourse. In this poem she writes:

> Instead of flowers,
> Our neighbors plant
> bombs and machineguns in their gardens.
> Our neighbors
> cover their tiled ponds,
> Turning them into
> Secret storerooms of gunpowder.
> And our neighbors' children
> fill their schoolbags
> With small bombs.[27]

Here, Farrokhzād's narrative turns outward with less emphasis on the intimate feelings that marked many of the poems in her previous collections. Farrokhzād's adherence to the prevalent metaphoric discourse becomes paramount in 'Kasi keh mesl-e hich-kas nist' ('One Like No Other'), which clearly demonstrates her new tendency to expand her narrative of life into a broader social discourse. In this poem, she pronounces a social revolt.

All of the previous disappointments are now replaced with hopes and wishes expressed in a dreamlike account, a dream in which a mighty, loving saviour arrives. And in her portrayal of this leader, Farrokhzād clearly employs the rhetoric of committed literature, demonstrating her newly gained vision, and exciting readers and critics already swept away by the power of revolutionary literature. According to this literary discourse, which frequently appeared in other works of the committed and Marxist authors, metaphors can be easily deciphered with little effort: the jail and the handcuffs refer to the state; the lack of equal distribution of food refers to society's injustice; and the red star and the fireworks foretell or express a desire for revolutionary change. This rhetoric is not exclusive to this poem; it is rife in the committed poetry of the time.

Here, her personal and social aspirations merge ingeniously, lending a new depth to the voice of the narrator and resulting in some of her most memorable lines: 'Birds are mortal / Remember the flight.'[28] Elsewhere, she presents hopeful glimpses of the future: 'Why should I stop, why? / I learned from a dead bird / to memorize the flight.'[29] Then on other occasions, a departure from personal rebellion about carnal love becomes most apparent when she writes, 'What is to me / the lengthy whimpering wildness / of animals' sexual organs? / What is to me / a worm's loathsome penetration / into a fleshy vacuum?'[30]

This brief review of her collections demonstrates the lack of cogency of the commonly held opinion that the shift in Farrokhzād's thinking, poetry and style of writing occurred in the space between *'Esyān* and *Imān biāvarim beh āghāz-e fasl-e sard*. A number of poems in these two volumes indicate that a delineation of her representational approach might not be as easy as has been assumed previously by others. Farrokhzād's poems in *'Esyān* might well indicate a personal rebellion against the traditional structure of society (or more precisely the family), but in them one can also sense a social consciousness that promotes a collective protest. The 'I' and the 'we' are both present. Conversely, in *Imān biāvarim*, one finds poems that recall Farrokhzād's early approach to life, social issues and male-female relationships, which also cast doubt on the belief that she adhered to a feminist ideology in her writings.[31] As will be explained, the shift is also less ideological than has been suggested. She did not become a pure promoter of any discourse, a propagandist of any political party or a strident feminist.

If all of this is true, one might even doubt the common belief that the poet's acquaintance with Golestān was the only or even a major reason behind the shift in her social and stylistic representations. 'Ābedi repeats this notion, this sort of cause and effect relation(ship), when he writes, 'Golestān had positive influences on Farrokhzād's artistic character.'[32] But clearly, Farrokhzād was, since her youth, a dynamic, sensitive and artistically ambitious person, who drew poetic inspiration from all events and relationships in her life. Her trips to Europe, her acquaintances with political activists in Germany, her reading and translating of German poetry, her studies of Persian poetry and her interaction with the leading poets of Iran at the time (e.g. Nimā, Shāmlu, Akhavān-Sāles, Tavallali and Sepehri) all played roles in her poetic and narrative changes. Those who see Golestān as a mentor who changed Farrokhzād ignore these facts and instead impose a so-called Rumi-Shams model on her relationship with Golestān, forgetting that the latter does not even feature in her writings.[33] Farrokhzād never wrotea Divān-e Ebrāhim Golestān. I believe this whole concept of *morshed* or *pir* versus *morid* or *sālek* (the spiritual ad viser, the wise guide versus the disciple, the devotee) needs to be reconsidered or revised because it is not a probable explanatory model for understanding causality.

Moreover, even if we safely assume that Golestān was to some extent influential in Farrokhzād's poetic progress, why do we never hear about Golestān's influence on Akhavān-Sāles and other poets who frequented his circle? Equally important, why is it always assumed that the 'influence' and 'guidance' flowed in just one direction? Regarding Golestān's influential role, Kessler and Banani write, 'It was a rare attachment of two artists that coincided with, and undoubtedly affected, a profound process of self-discovery and growth in Forugh Farrokhzād.'[34] The authors fairly describe both Golestān and Farrokhzād as highly talented. In that case, should we not perhaps begin to look at traces of Farrokhzād's poetic influence on Golestān's work? In fact, many of the contributors to an edited volume on the cinematic works of Farrokhzād describe her film as poetic.[35] Her film that contains rhythmic and equal 'stanza' in its dialogue and in the sequencing of the scenes was indeed a new notion that she brought to Golestān's studio.[36]

The above analysis also shows that there were many men in Farrokhzād's life before (and alongside) Golestān. Some of them were affiliated with important journals of the time and apparently had a strong presence in her poetry, indicating a long-lasting effect on her poetic development. Among them, Parviz Shāpur, of course occupies an exceptional place. Reading her love poems, one is tempted to imagine the young woman falling in love with this controlling and much more mature man, himself an accomplished author, who becomes her husband almost overnight. The experience changes her profoundly. Even when separated from him, she restates her love: 'Do you know that in my heart / I had hidden a picture of your love? / Do you know that from this love / I had a burning fire in my soul?' Farrokhzād also dedicated her second volume of poetry to him. Her short stories often reflect the significance (and the singularity of the significance) of Shāpur in the formative stages of Farrokhzād's poetic career. Her letters are the most telling of all. In them, we can find a very clear picture of Farrokhzād's poetic approach to life, love and her relationship with Shāpur. After all, one of the most dramatic events of the poet's life was falling in love with the future father of her child. Golestān's influence, even if we must admit to a degree of it simply because they were lovers for years, is not then as clearly visible and attributable since Farrokhzād's poems do not reveal praise for Golestān and his wisdom in the same way she acknowledged the impact of Shāpur's love on her own life.

The next myth to dispel concerns Farrokhzād's supposed advocacy of feminism, keeping in mind that stating that Farrokhzād was not a feminist is not tantamount to devaluing her poetic ability or denying her amazing female sensibilities or her influence on other writers, both male and female. In their pioneering works, Milani and Hillmann have to some extent analysed Farrokhzād's poetry from a feminist perspective.[37] Reading her works through feminist literary theories is in fact a valid and necessary approach. However, as a result of scholars adopting this approach, a popular notion has taken shape that Farrokhzād, especially in her poetry, was a staunch feminist who spent her career advocating women's causes.[38] I have written elsewhere that even Farrokhzād's early poetic efforts did not lead to the creation of a literary movement or to the inspiration for feminist literary activities. The recent emergence of previously unknown information about her life, some of which has been discussed above, further substantiates this stance.[39] Retrospectively writing about a woman's daily experiences in the mid-twentieth century may be considered a feminist practice. However, Farrokhzād never placed those daily experiences in a broader socio-political or gender-role framework; she never conceptualized her agonies in explicit feminist terms. Feminist discourse, after all, consists of certain beliefs and practices that help to legitimize and implement women's rights and sexual equality. And in order to have *feminism*, there has to be theory, advocates, organization and social resources and all be devoted to the implementation of social equality of the sexes and the promotion of women's rights and to efforts against the historical distortion of those rights. It is within such a context with such conditions that feminist literary activists can appear on the social or cultural scene, exert influence and inspire humanist responses to their cause. In pre-revolutionary Iran, the efforts of many pioneering women activists to promote women's social participation were, in the final analysis, a complement to the state's attempts to modernize the country.

Both Farrokhzād's poems about her emotions and sensibilities and her poems about social issues and the construction of a new identity, presented in terms of a revolt against social norms and the political status quo, have inspired more women to feminist causes in recent decades than in her own time. This is due to the rise of feminist literary discourse *after* the revolution, in opposition to the new regime's efforts to reverse the pre-revolutionary progress in women's social and legal situations. Renewed interest in a poet's work is not a new phenomenon. The works of Rābe'eh, Tāhereh Qorrato'l-'Eyn and Zhāleh Bakhtiāri have arguably attracted more attention in the post-revolutionary period than ever before. Elsewhere, many women authors and activists still find the works of the ancient Greek female poet, Sappho, inspiring.

To provide textual evidence for the above arguments, the poem 'Sin' is significant, especially when we read it as a confessional poem. In addition to a woman talking about a taboo subject, the poem also inserts a real female 'I' into the still decidedly male-oriented literary scene. Yet, it is daunting that the 'I' is so filled with guilt, a notion that keeps repeating throughout the poet's works. She chastises herself on behalf of men, writing, 'A smile danced across his lips / "Oh lustful; do you know me?"'[40] The 'sin' shows up frequently in *Asir*.[41] Her second collection, *Divār,* opens with the poem 'Gonāh' with the word 'sin' occurring twice in it. At least two other poems in the volume contain the word (again, sometimes more than once).[42] The word also appears in some poems in her subsequent collection, *'Esyān*.[43] In contrast to Farrokhzād's first three collections, in which the word *gonāh* appears a few dozen times, in her last two collections, *gonāh* appears only once in 'I Feel Sorry for the Garden', and even then in an entirely different context (in association with the Mother's religious beliefs): 'My mother thinks that a sinful infidelity has tainted the garden / My mother prays all day long / my mother is a natural sinner.'[44] The use of the concept of sin, then, further proves my previous point about the shift in the poet's focus. It also says something more about Farrokhzād's worldview. According to memoirs of the pre-revolutionary political activists and the literature of martyrdom produced by the revolutionary organizations about their fallen warriors, failing to support the dominant revolutionary discourse in the late sixties and the seventies was treasonous.[45] The texts that supported action imposed a sense of guilt upon the readers for inactivity. On the other hand, individualism, and any other 'worldly' and materialistic inspirations were considered even more sinful. Perhaps if the leftist discourse and Marxist advocates had been conscious of women's rights and the significance of gender and sexual equality in society vis-à-vis the issue of political change and revolutionary idealism, the female as well of the male poets would have been more capable of merging the self and the social, and gender and the culture all at once.

Farrokhzād's 'She'r-e safar' ('Leaving: The Poem') provides more evidence and is a good example of the anomalous poems from the collection *Tavallodi digar*. It represents those poems that challenge the notion of the existence of feminism in Farrokhzād's oeuvre, a claim now substantiated by the analysis of her letters and short stories. As explained elsewhere, the poem displays Farrokhzād's personal approach toward gender relations and is perhaps a reflection of her own romantic experience.[46] The protagonist of the poem spends a night with her lover. Even though she deeply wants him to stay with her the next day, she succumbs to tradition because staying could compromise him. She advises herself to 'Let him go, my eyes will follow him / Let him go, my love will guard him.'[47] She makes every sacrifice because 'She who gives her heart to her love never thinks of hurting him.'[48] This combination of her love and her sacrifices does not leave a good impression on her soul, causing myriad enunciations of her unhappiness, her sense of having committed a sin and her feelings of guilt.

In the final analysis, in her expression of love and relationships, Farrokhzād adheres to the traditional notion that a woman should sacrifice herself for her love – that is, a man – and later feels no more guilt when her advocacy for social equality or, rather, her objections to social inequality drive her poetic efforts. The poetic character returns to a somewhat traditional notion even in her last volume in the poem titled 'Vahm-e sabz' ('Green Illusion'). In it Farrokhzād writes, 'Shelter me, o simple perfect women.' In this poem, the protagonist does not seek to change anything; she simply 'cries all day in the mirror' and craves a return to the traditional, safe and simple life.[49] The notions underlying this poetic expression often display a close affinity with the cultural context of male domination that promoted sacrifice for another person or for the revolution. Or to be more optimistic, such notions might be driven from the fact that she had no major disastrous experiences with the men she loved; after all, she dedicated two of her books to them. Though, she does not seem to have been sincerely loved by the men portrayed in her work or referred to in her letters.[50] Yet, she also blames herself for this. That is, in her writings, she may occasionally blame certain men for a certain situation, but she also scorns herself for her predicaments.

Her understanding of love is also somewhat in line with traditional culture. She writes to Shāpur:

When I see young men and women sharing the prettiest or darkest moments of love in the public parks [in Rome] in the most natural manner, I wish to shout. Here, the love is a conquered summit, a read book. Excitement has no meaning and love is in its ultimate state of triteness.[51]

Her short stories, often confessional, further substantiate this claim. In one of them, 'Shekast ('Defeat'), the female narrator confirms, 'One should not expect loyalty from any man.' And in another, 'Bi-tafāvot' ('Indifferent'), she concludes, 'What bothers me is nothing to do with him; it is something in me, stuck to my dark world.'[52] She finally says, 'Hold my hand and take me with you wherever you want; perhaps I might be able to arrive there with you.'[53] And in another story, when he leaves her behind, she pronounces, 'Love is ridiculous.'[54] These portray an indecisive, fragile, and dependant person.

In the short stories that follow, the female narrator also constantly expresses her desire to love, and to be loved. In almost all of them, the love relationship remains unfulfilled. Reading her love poems and short stories comparatively, one can conclude that there was always a barrier between Farrokhzād and the fulfilment of love. She never blames it on the culture, the men in her life or her circumstances. Often, she blames herself. Obviously, another meaning of *gonāh*, besides sin, is guilt, and she does use the word to convey this second meaning to blame herself for her adventures and for the lack of love in her life. It is a complex issue; in a society that lacks a genuine and serious discourse on sexuality in its modern sense and in a culture where all issues related to sex were and are still taboo, engaging in sexual acts and talking about them are both inevitably associated and ridden with guilt. This is particularly true in the case of the revolutionaries and intellectuals. The very culture that does not recognize women's sexuality controls any expression and feelings about it as well. Thus, despite the strong, esoteric and independent character of the poet, in some of these confessional and autobiographical writings, she is not narrating; rather she is narrated.

Another way to look at this question is to examine the role of literary agency in her writings. Agency and agent may be compared to the relationship between acting and actor. A literary actor performs the actions, whereas an agent may act but also cause the action. Therefore, an actor can be the object of an act but an agent cannot.[55] The female speaker in Farrokhzād's poetry speaks of some aspects of sexuality but she often acts in a subordinate capacity. She hardly represents the sexual agency because the narrator asserts her desires as the sexual object and in terms of sins and wrongdoings. The absence of agency is particularly evident in the poem 'One Like No Other.' Farrokhzād's presentation of this 'someone' reflects the dominant discourse because it follows the pattern of male authority with a dependent female figure. It reflects the stereotypical view of male and female roles – one gives, one takes. He is 'someone' who is 'better', 'taller', 'braver' and able to bring light and justice. She, on the other hand, has to wait to receive her share. This hierarchy was also present in 'Leaving; The Poem', in which the woman must accept the man's decision to leave, while she remains at home behind a window from which she looks out and mourns her loss. Like the works of other committed authors, 'One Like No Other' displays sympathy for Islam extolling the 'neon Allāh sign' and 'Qāzi ol-Qozāt' ('The Judge of the Judges'; the Promised Mahdi). Therefore, even though the poem is highly social and political, the woman in it is merely acted upon.

It is true that Farrokhzād's poems about women's emotions and feelings are straightforward. She brings love to relationships between men and women. In her poems and her deeds, she destroyed the walls of her confined life. Yet her overall literary discourse does not revolve around the problems of gender hierarchy. She refuses to express any thought about what constitutes a man or a woman's poetic differences, let alone their sexuality. Her approach for evaluating the men in her life is limited by the way in which she is perceived by them during their brief encounters. She does not offer any understanding of the extent to which women can be independent in their thoughts and actions. She, instead, only denounces a family who disagreed with her about her choice in marriage and who in retrospect might have been rightly concerned about allowing a young girl to marry a much older man and to travel to another city. Then, she ends up connecting her fate to the fate of those whom she dates; literally or poetically, feeling good about them or feeling guilty. Her most important works speak to social rather than gender issues. All this is evident in the interview where Farrokhzād stated:

If my poetry has a degree of femininity, it is quite naturally due to the fact that I am a woman. I am fortunate to be a woman. However, if my poetry is judged in terms of artistic criteria, then I do not think gender can be a determining factor. . . . The essential issue is the human being. To be a man or woman is not the issue.

She believes that 'discussing this matter is not right in the first place', and thereby complies with the committed literary notion that honours sexually objective and indifferent criteria in literary criticism and literary activities.[56] In other words, her poetry engaged in a non-traditional view of human beings, whether male or female, a departure from the old tradition of male domination. She derives her artistic values from a humanistic notion of life and literature freed from the bindings of gender conditioning. This can at best correspond to Showalter's definition of the feminine stage in Western women's writings.[57]

In an uncanny way, Farrokhzād's approach to male-female relationships also calls for a comparison with that of Sādeq Hedāyat in *The Blind Owl*. Gender relations in Hedāyat's novel are historical, and historically dysfunctional. All the males resemble each other and each is a mockery of a man. All females resemble each other and each is the subject of male contempt. For Farrokhzād, even though boys and girls live in a better time, they are not capable of maintaining a meaningful relationship either; the only glimpses of happiness are expressed in a nostalgic sense. The reason for this ineffectuality is sometimes immaturity of emotions and sometimes the maturity of cautious parents. Both authors turn inward and become dejected intellectuals who seem tremendously out of place and time. Both gained a healthy understanding of modernity and its core concept of creativity but none offered solutions to social predicaments. For both, death became a viable solution (sensitivity, creativity and depression are not, after all, incongruous concepts). At the end, their answer to the problems of Iran's modernity and its hobbling by a long-lasting traditional culture was different, but the work of both transcended the restrictive nihilism that ruled over intellectual communities and the few coffee shops and bars that existed during those few decades prior to the 1979 revolution.

Finally, I would also like to address the commonly held opinion that Farrokhzād was harshly treated and criticized for her poetry and character. Many have even argued that she was marginalized because she was a woman stepping into the realm of men, when she wrote new poetry.[58] Others have said that she was chastised for writing about personal and sexual aspects of her life.[59] None has provided examples of this alleged brutal treatment and they simply repeat an anecdote.[60] The few critical remarks that I managed to locate in some obscure publications cannot be taken seriously.[61] As mentioned, Farrokhzād herself was a harsh critic of her own early works. All of this indicates that the evidence is not sufficient to support the notion that Farrokhzād was 'highly' or 'too harshly' criticized for her poetry or for her liberated spirit.[62] In fact, during a time when a woman could not easily enter the male-dominated literary communities, there is plenty of evidence that she was highly praised during her entire career.[63] A volume of *Ārash* was once dedicated to her work and the same journal published six of her poems in one issue.[64] Early on, a book was published about her that included a selection of her poems. Other books about famous women writers included entries praising her.[65] Early in her career, she published the second printing of her first collection, *Asir*, with an introduction written by Shojā'oddin Shafā, an important literary authority at the time. She soon became a literary, and I would even say, a cultural authority in the intellectual community. She helped launch a number of poetic careers, approved or disapproved of other poets' works and effectively campaigned on behalf of a group accused of plotting to assassinate the king.[66] Almost all major poets and literary critics including Shāmlu, Hoquqi, Rahnemā, Sepānlu, Roshangar, Tahbāz, Royā'i and Moshiri (who helped her publish her poem 'Sin' in *Roshanfekr*) praised her during her time or soon after her death. Many artists and officials attended her state-sponsored funeral. Many more famous personalities wrote and have continued to write about her in interviews, articles and books.[67] The number of her interviews seems, even by today's standards, impressive. In some of these interviews, she actually criticized other contemporary poets such as Nāderpur, her close companion for a short while. This incredible acknowledgement, support, and sympathy did not materialize overnight.

It is, in fact, pleasantly surprising that she was not criticized for her poetic innovation by, say, Hamidi Shirāzi, as harshly and systematically as, say, Nimā

Yushij was. Earlier, Hedāyat and Jamālzadeh were more brutally criticized for their 'blasphemies'. Women authors such as Tāhereh Qorrato'l-'Eyn, Parvin E'tesāmi and Shahrnush Parsipur suffered because of the absence of a serious and genuine discourse on sexuality and the lack of freedom for women's self-expression. Farrokhzād, on the contrary, gained fame nationally and internationally (through her film and translated poems). I believe portraying Farrokhzād as a victim is not productive and is indeed a disservice to her legacy.

Thus, reading Farrokhzād's poetry, short stories, interviews, travelogues and letters as integral parts of her narrative of life helps to clarify what is meaningful to her, and illuminates many aspects of her character as a woman constantly in search of love, friendship and progress. She was an urban, iconic, a young and eventfully leftist woman who presented a poetic version of a woman's life as she lived it. This contextualization of her work and life story helps picture a woman who is ambitious, committed to her arts, who is willing and able to use all sources and experiences available to her in order to improve. This study shows also that many long-held assumptions about her worldview, her sources of inspiration and her influences have not been completely factual. It is not surprising that a praiseworthy woman's narrative of life has, under patriarchal influences, been checkered by distorting assumptions. It is perhaps time to transcend the mentality that portrays her as a victim and rather focus on and celebrate her contributions and her life as a woman who was able to shine in the literary scene of Iranian society with a modern message that remains even more pertinent today.

Chapter 7

Garden in Motion: The Aesthetic of the Space Between

Michael Beard

It is traditional to define certain poets through the intensity of their pain. This is, I suspect, a global phenomenon: Leopardi's melancholy is what we may remember about his last poems. The childhood memories the great Iraqi poet Badr Shākir al-Sayyāb evoked in his last days, while he was dying in Kuwait, combine beauty and an elegiac intensity in a miraculous balance. In anglophone poetry, the tortured last poems of Sylvia Plath may represent a limit to the amount of pain which can be contained by the boundaries of the genre. It is traditional to say of such poets that the experience of pain shapes their poems, and in turn the poems work as conduits for pain. In Forugh Farrokhzād's case the pain is particularly accessible today. In our own historical moment, we can locate in her work a feminist vision, written against the background of a society out of synch with her personal values and we can hear her determination to live as she wished, to turn that sadness into beauty. I believe this is true, and yet I hesitate to discuss Forugh Farrokhzād in these terms. It is not just because of a last name that suggests happiness and satisfaction; an experience which entered her life only intermittently. I hesitate because I suspect the intensely beautiful sequence of styles we feel as we watch her art evolve, as the poems deepen and glow with control, is quite separate from the themes which characterize her life. If we see her as a machine for suffering, how do we account for her exuberance?

I use the word 'themes' with a polemic intent. Our lives are marked by themes, by repeated events which create trajectories, characteristic experiences that define our identity. Our writing expresses themes, inevitably drawn from experience: we call them 'content'. And one of the first rules of aesthetics is that a poem is not identical to its content, no matter how powerful, moving or brave. Those themes are not what make Farrokhzād a great poet.

And yet. What extraordinary bravery we find in her choice of themes. They threaten propriety; they threaten her reputation; they needle conservative readers and they welcome new emotional realms, perhaps in the hope that her vision might some day be more widely spread. Imagine, as early as 'Gonāh' ('Sin') in the collection *Divār* (*The Wall*, 1956), opening a poem with the phrase *gonah kardam gonāhi por ze lezzat* ('I've sinned, a sin full of pleasure').[1] It's not as if we could miss what she's talking about. Even a simple pair of lines like these from *Tavallodi digar* (the poem is 'Joft',[2] translated as 'Mate' in Ahmad Karimi-Hakkak's translation) can reach way beyond the boundaries of propriety:

بعد دو نقطهٔ سرخ
از دو سیگار روشن

Then two red dots
from two lighted cigarettes[3]

It's indirect, but it's an unmistakable reference to the unsayable, the moment after making love (thus *ba'd*, 'after,' 'afterwards' – we needn't ask after what). And even as an indirect reference it shocks; an allusion which is even less sayable from a woman's point of view.

I suggest that even powerful themes don't create powerful poetry, not in themselves. Once we have those thematic building blocks they have to be set in order somehow. I suggest focusing on the mortar holding them in place, which can connect in various ways, perhaps with the linkage of cause and effect, perhaps an adhesion where premise is followed by example, or the other way around, with examples followed by conclusion (as in most sonnets, most *ghazal*s). There are narrative poems too, in which one event follows another, but it is hard to imagine a narrative poem without a reiterated mood, a chorus or leitmotif. And then there are poems which are just lists (Allen Ginsberg's 'Howl'), where the listener or the reader is forced to supply the links. (This is probably the place to add that an unusually challenging proposal by the late Michael Riffaterre[4] defines lyric as a genre which reiterates a kernel statement – see particularly his essay 'Interpretation in Descriptive poetry', in which he reads a seemingly rambling Wordsworth poem and demonstrates how seemingly disparate parts return invariably to a single image. The reader is likely to see the mark of that essay throughout this essay.) It may be that 'building blocks' are not quite the image I want, since building blocks abut on one another. Farrokhzād's poetry often seems to assemble the component parts in the form of a list, but I think in every one of her greatest poems something else is happening: the point is that the component parts, the building blocks, the congealed thematic matter (or the variations on a kernel statement) lie apart from one another. They float in space.

In a simple form you can watch a short lyric broken into just two parts. The poem 'Joft', which we glimpsed above, is for eight initial lines simply a series of descriptive terms for night framed explicitly as a list: evening comes, and with it, darkness, and after darkness, hands, breathing and the sound of a dripping faucet. It is only after a break (marked by asterisks in the Persian text[5]) that the unfocused night-time scene resolves as a love scene, in the image of those two lighted cigarettes cited above. If the kernel image is loneliness between alienated people, it is only hinted in the first section (by the word 'hands' – line six), it resolves elegantly in the five lines which follow the asterisks.[6] What makes it a poem is the shape which separates the two modes in which the scene is described.

Another poem, 'Delam barā-ye bāghcheh mi-suzad' ('I Pity the Garden'[7]), could be read as a sequence of images or a sequence of transitions – that is, of spaces between. The poem opens with a series of emotive observations which seem to have been generated by the title, a *bāghcheh* ('garden') personified as someone expiring, dying alone. This overture (the first two stanzas) seems to hint at a kernel statement which is a little too simple. It will take on full meaning only through its variations. We are perilously close to a facile binary opposition: natural world (garden) opposed to unnatural constraints (the unobservant, the ones who don't think about the garden). Freedom versus non-freedom. Nature threatened. So far it is a legitimate emotive anxiety, but a predictable one, not a poem. There is a slight variation at line ten when we learn that it is the garden of 'our' house, but the process of personalizing the scene is likely to pass unnoticed. The 'our' in the phrase *Hayāt-e khāneh-ye mā* ('the courtyard of our house') is unmarked, unemphasized, though already it has subtly set up what follows. What follows is that startling and beautiful moment in line twenty: *Pedar miguyad / az man gozashtehast* . . . 'Father says / "My days have gone by . . ."'.[8] We have become so used to an impersonal narrator identifying with the garden that we have been given no reason to expect a dialogue, and yet the appearance of the father is exactly that – a second voice located *dar otāq-ash* ('in his room'), thus giving us a new polarity (garden versus house). So this isn't an abstract statement about nature. It's about families. The father, in the house, reads heroic texts about the past. (At this moment a whole other dimension peeps in, at least for a moment – a sketch of Farrokhzād's own aesthetic commitments, splitting them off from the big epic statement. Epics are for daddies.) Between the pale opening statement and the moment we begin to hear the father, super-annuated, dreaming of the past, is an edge, and that edge between the two voices is definitive, stronger because it has arrived unannounced.

Then we run into a second transition. We've heard from Father, and now three stanzas characterize Mother, introduced appropriately as a listener, object of his opinion. *Pedar beh mādar mi-guyad . . ./* 'Father says to Mother . . .'. In retrospect her syntactic position is logical and natural, but what reader sees it coming? I'd call it a second leap. And within the lingering portrait of the mother (to whom life is simply prayer: *sajjādeh-ist gostardeh . . .* 'a prayer rug unrolled' . . .). The stanza which sums the mother up is itself another surprise: *Mādar gonāhkār-e tabi'i-st* ('Mother is a sinner by nature').[9] Does it mean that she is so pious she thinks herself a sinner simply because she is human? Maybe, but the tone of the poem suggests otherwise, that she is indeed guilty, a member of that camp aligned against the garden, an identity remoulded by the father's values. A collaborator.

Once we have moved past the portraits of the older generation and we get to the brother and sister we know what to expect, and at this point the breaks will start to wedge themselves into surprising locations, for instance the middle of a section. There are no surprises in the portrait of the brother (a bully, prodded internally by his despair), and by the time we get to the sister, *keh dust-e gol-hā bud* ('who used to be the roses' friend') a more complete characterization erupts. What we are not really prepared for is the sudden shift into specificity: a momentary scene where Mother hits her, a marriage after which she has moved to the other side of town (*ānsu-ye shahr*) and an aftermath in which she has the family over to formal tea parties. At this point we are expecting the repetition of the word *masnu'i*, 'artificial' – that her artificial house has its artificial goldfish, an artificial husband, but she 'makes' (*mi-sāzad*) babies, which are natural (*tabi'i*). It is a small surprise, but it is like a little signature to remind us that we are reading a poem built of unannounced shifts.

In a last sequence the lone, authoritative voice of the opening stanzas returns but taking in a wider scene. In an escalation of the opening mood she speaks in the manner of a prophet, insisting she fears an age which has lost its heart (*zamāni / keh qalb-e khod-rā gom kardeh ast*).[10] It is an escalation, but the term *qalb* ('heart') also allows a brief return to the 'heart of the garden' (*qalb-e bāghcheh*) in the fifth line. We are back at the opening binary. (Pardon a semiotic term; it's been implied all along.) But the opposition between the threatened garden and the unhappy family which lets it die has returned stronger and more emphatic, characterized as a symptom of something wider, a degraded moment in history. If we accept the notion that one idea gradually emerges, and if it is a poem which widens as it gathers force, what allows it to deepen and accelerate is only incidentally a matter of thematic pain. What makes it a poem is the space between parts, the gear changes which give it its speed. Yes, there are themes which transgress propriety, but Farrokhzād's real risk is elsewhere. Each segment flirts with the danger of a descent into the predictable: lists which are just lists, lamentation which simply depresses, forced exuberance, shallow emotion. This puts real pressure on the moment when we pass from one segment to the next, the moment of a shift in register (in point of view, in subject matter, in tone or mood). The task is to surprise, and she sets up one poem after another which require surprises to keep it in motion. These are effects which are visible in the big units of rhetoric. (There are Iranian poets whose effects require a close attention to nuance, levels of formality, culturally sensitive vocabulary or choice of the precise word. These are not the only effects available.) In Farrokhzād's poems there is an emphasis on the big units of meaning, which I suspect is one reason why there are so many fluent and accessible translations of her work. But she buys that accessibility at a considerable price. A direct, conversational language always risks a descent into the commonplace.

In the title poem of *Tavallodi digar* occurs perhaps the most elegant transition in her oeuvre, and if I have made myself clear in the previous discussion, it can be sketched rather quickly. The opening move of the poem sets a high level of risk: *Hameh-ye hasti-ye man āyeh-ye tāriki-st* ('my being is all one dark *āyeh* . . .'). The most obvious risk is thematic, since *āyeh* (Arabic *āya*) is a privileged word in theological discourse. It is of course something like English 'verse' in Bible scholarship. But 'verse' in English also has a secular meaning. *Āya* doesn't allow so much leeway. A sura of the Qur'ān is divided into phrases or sentences (sometimes longer grammatical units) called *āyāt*: and since *āya* is also the term for 'miracle', there is a built-in theological penumbra surrounding the term. (This is one reason that Salman Rushdie's *Satanic Verses* looked blasphemous in translation, even to people who hadn't read it. All they had to see was the title.) The only way to translate English 'verses' in Rushdie's context was with the word *āyāt*, and thus the title becomes *Āyāt-e shaytāni* – carrying a narrow specificity of reference left open in the English original. 'Verses' by comparison is a pretty tame word. Etymologically, the opening move of the poem 'Tavallodi digar' makes her life not just a verse but something divine, thus co-opting a familiar religious term. The list which follows (Perhaps life [*zendegi*] is . . . or perhaps life is . . . etc.) is a risk in formal terms: it resembles the generic lists of an ironic, apocalyptic poetry which traces back for Western readers to Rimbaud, Lautréamont, T.S. Eliot, Hart Crane, until it grows pale and predictable in recent generations. It is always hazardous to follow in the footsteps of an oversize mode of speech. Here the risk is a poetry which overstates, which takes on big claims and reduces them. And yet, even if we feel that the statement of the extreme and apocalyptic list is outdated and worn out, we have to admit that each definition surprises us. The definitions are in fact a series of moods: life is a street down which a woman walks every day, a rope with which a man hangs himself, a child come home from school, perhaps two cigarettes lit after making love (an image we are already familiar with), or two people saying a formal hello as they pass in the street, and finally life may be when the lover's eyes fall into ruins (*virān mi-sāzad*). It is a list, but a deceptive list because it is really a set of variations – ironic, musical, always framed by surprise. (I would argue that moving from the two cigarettes to a scene of two acquaintances passing in the street surprises, and in retrospect the one, innocent and familiar, comments on the other, the dangerous image of making love.)

By this stage in the evolution of her poetry, we should probably speak of the segments of the poem as movements in classical music. The third movement shifts to another key – the speaker as a lover remembering the past in a deserted room. And here we find another list: the repetition of 'life' recapitulated in another key, by the repetition of *sahm* (*sahm-e man in-ast*) this is my *sahm*, my 'lot', 'portion', 'allotment' (in context, 'fate'). Her *sahm* is a sky closed off by a curtain, her *sahm* is descending a deserted staircase (*pelleh-ye matruk*), a walk in the garden of memories. It is as if the scene narrows and narrows (with a list of childhood memories); all the sadder because the concluding list is like a compendium of privileged terms in her previous poetry. Up until the last eight lines we may feel that we are reading a retraction – that her whole life, her poetry come to nothing. But when we hit those last eight lines we are in a different world altogether:

من

پری کوچک غمگینی را

میشناسم که در اقیانوسی مسکن دارد

I know
a sad little fairy
whose home is in an ocean . . .[11]

The shift of registers is as powerful and moving as any transition in any poem I know. I may be understating this. What began as a list of existential complaints, restated in variations which risk a painful claustrophobia, suddenly takes an unpredictable sharp turn not just into a folkloric image but a shift from the tentative tone of all the lists to a simple assertion. Persian syntax allows the postponement of the verb, so that the diminutive, sad fairy is in front of us before we hear that the speaker is acquainted with her. (I'm making an assumption here that we are looking at a woman *pari*). The word *mishenāsam* ('I know') allows us to feel that what follows is a kind of secret: here's something else I know:

و دلش را در یک نی لبک چوبین
مینوازد آرام ، آرام
پری کوچک غمگینی
که شب از یک بوسه میمیرد
و سحرگاه از یک بوسه به دنیا خواهد آمد

. . . and who softly, softly
pours her heart out into a flute,
a sad little fairy who dies at night with a kiss
to be reborn at dawn with a kiss.[12]

We know that *pari* too. She reiterates the speaker of the poem, who plays a more complicated flute. Since she was introduced to us as 'little' and 'sad', her song evokes the same sadness we have read before, but transformed completely. She may be sad, but the poem locates her in a corner where we feel privileged to glimpse her. Or to hear her. By now a commentator feels a little embarrassed because the process of transition will be so obvious. That extraordinary subtle pivoting motion at the terminal point, absolutely unexpected but in retrospect so simple, may be the most startling moment in Farrokhzād's startling career. Sometimes all a commentator can do is point.

Chapter 8

Forugh Farrokhzād's Apocalyptic Visions

Sirous Shamisa

Translated by Dominic Parviz Brookshaw

Introduction

In my book *Negāhi beh Forugh* (*A Look at Forugh*),[1] I showed that Forugh
Farrokhzād, in some of her poems, plays the role of a prophetess, prophesying
certain future events. Here, my intention is not to collate all these prophecies,
although I will present some examples. What I will examine is the source for
the inspiration behind these prophecies, many of which were realised after her
death. She lived in a time when intellectuals had not sought refuge in caves,
mothers did not give birth to headless babies, and men did not molest sleeping
children on beds made of blood.[2] These apocalyptic prophecies are similar to
what is related about the Day of Judgement (*ruz-e qiyāmat*), when the world
will be filled with oppression and injustice until such time as the Promised One
(*mow'ud*) appears. But Farrokhzād, to all appearances, was not a religious
person, however, as an Iranian (and in particular as an Iranian woman)[3] it is
possible that in the deepest depths of her being there existed residual religious
elements. In any case, there are two questions which occurred to me when I
was writing my book, and which still intrigue me. The first is: What was the
source of these terrifying visions, and what was her inspiration for these
depictions (and how is it that in the poetry of her contemporaries there is no
sign of such visions)?[4] And: How is it that some of these prophecies came true?

One answer might be this, that Farrokhzād lived at a time when the 'file' of
traditional society was being closed in Iran. A long period of history was
coming to an end; its millennium was approaching. It was time to expect a

This essay was translated from the original Persian by Dominic Parviz Brookshaw.

Day of Judgement or Resurrection (*qiyāmat*), and Farrokhzād in her poetry prophesies the events that will occur when that traditional society will have come to an end.

But it could be said that, with her strong, prophetic sensibility, Farrokhzād foresaw the contradictions and the lack of harmoniousness between the traditional segment of society (which was its largest component), and a superficially modernised stratum. In 'Delam barā-ye bāghcheh mi-suzad' ('I Feel Sorry for the Garden'),[5] Farrokhzād foretells the emergence of armed movements, and says neighbours are hoarding gunpowder in the pools of their courtyards, and have hidden machineguns in their gardens. She sensed that this situation was one of crisis. The heart of the garden was swollen. Mayhem and killing would ensue, and a period of unrest and disarray was set to give birth to a new, alien generation.

Perhaps Farrokhzād, like many others, thought that Iranian society had been in a constant state of disarray following the Constitutional Revolution (1905–1911), and that politicians and government officials had stolen the values of the constitutional movement. For many, Iranian society was not on the right path to progress. This is why, she says, '[her] trust was hanging from the loose thread of justice',[6] that she was not consoled by 'the lullaby of civilisation and culture' in 'the land of poetry, the rose, and the nightingale'.[7]

Farrokhzād's home is a typical middle class, Iranian home. Father, who is contented with his pension, reads *Nāsekh al-Tavārikh* and the *Shāhnāmeh*. Mother is constantly seated on her prayer rug. Brother, who gets drunk, is addicted to philosophy, and he believes that until everything is destroyed, it cannot be made right. But Farrokhzād believes that the garden can be taken to hospital. This belief, on the part of the poet, that the 'garden' (i.e. Iranian society) can be taken to hospital – can be healed – is an important one in light of the history of political theories about contemporary Iran, as I shall show in this essay.

In brief, the existing situation is, in Farrokhzād's eyes, a sick one. It is true that in all of Iran's towns and cities beautiful swimming pools and fountains have been built, but around the edges of these pools and fountains stand little criminals (*jāniān-e kuchak*).[8] The public enjoy watching executions. The poet observes the age in which she lives with precision, and sees it for what it truly is. She assesses her society, and with her poetic genius prophesies its future. This voice of hers has lasted in contemporary Iranian history. Everyone is waiting for someone who should come and share out the bread and water, but it is not clear who that someone is, because he is not like anyone else.[9] For Farrokhzād, Iranian society is not homogeneous. A huge gulf (whether material, spiritual or cultural) divides it in two. That is why that someone who must come has two faces: on the one hand, he is the Promised One (*mow 'ud*) awaited by the religious, and on the other hand, he is Lenin.

Apocalyptic literature

Apocalyptic literature is a genre within ancient Jewish and Christian religious literature. These texts are full of symbols of darkness and horror. Examples of such texts in the Torah can be found in the books of the Prophets Isaiah, Daniel and Ezekiel. The last book of the New Testament is the Revelation of St. John the Divine, about which numerous interpretations have been written. In such apocalyptic revelations, there is much talk of killing, destruction, fear and oppression, but they can also contain news of the ultimate triumph of good over evil, as is the case with the Revelation of St. John. This is similar to the way the Day of Judgement (*ruz-e qiyāmat*) and the fierce, epic battles at the End of Time (*ākhar al-zamān*) are referred to in classical Persian literature. It echoes the writings of Virgil and Nostradamus, who claimed to have seen visions of future calamities, and who are sometimes referred to as seers. These seers were people who were informed of the hidden world (*gheyb*) and the world of spirits. There is a passage in 'Attār's *Elāhi-nāmeh* which illustrates this.[10] 'Attār tells the tale of such a seer who was taken to the grave of 'Omar Khayyām and who declared that he had seen in a revelatory vision that Khayyām was 'incomplete' (*nā-tamām*). Another well-known example of apocalyptic literature in Persian is the famous poem by Shāh Ne'matollāh-Vali, which has the *radif* (refrain at the end of each line), 'I see' (*mi-binam*).[11] In this type of text, there is a high occurrence of phrases such as, 'I have seen', 'I see', and 'I see that . . .'. In mystical, Sufi terminology we also have 'the event' (*vāqe'eh*), where a mystic has a vision of an event that will inevitably come to pass.[12] I believe such revelatory literature should be divided into two sub-genres: (a) apocalyptic literature which talks of the End of Time (*ākhar al-zamān*) and which depicts darkness, destruction, killing, pillaging and terror (Farrokhzād has at least one whole poem of this type: 'Āyeh-hā-ye zamini' ['Earthly Verses']); and (b) revelatory or prophetic literature which, to a certain extent, is also related to killing and disorder, but which can also foretell the triumph of good over evil. (Farrokhzād has several poems of this kind, but none of them are optimistic in tone, except for 'Kasi keh mesl-e hich kas nist' ['Someone Who is Like No Other'], in which the narrator is *jonub-shahri*, an ordinary person from the rough, south side of town.)

Farrokhzād's 'Earthly Verses' is the best example of an apocalyptic poem in contemporary Persian literature. In this poem, Farrokhzād speaks as a sad and despondent prophetess about a dark and dismal future. What is amazing is that the events described in Farrokhzād's poem (which are depicted as occurring at the End of Time) can be said – in some form or another – to have come about gradually, one by one, following the poet's death. It seems there were signs, during the poet's lifetime, which she picked up on with her strong sense of precognition. Farrokhzād somehow foretold future events. 'Earthly Verses' opens with the following lines:[13]

آنگاه
خورشید سرد شد
و برکت از زمین ها رفت

و سبزه ها به صحراها خشکیدند
و ماهیان به دریاها خشکیدند
و خاک مردگانش را
زان پس به خود نپذیرفت

Then
The sun grew cold
And blessing left the lands

And the green shoots on the plains withered
And the fish in the seas dried up
And the earth, from then on,
No longer accepted the dead unto itself

In this most effective and moving poem, Farrokhzād sketches a terrifying scene. The sun has turned cold, and the fields have become barren. The new shoots have dried up and the fish – although they remained in the sea – have died. The earth will not accept the corpses of the dead and, in the absence of the sun, the night reigns supreme. In such circumstances, no one thinks any more of love or conquest. People are crawling in the darkest depths of the caves of loneliness, and their only occupation in this isolation is smoking opium and hashish. Women give birth to stillborn babies; what a dark, bitter age it is! Even the prophets – cursed by misfortune – are starving. Those lost souls who venture from door to door no longer hear the soothing voices of their spiritual leaders. The mirrors reflect things in 'reverse'. For example, they show halos shining above the heads of whores and fools. Intellectuals lie drowning in swamps of alcohol, while books containing ancient wisdom lie unread. The sun has been absent for some time, and so the young have no concept of tomorrow. The children's distorted understanding of tomorrow causes them to represent it in their drawings with blobs of black ink. The dead launch attacks against one another without thinking, slitting each other's throats, and in beds made of blood they lie with prepubescent girls. When someone is hanged, everyone gathers, and – watching with bulging eyes – they think lustful thoughts. But what is strange is that the speaker says small criminals sometimes could be seen around the edges of the town square, looking towards the fountains. Perhaps, behind their blinded eyes and in their dead hearts, there was still something that wanted to believe in purity, life and hope? Farrokhzād, in an interview, said about this poem:[14]

There is certainly no negative (lit., 'ugly') perspective in this poem, in particular in relation to human beings. In fact the whole of this poem is a description of the atmosphere (fazā) in which humans live, not the actual humans themselves. [It's the description of] an atmosphere that draws humans towards ugliness, absurdity and criminality.

The societal background

The key word in the above quoted interview is 'atmosphere' (fazā). What Farrokhzād means is the societal background of the period in which she lived. It is a given that Farrokhzād's prophecies emerged from the society in which she lived, and from her particular situation in that era. In the same interview she says, 'I had in mind that crime-nurturing seed. Otherwise, humans are innocent (bi-gonāh; lit., 'sinless')'. Farrokhzād saw that traditional Iranian society, in the absence of any sort of cultural preplanning, was moving towards a form of hollow modernity. Behind the ironed suits of the tie-wearing peasants, she sensed savagery, harshness and a lack of culture. This civilised veneer was, in her eyes, extremely superficial. On the other hand, she believed the intellectuals of her age to be merely imitating intellectuals. In Farrokhzād's opinion, they espoused empty slogans in their search for fanciful ideals. Their analyses in many cases were unsound.[15]

Via her family (in particular her mother) and via those who lived in her neighbourhood of Tehran, Farrokhzād was in touch with many traditionally minded Iranians, whereas through her artistic activity, she was equally in contact with the intellectuals of her day. She knew the poverty, misfortune and superstitions of the first group, as well as the hollowness and despair of the other. When she says, 'the blood smelled of hashish and opium', or when she speaks of 'hungry and unfortunate prophets', or 'swamps of alcohol',[16] these are all associated with the intellectuals of her time. Her representations of intellectuals in her poetry are all negative and disheartening. Here are two examples, the first from 'Didār dar shab' ('Meeting at Night'),[17] and the second from 'Tanhā sedā-st keh mi-mānad' ('Only Sound Remains'):

پس این پیادگان که صبورانه
بر نیزه های چوبی خود تکیه داده اند
آن باد پا سوارانند؟
و این خمیدگان لاغر افیونی
آن عارفان پاک بلند اندیشند؟

همکاری حروف سربی بیهوده ست
همکاری حروف سربی
اندیشه ی حقیر را نجات نخواهد داد.

So these foot soldiers who lean patiently
on their wooden spears
are those swift riders?
And these stooping, emaciated heroin addicts
are those pure, lofty-minded mystics?

Cooperation of lead letters is futile
Cooperation of lead letters
will not save worthless thoughts.

The passage of time bore out the truth of Farrokhzād's assessment of her age. Iran's intellectuals did not have an accurate perspective on their society, culture or world history. They lacked both sound ideas and accurate analyses. Farrokhzād depicts her brother as one of these petty intellectuals, who has grown up in a traditional, religious family, where the mother prays continually and the retired father reads Ferdowsi's *Shāhnāmeh* (from 'Delam barā-ye bāghcheh mi-suzad', 'I Feel Sorry for the Garden'):

برادرم به فلسفه معتاد است
برادرم شفای باغچه را
در انهدام باغچه می داند
او مست می کند
و مشت می زند به در و دیوار
وسعی می کند که بگوید
بسیار دردمند و خسته و مأیوس است

My brother is addicted to philosophy
My brother sees the garden's cure
in its destruction

He gets drunk
Beats his fists against the walls
And tries to say
how very pained, tired, and despondent he is

The socio-political circumstances of Farrokhzād's era

From the Constitutional Revolution onwards, Iran transformed into an unsettled and politicised society. During the poet's lifetime, three important political events took place in Iran: the ousting of Reza Shah in 1941, the Coup of 1953, and the events of 15th Khordād 1963. Farrokhzād died in February 1967, and after her death the tensions between the two main factions – the Islamists and the Leftists – increased considerably.

Some of the events that took place shortly after Farrokhzād's death had a considerable impact on Iran's literary community and on the country as a whole: the founding of the Iranian Writers' Association (Kānun-e Nevisandegān) in 1967; the death of Samad Behrangi in 1968 (of course, the rumour was that he had been killed); the Siyahkal operation of 1970; the celebrations of 2,500 years of Persian monarchy at Persepolis in 1971; the death of Dr Shari'ati in 1977; and the Goethe poetry evenings of 1977 (which, in contrast to the Khusheh poetry evenings of 1968, were very political). In addition to these events at home, news was reaching Iran of numerous social and political movements abroad, and of such monumental events as the Cuban Missile Crisis (1962), the Vietnam War, Mao's Cultural Revolution in 1960s China, and the Algerian War of Independence (1954–1962).

After Farrokhzād's death in 1967, the two main factions of the Islamists and the Leftists became much more defined. Individuals such as M. Azarm, Musavi-Garmārudi, Tāhereh Saffārzādeh and even Shafi'i-Kadkani were in the pro-religion front, and individuals such as Sa'id Soltānpur, Kasrā'i and Golsorkhi were pro-leftist. The literature produced at the time by these two factions is collectively known as 'resistance literature' (*adabiyāt-e moqāvemat*). No one of the five great poets of contemporary Iran (that is, Nimā Yushij, Mehdi Akhavān-Sāles, Ahmad Shāmlu, Sohrāb Sepehri and Forugh Farrokhzād) had any inclination towards either of these groups. But all of them (with the exception of Sohrāb Sepehri) were political poets and opposed the regime. At this time, poems by important non-Iranian political poets such as Lorca, Aragon and Neruda were being translated into Persian. The poets who had come before Nimā Yushij (such as 'Āref, 'Eshqi, Farrokhi, Lāhuti and Bahār) had also been political poets. (Up until the Constitutional Revolution, for almost a thousand years, Persian poets had – bar a few rare exceptions such as Ferdowsi and Hāfez – avoided discussing political matters, but following the constitutional movement, Persian poetry on the whole became socio-political in nature.)

Farrokhzād was a pioneer, in the sense that her poems are some of the earliest examples of revolutionary poetry in Iran to foretell the impending rise of the armed militia. Farrokhzād observed the traditionally minded people in the old neighbourhoods of Tehran whose children – whether Islamist or Communist – were stockpiling weapons. She also saw the Shah's secret police (the SAVAK), which, unconcerned as to the root causes of this phenomenon, was in continual pursuit of the weak:

تمام روز

از پشت در صدای تکه تکه شدن می آید

و منفجر شدن

همسایه های ما همه در خاک باغچه هاشان به جای گل

خمپاره و مسلسل می کارند

All day
from behind the door comes the sound of shattering and explosions
All our neighbors, instead of flowers,
plant mortar and machineguns in their gardens

Following the Constitutional Revolution all Iranians waited expectantly, but what they had wished for was never fully realised. Some awaited the appearance of the Lord of the Age, the return of the Hidden Imām (*zohur-e imām-e zamān*), while others waited for a Lenin figure to appear, one who should manifest himself in a neighbour's house, where a cock has not crowed for a very long time.[18] This mixed perspective on Iranian society which, after Farrokhzād, divided into two separate parts, is already clearly visible in the poem, 'Someone Who is Like No Other'. The personage described in this poem is both the Imām of the Age *and* Lenin; he is the one awaited by the religious people in society, as well as by the leftist youth, and the intellectuals:

من خواب دیده ام که کسی می آید

من خواب یک ستاره ی قرمز دیده ام

...

...

من خواب آن ستاره ی قرمز را

وقتی که خواب نبودم دیده ام

کسی میآید

کسی میآید

کسی دیگر

کسی بهتر

کسی که مثل هیچ کس نیست، مثل پدر نیست، مثل انسی
نیست، مثل یحیی نیست، مثل مادر نیست
و مثل آن کسیست که باید باشد
و قدش از درخت های خانه ی معمار هم بلندتر است
و صورتش
از صورت امام زمان هم روشنتر

...

و اسمش آنچنانکه مادر
در اول نماز و در آخر نماز صدایش می کند
یا قاضی القضات است
یا حاجت الحاجات

...

کسی می آید
کسی می آید
کسی که در دلش با ماست، در نفسش با ماست، در
صدایش با ماست

...

...

کسی از آسمان توپخانه در شب آتش بازی می آید
و سفره را میاندازد
و نان را قسمت میکند
و پپسی را قسمت میکند
و باغ ملی را قسمت میکند

...

و سهم ما را هم میدهد
من خواب دیده ام

I've seen in a dream that someone is coming
I've dreamt of a red star

. . .

I dreamt of that red star
when I wasn't asleep
Someone is coming
Someone is coming
Someone else
Someone better
Someone who is like no other: not Father, not Ensi, not Yayha, not Mother
He's like the one he must be
He's taller than the trees in the architect's house, and his face is

brighter than the Promised Imam's

. . .

And his name, just as Mother calls him
at the beginning and end of her prayers,
is either 'Judge of judges'
or 'Need of needs'

. . .

Someone is coming
Someone is coming
Someone who in his heart is with us
Who in his breath is with us
Who in his voice is with us

. . .

Someone is coming from the sky of Tupkhāneh Square on fireworks' night
He'll spread the table, and divide up the bread
And share out the Pepsi
And divide up Melli Park

. . .

He'll give us our share too
I've dreamed a dream

This poem is narrated using the voice of the common, religious, poor stratum in Iranian society, and Farrokhzād uses the register and vocabulary of that class of Iranian society in this poem.

Farrokhzād's developmental and educational background

Farrokhzād lived in a society in which most people were traditionally minded and religious. They were being driven towards a form of modernity, the foundations of which had not properly been laid. She lived in a house in which she saw her mother continually praying and asking for God's forgiveness (from 'Delam barā-ye bāghcheh mi-suzad', 'I Feel Sorry for the Garden'):

مادر تمام روز دعا می خواند
مادر گناهکار طبیعی ست
و فوت می کند به تمام گل ها
و فوت می کند به تمام ماهی ها
و فوت می کند به خودش
مادر در انتظار ظهور است
و بخششی که نازل خواهد شد

Mother prays all day long
Mother is a natural sinner
And she breathes on all the flowers
And she breathes on all the goldfish
And she breathes on herself
Mother is waiting for the Coming of the Imam
And for a forgiveness that will be sent down

On the other hand, the poet lived in Iran's incomplete, post-Constitutional Revolution society; a society in which every day people waited for something to happen:

بعد از تو ما به میدان ها رفتیم
و داد کشیدیم
زنده باد
مرده باد

After you, we went into the squares
And shouted:
Long live . . .!
Death to . . .!:[19]

This is why in her poetry Farrokhzād is not only pessimistic about the socio-political state of Iran itself, but also disapproves of the socio-political trajectory of the world as a whole. In her view, although mankind makes new discoveries and devises novel inventions on an almost daily basis, in reality, the world is not on the straight path to true happiness. In other words, Farrokhzād did not accept the idea of progress:[20]

پیغمبران، رسالت ویرانی را
با خود به قرن ما آوردند
این انفجارهای پیاپی،
و ابرهای مسموم،
آیا طنین آیه های مقدس هستند؟
ای دوست، ای برادر، ای همخون
وقتی به ماه رسیدی
تاریخ قتل عام گل هارا بنویس

The prophets brought with them
into our century their message of ruin
These continual explosions

These poisoned clouds
Are they the echoes of holy verses?
O friend, o brother, o relative
When you reach the moon
Write down the date the flowers were massacred[21]

In the poem, 'Ey marz-e por-gohar' ('O' Bejewelled Realm'), Farrokhzād derides the socio-political and administrative systems in Iran which are run by leading men who appear on the surface to be 'modern' but who are, in essence, backward and superstitious.[22]

The despondent and sad poet

Farrokhzād can be categorised as belonging to the subgroup of poets sometimes referred to as 'Dionysian poets', who are understood to employ 'dark', 'stormy' or 'turbulent' imagery in their poems, as opposed to 'Apollonian poets', whose works are considered more 'sunny' or 'serene'. Farrokhzād arguably also qualifies as Dionysian in that she is a naturalistic poet. In an interview, when answering the question why she sometimes sees life and people as ugly or grotesque in her poetry, she says:[23]

> This is not a grotesque or ugly perspective, but rather a natural one. Every living person, when he or she looks at existence as a single unit – which is him or herself – suffers from this sense of despair and painful pessimism. I am indeed something meaningless and unfortunate if I am not part of life itself. I am as empty as the image depicted in the poem, 'Dar-yāft'.

This weariness, sadness, despair and sense of grief run throughout her poetry. In the poem, 'Jom'eh' ('Friday'), Farrokhzād depicts the life of a lonely woman (perhaps herself) on Fridays in Tehran in the following way:

آه، چه آرام و پرغرور گذر داشت
زندگی من چو جویبار غریبی
در دل این جمعه های ساکت متروک
در دل این خانه های خالی دلگیر
آه، چه آرام و پرغرور گذر داشت...

Oh how calmly and full of pride my life passed like an alien stream
through those silent, abandoned Fridays

through those empty, depressing houses
Oh how calmly and full of pride it passed![24]

Farrokhzād is in many senses a poet who looks to the past; a poet who is, essentially, pessimistic about not only the present, but also the future. The opening poem in her immortal collection, *Tavallodi digar,* called 'Ān ruz-hā' ('Those Days'), shows how her mind is tied to the past.[25] In relation to the future, I have shown that Farrokhzād presents terrifying, apocalyptic imagery in her poetry, but the way in which she describes her present state in this poem touches the heart of every sensitive reader. At the end of the poem, 'Dar āb-hā-ye sabz-e tābestān'[26] ('In the Green Waters of Summer', actually in the penultimate stanza, although Farrokhzād herself said the last four lines of this poem were superfluous)[27] she says:

$$\text{ما بر زمینی هرزه روئیدیم}$$
$$\text{ما بر زمینی هرزه میباریم}$$
$$\text{ما ((هیچ)) را در راهها دیدیم}$$
$$\text{بر اسب زرد بالدار خویش}$$
$$\text{چون پادشاهی راه می پیمود}$$

We sprang from vile land
We rained down on vile land
We saw 'Nothing' on the roads,
mounted on his winged, yellow horse,
following the road like a king

'I Feel Sorry for the Garden'

'I Feel Sorry for the Garden', which Farrokhzād wrote near the end of her life, is one of the poet's most important poems, and was published posthumously.[28] It is after this poem that she has a vision in which she sees the Promised One coming.[29] 'I Feel Sorry for the Garden' is one of Farrokhzād's most symbolic poems, in which the 'garden' (*bāghcheh*) stands for Iranian society as a whole. For Farrokhzād, every family home is an essential part of the whole country. The 'flowers' are the children and youth of Iran; the 'goldfish' are those in society who seek freedom.[30] In Farrokhzād's vision of Iran, the garden, no one wants to accept the fact that the garden is dying and that society is little by little losing its verdure, and is being emptied of its lush, green memories.[31] The poet depicts people waiting expectantly for an 'unknown cloud' to save the garden by delivering life-saving rain. The 'small, inexperienced stars' mentioned in the poem (which are described as falling from the height of the trees onto the dust) are the young men and women involved in the political struggle. In this poem Farrokhzād presents a detailed and accurate picture of contemporary Iranian society. She depicts four 'types', described by a narrator who has adopted an isolated, solitary tone. It is the voice of this lone speaker which is perhaps the most interesting element here.

The first 'type' is the Father, who represents those in society who say that their time is up, that they have done their share. They are happy that they have reached retirement age peacefully, and they busy themselves at home reading books. It is interesting that Farrokhzād depicts this type of person reading history books (namely the *Shāhnāmeh* and *Nāsekh ol-tavārikh*, which espouse two diametrically opposed worldviews). Perhaps her point is that they content themselves with mythical illusions or lies about the supposed glory and majesty of the past? The Father is furthermore upset with the free thinkers and political activists: he curses the birds and the fish, who, he feels, cause him trouble. He asks why it should make any difference to him what will happen to the garden when he dies.

The second type is the Mother who represents the traditionally minded, religious stratum of Iranian society. The Mother is constantly preoccupied with the thought that she might sin or transgress in some way. In her opinion, it is the sins and moral corruption of ordinary Iranians that have caused the 'garden' to fall into its present, decrepit state. She prays and blows on the 'flowers' (the young people of Iran) and on the 'fish' (Iran's freethinkers) who seek a better, less constrained life. The Mother is hopeful, and is content to spend her life in anticipation of the advent of the Promised One (*zohur-e mow'ud*).

The third type is the Brother, who represents Iran's intellectuals. He is continually moaning, and has his own pessimistic vocabulary and expressions. For example, he calls the garden 'the graveyard' (*qabrestān*). The Brother engages in philosophical debates and, like all other Iranian intellectuals of the time, is leftist. That is why he believes the garden can only truly be healed if it is first destroyed. He gets drunk, shouts and screams, and likes to show himself to be despairing and weary. Farrokhzād shows her contempt for this group in society through the tone she uses to describe the Brother.

The fourth type is the Sister, who represents the affluent members of Iranian society, those living in the new suburbs of Tehran, who are not from old, established families, but rather are nouveau riche, and therefore do not have the cultured ways of the true upper classes, although they attempt to mimic their mannerisms. The Sister's home is on the other side of town, perhaps northern Tehran (the Farrokhzād family home was located in southern Tehran). These newer, more affluent homes are, in the poet's eyes, 'artificial' (*masnu'i*); they have all the glitz of American or European homes (the most expensive tables and chairs), but life within their four walls has not changed one bit: the occupants still sit on the floor to eat their meals. This affluent Sister, whenever she comes to visit her family in southern Tehran expresses repulsion at the rundown neighbourhood and its inhabitants:

او
هر وقت که به دیدن ما می آید
و گوشه های دامنش از فقر باغچه آلوده می شود
حمام ادکلن می گیرد

Whenever she comes to see us,
and the hem of her dress becomes soiled by the garden's poverty,
she bathes in eau de cologne

I would argue that Farrokhzād's depiction of the last two types, i.e. the 'Brother' – the vacuous intellectual – and the 'Sister' – the nouveau riche social-climber – are the two that she despises the most. As for the 'Mother', the poet expresses something bordering on sympathy, and as for the 'Father', she seems largely disinterested. But what is Farrokhzād's own view on the state of the garden? Her lone, isolated voice declares that their courtyard garden is 'alone' and 'lonely' (*hayāt-e khāneh-ye mā tanhā-st*). It is in this state of loneliness that Farrokhzād realises the garden of Iran is a time bomb waiting to explode. The neighbours, instead of planting flowers, are planting mortar and machineguns; they are hiding weapons in their pools, and their children's pockets are stuffed with hand grenades. Farrokhzād feels dizzy and terrified; she is frightened by the future of her society and its unstable condition. She fears all these hands and mouths that cheer in vain and shout out slogans. She views all faces as those of strangers. She expresses how isolated she feels amidst all this with a novel and powerful simile: she is like a school pupil who is madly in love with her geometry classes. We know how rare such schoolchildren are, and how exceptional and strange she therefore must be.

It could be argued that here the poet represents the true Iranian intellectual, who is isolated in her views, who does not espouse any particular ideology, and who does not belong to any political party – and who is therefore truly alone. That lone voice in the poem concludes by saying that she believes the garden can be taken to hospital; that, with the right reforms, it would be possible to turn around this sorry state of affairs, and avoid what appears to be an inevitable, impending catastrophe.

This talk of 'reforms' is something that belongs to more recent political language. Such a discourse was not current when Farrokhzād wrote this poem (around 1965). Gadamer, in relation to the dialogue between the text and its interpreter, says that first of all, we understand the text in a contemporary fashion, and it is only after that that we understand the text within its historical context, employing a true sensitivity for the contemporaneous meaning of the language and expressions used in the text. Now when I read, 'And I think that the garden can be taken to hospital', I understand this to be an allusion to political and social reforms, but I surely would not have drawn this conclusion when the poem was first published.

Farrokhzād says she is continually thinking about the state of the garden and she repeats four times, 'I think' (*man fekr mi-konam*), but the only thought that she expresses is that the garden can be taken to hospital. With hindsight, the import of these simple words seems clear to the reader today.[32] At the end of the poem, after all that thinking, the poet repeats two of the most symbolic lines from the beginning of the poem:

و ذهن باغچه دارد آرام آرام

از خاطرات سبز تهی می شود

And the garden's mind is, little by little
Being emptied of green memories

Iran for Farrokhzād was losing a period of peace, beauty and goodness. The colour green in Farrokhzād's terminology carries a wide range of positive connotations. It is perhaps interesting to note that Ebrāhim Golestān has a short story entitled, ''Eshq-e sāl-hā-ye sabz' ('Love of the Green Years').

Chapter 9

Capturing the Abject of the Nation in *The House is Black*

Nasrin Rahimieh

Forugh Farrokhzād's visionary documentary, *The House is Black* (1962), was commissioned by Anjoman-e Komak beh Jozāmiān (Society for Aiding Lepers) to generate support for Iran's victims of leprosy, although the Society had no input in the substance and direction of the film and its involvement was limited to providing only partial funding. Farrokhzād became involved in the project through her work at the Golestān Film Studios, where she had gained experience in cinema. The film was shot over a period of twelve days in a leper colony in northwestern Iran. The small film crew included Farrokhzād, a cameraman and a soundman. Farrokhzād completed the editing upon the team's return to Tehran and produced a unique documentary, blending images of everyday life in the colony with a poetic voice-over composed by her and delivered in her own voice.

The House is Black takes its viewers on a difficult journey into the colony, and directs their gaze on to the terrible and visible deformities caused by leprosy. There is little in the physiognomy of the inhabitants of the colony that could be aligned with normative concepts of beauty; the faces and bodies captured on the screen have been ravaged to varying degrees by the disease. The voice-overs reinforce the harshness of the visual essay. The film's relentless emphasis on the impact of the disease on its victims demands that the viewers become accustomed to the unpleasant sights and to accept them as part of the social fabric of their society and nation. The challenge Farrokhzād levels at her viewers, as she pointed out in a comment she made about the documentary, is to view the film as if they were looking at their own lives reflected in a mirror.[1] But the image reflected in the mirror does not invite easy identification. Apart from the visible effects of leprosy there is the underlying fear of contagion associated with the disease. The images we see on the screen become the personification of the abject,[2] that which 'disturbs identity, system, order' and 'does not respect borders, positions, rules.'[3] The abject, as theorized by Kristeva, does not merely signify but confronts us with death:

> No, as in true theater, without makeup or masks, refuse and corpses *show me* what I permanently thrust aside in order to live. These body fluids, this defilement, this shit are what life withstands, hardly and with difficulty, on the part of death. There, I am at the border of my condition as a living being.[4]

This foregrounding of the abject and the accompanying unsettling of the self constitute a critique of ways of seeing and making meaning of the discarded and the stigmatized. Even more importantly, the incorporation of images of lepers into the viewers' field of vision dissolves the border separating the viewer from the victims, who despite having been relegated to a *jozām khāneh*[5] trespass, albeit temporarily, into other spaces of interiority to which the nation has denied them access. The 'home' the victims of leprosy have been assigned is a far cry from the spectators' concept of home.

This re-evaluation of what constitutes the 'home' and by extension the nation, implicit in *The House is Black*, is part and parcel of the ethos of this particular moment in Iranian cultural history. The decades immediately following the 1953 CIA-backed coup, staged to topple the democratically elected prime minister, Mohammad Mosaddeq, and to bolster the ruling monarch, Mohammad Rezā Shāh Pahlavi, although imbued with disillusionment, gave rise to intellectual, social, political and religious movements preoccupied with the nation's apparent total capitulation to foreign powers and the loss of national autonomy.[6] This era inaugurated an age of introspection and a re-evaluation of how Iranian national identity was imagined and what it elided in the process of projecting an image of modernity and progress. Intellectuals, artists, writers and poets of the time were equally attuned to the contradictions and tensions that pervaded the country. The malaise haunting the nation is evident in the work of some of Farrokhzād's literary cohort.

The most prominent articulation of the concept of an ailing nation is Jalāl Āl-e Ahmad's famous 1962 treatise, *Gharbzadegi*,[7] in which he deploys the metaphor of the disease to describe the prevailing social reality of Iran in the early 1960s. While Farrokhzād's film zeroes in on the decayed exterior, Āl-e Ahmad's treatise speaks of a seemingly whole surface covering a hollowed shell. In the opening paragraph of *Gharbzadegi*, Āl-e Ahmad likens the disease affecting his compatriots to cholera, before opting for another analogy:

> It's at least as bad as sawflies in the wheat fields. Have you ever seen how they infest wheat? From within. There is a healthy skin in place, but it's only a skin, just like the shell of a cicada on a tree.[8]

Āl-e Ahmad proceeds with an analysis of the economic, social and cultural conditions he believes have robbed the Iranian nation of its sense of 'authentic'[9] self. In contrast, Farrokhzād holds a mirror up to her viewers and forces them to see what they have refused to see as part of themselves: the disenfranchised, deformed and disabled.

By foregrounding this underside of Iranian life, the poet-filmmaker questions the assumption that the nation's house is in order. In this sense, *The House is Black* is not different in approach from much of Farrokhzād's poetry in which, as indicated by Farzaneh Milani, she:

> presents the voice of the Other in modern Persian literature. By speaking as a woman, she literally creates an-other voice . . . throughout her poetry, she puts herself as well as her vision of men into the text, and contradicts prevailing notions of the feminine and the masculine. She is neither silent nor concealed, neither chaste nor immobile. She refuses to suffer and not complain. She does not endure restrictions and prohibitions with fortitude. . . . Her poetry reveals the problems of a modern Iranian woman with all her conflicts, painful oscillations, and contradictions. . . . It explores the vulnerability of a woman who rejects unreflective conformity with the past and yet suffers from uncertainties of the future.[10]

This defiance of boundaries is the force that propels the camera's movements into the living spaces occupied by lepers who are otherwise closed off from the viewers' field of vision. Farrokhzād's camera pans the *jozām-khāneh* and makes this site of abjection into a space of the familial and the familiar. The film captures moments of domesticity and familial interaction. Such scenes are undercut by the dejection and the isolation of the visual and verbal narrative and, along with the film's ending, highlight the limits of the film's transgressive potential. In the final sequence of the documentary we see a group of lepers walking toward the colony's gate as it shuts on them. The inscription on the gate, *jozām-khāneh*, reminds us that they cannot cross over the physical barriers separating them from the spectators. The camera's pulling away from the colony reasserts the boundaries, rearticulating the uncertainties Milani finds reverberating in Farrokhzād's poetry. The relegation of the lepers to the space behind the closed door of the colony forecloses the possibility of anything more than a temporary transgression. The film thus records its own limitations and captures a remarkable self-awareness on the part of the artist.

Hamid Dabashi sees a different kind of self-awareness at work in *The House is Black*. In his view, the film is an interrogation of Iranian culture as a whole:

> In the ravaged faces and bodies of the lepers, Farrokhzad saw the deranged layers of Iranian culture; for her they were a mirror of a brutalized history. She looked into that mirror and reflected those faces neither in sympathy nor in empathy. She probed the distorted features of those bodies in search of the most hidden horrors and exposed them.[11]

Dabashi conflates the figure of the leper with Farrokhzād's self-image and situates her film in her identification with the lepers she encountered in the process of making the film:

> In lepers and their predicament, Farrokhzad saw her own projected image: ashamed of yet attached to a guilt falsely carried. In the face of the lepers, Farrokhzad saw her own face, and that is why and how she identified with them – other people literally marked with a shameful sign, a people moved to the dark, the grotesque, the frightful, the feared, and the despised side of humanity. When through her camera Farrokhzad looked at the lepers' physically deformed faces she saw what the patriarchal pathology she defied had cauterized on her morally defamed face – a defacement she could until then imagine but not see. The leper was Farrokhzad's vilified public persona, to which she now lent her defiant poetic vision. Farrokhzad had a culturally contracted leprous scar on her face – code-named dagh-e nang – long before she visited the leprosarium. That is why she could identify with the lepers so immediately.[12]

In Dabashi's argument,

> A leprosarium is a transgressive space – a grotesque, forbidden space where bodies ruined by disease are locked away so as not to disturb the legislation of bodily normalcy. Opening the door on a defiant semiotics of the grotesque, Farrokhzad releases a disruption of the semantic legislation of the body.[13]

As I have argued, the film's ending, which depicts a closing gate, rules out such a complete rewriting of the 'legislation of the body'. What the film successfully disrupts is the assumption of the wholeness and wholesomeness of the nation. Not unlike Āl-e Ahmad, Farrokhzād asks her audience: 'How can a home whose foundations are in the process of disintegration serve as a foundation . . .?'[14] Her film shines a light on some cracks in the foundation and destabilizes the security of the home. Making room for the faces and bodies of the victims of leprosy in the nation's self-image is part of the film's objective and its attempt to allow the lepers entry into a realm of humanity from which they are otherwise barred.

I should add that, unlike Dabashi, who sees Farrokhzād's optics as falling outside the range of humanism,[15] I am less preoccupied with the co-optive potential of the grand narratives of humanism[16] and their much feared universalizing tendencies. I believe we can counteract such possible adverse effects by focusing on the specifics of cultural practices and attitudes foregrounded in Farrokhzād's documentary. Uncovering the human in the lepers is to unsettle cultural assumptions about the need to fear and abhor disfigured, disabled and diseased bodies.

One of the challenges Farrokhzād's film poses is to question the practice of mistreating those who have been disabled as a result of a disease, even worse, condoning such mistreatment and ostracization as culturally normative. To make the film, Farrokhzād herself had to learn a new mode of seeing and part of what she conveys to her viewers is how to inhabit a world riven by disease and deformity. In an interview Farrokhzād gave a year after the making of *The House is Black*, she spoke about her entry into the leper colony and the process by which she gained access to the scenes she filmed:

> The first day that I saw the lepers I was deeply moved. . . . It was terrible. In the leper colony a number of people live who possess all the qualities and feelings of a human being minus a face. I saw a woman whose face was only a hole through which she talked! . . . [To make a film truly portraying these people] I was obliged to win their confidence. These people had not been dealt with squarely before. Whoever visited them had looked at their flaws. But I . . . sat at their tables, touched their wounds, felt their feet, the toes of which were ravaged by the disease. It was through such equal treatment that the patients came to trust me [and I was able to show them as they were]. . . . Even today, after one year from the visit, some of them still write me . . .[17]

What we glimpse in this statement is Farrokhzād's own ability to inhabit their space and to accept the human beneath the ravaged body. By overcoming her distaste for the disfigured victims, she could look at her subjects not merely as diseased and disabled bodies but grant them communal and social agency.

As Benedicte Ingstad and Susan Reynolds Whyte argue in *Disability and Culture*, 'Cultural assumptions about the body and personhood must be seen in the context of ordinary social interaction.'[18] By capturing daily routines in the leper colony, Farrokhzād introduces a new vision of the diseased and disabled. She creates conditions for the lepers to be imagined as persons in their own right, albeit part of a hitherto unimagined category of existence:

> 'Radical relativism' seeks to reveal basic assumptions about what it is to be a person, and what kinds of identities and values exist in given social contexts. How important is individual ability as a source of social identity? What is it people are trying to achieve? The strong version of relativism questions the terms of analysis and attempts to uncover the categories implicit in other worldviews. The concept of disability itself must not be taken for granted. In many cultures, one cannot be 'disabled' for the simple reason that 'disability' as a recognized category does not exist. There are blind people and lame people, and 'slow' people, but 'the disabled' as a general term does not translate easily in many languages.[19]

The House is Black translates for its Iranian viewers the very absence of a word for disability in Persian. Yeganeh Salehpour and Narges Adibsereshki note in their study 'Disability and Iranian Culture':

> Our first finding has to do with the absence of the general word 'disability'. The equivalent chosen for the word 'disability' in academic literature is 'natavan' in Farsi. However, in Farsi literary works, 'natavan' usually refers to the elderly or the poor ... In Farsi folklore, ... the writers refer to specific impairments of blindness, deafness, impairment of speech, physical impairments (usually impairments in one's legs, 'lang'), and in a few instances, intellectual and emotional impairments.[20]

The authors of this study further observe:

> the uni-dimensional aspect of the attitudes conveyed through repeated use of the concept of 'mercy'. Iranian people, time and again, through their stories, poems, and proverbs communicated the importance of showing 'mercy', and 'patience' in dealing with people with disability. In addition, our reviewed material portrays the disabled themselves, especially the blind, requesting and pointing out their need for people's mercy.[21]

We find such an example of the negative construction of disability in Irān Darrudi's autobiographical reflections in *Dar fāseleh-ye do noqteh* and her memories of how her appearance was the source of constant ridicule in the family:

> I, the second daughter of this family, was born with a face that was described by others as not particularly graced with beauty and eyes whose directions could not be followed. After seeing me, my father's step-mother told my mother: 'Why did you have so much pain for giving birth to this wall-eyed girl?' This harsh judgment passed on the appearance of a child who had just entered the world became entrenched in family memory.[22]

When we consider the fear of contagion that accompanies leprosy, we can better appreciate the radical and innovative nature of Farrokhzād's gaze. While the spread of leprosy can be contained through proper hygiene and medical treatment, victims of leprosy, at least at the time the documentary was made, were nevertheless shunned as carriers of the disease. The documentary not only makes us look at the lepers and their lives in the confinement of the colony, but also intermingles the disfigured faces and bodies with moments when those very bodies are engaged in play and celebration. This juxtaposition of the abject and the playful urges the viewer to see beyond the surface of the disease. As if to underline the film's emphasis on seeing differently and clearing away preconceptions, the documentary begins with a blank screen.

Before we see the first image in the film, we hear a man's voice setting the tone for what we are about to see:

> There is no shortage of ugliness in the world. If man closed his eyes to it, there would be even more. But man is a problem solver. On this screen will appear an image of ugliness, a vision of pain no human should ignore. To wipe out this ugliness and to relieve its victims is the motive of this film and the hope of its makers.[23]

Projected onto a black screen, the verbal here acquires supremacy before we are launched into the visual.

As the camera enters the interiors of *jozām-khāneh*, our eyes are immediately confronted with a sequence that dwells on the bleakness that will engulf our vision. The opening sequence is composed of a woman looking into a mirror. In a medium shot, we see what she sees in the mirror: her partially covered, disfigured face. The scarf covering the woman's head and part of her face could well be seen as indicators of her modesty and adherence to the Muslim dress code. But the movement of the camera soon undercuts the possibility of seeing the woman's head cover as only religiously motivated. The camera guides our gaze by travelling closer to zoom in an extreme closeup. The camera then freezes, almost rendering the image into a still shot. This focus reveals disfigured aspects of the face we see partially because the scarf covers half of her face. The progression from movement to stillness and the presence of the mirror suggest that our gazes cannot be averted from the grotesque image before us. The mirror, like the camera, mediates between the observer and the observed and acts as the medium through which the gazes are exchanged. One reviewer finds this opening shot representative of Farrokhzād's empathetic embrace of the subjects she films: 'The viewer not only looks at the woman, but *shares* the woman's gaze at herself, a mark of the film's implicit empathy.'[24]

This opening sequence of the film also invokes the prototypical image of a woman looking at herself in the mirror, normally associated with self-beautification. In this case, the subject gazing into the mirror finds progressive erasure and erosion of the tissue, nerves, cartilage and bone – the constituent parts of the type of face that would be gazed upon. Instead we see, at least partially, the absence of the components and our attempt to orient our gaze aesthetically is arrested. What is interesting here is that the camera insists on capturing the woman in this typical scene not merely for shock value, though shock is a byproduct of this opening shot. By pausing on this face, the camera draws us in and invites us to learn to see what we have closed our eyes to. This is a reflection of what we have heard in the voice-over in the beginning: that there would be more ugliness if humanity closed its eyes to it.

On the most immediate and obvious level, the film and the opening statement are means to incite individuals to offer help and to recruit more support for the prevention and treatment of leprosy. Not closing our eyes is the first step toward acknowledging the ravages of a disease which, as we are told in a later, more scientific or factual commentary, is curable.[25] But beyond this utilitarian message of the voice-over lies the possibility that letting our gaze roam through the house of leprosy will teach us to see reality differently, thus unsettling the normal associations of the beautiful and the ugly.

That the categories and concepts have been displaced and even inverted for the individuals living within the leper colony is poignantly delineated in the classroom exchanges between the teacher and his pupils. The teacher asks one pupil: 'Name a few beautiful things.' The pupil to whom this question is directed responds: 'The moon, the sun, flowers, and playtime.' The teacher then turns to another young boy and says: 'Now name some ugly things.' This time the answer which is followed by a round of giggles is: 'Hand, feet, head.'

This child's notion of the ugly is informed by observing the effects of leprosy on the human body. The contrast between nature, untouched by disease, and human deformity is sharply drawn out for these children, but their laughter inscribes playfulness in the answer. The young boy knows hands, feet and head are not necessarily synonymous with ugliness, hence his laughter. But his assertion also underlines the reality that for those who live in the leper colony the normal and the normative have been troubled and redefined.

An even more forceful reminder of how much life in the colony deviates from what is taken for granted by others living outside it also appears earlier in this classroom sequence. After students hear passages read aloud from a school primer reciting reasons for which a child would offer thanksgiving, the teacher asks one pupil why he should be thankful for having a father and mother. The youngster he pinpoints for an answer says without any apparent emotion: 'I don't know. I don't have either.' This factual response brings a secondary awareness that the leper colony is also an orphanage.[26] Yet the children entrusted to this orphanage do not have access to a language and means of understanding and expressing their reality. The school primer intended to socialize and educate young Iranians allows no room for a child deprived of parents and home.

Such moments of stark recognition are captured by Farrokhzād's own poetic voice-overs. They encapsulate a suffering and anguish beneath the daily routine, moments of joy and lightheartedness:

> I speak of the bitterness of my soul
> When I was silent my life was rotting
> From my silent screams all day long
> Remember that my life is the wind
> Like the pelican of the desert
> The owl of the ruins,
> And like a sparrow I am sitting alone on the roof[27]

But the visual and verbal also bring together diametric opposites. The next segment in the classroom is the one in which the young boy equating human body parts with the ugly breaks down into giggles. The two moments together make up the totality of the experience of living in the leper colony: disfigurement and depravation, coupled with an irrepressible desire to adhere to daily rituals and forms of pleasure.

Among the most striking instances of observing rituals is the sequence shot in the prayer room. The badly disfigured hands raised in prayer stand in stark contrast to the words of thanksgiving intoned in the prayers. To echo

Dabashi's views, the scenes of prayer and expression of gratitude transcend cultural specificity:

> By stretching beyond the Qur'anic and reaching for the biblical (Farrokhzad was always fascinated by the Persian translation of the Bible), Farrokhzad embraces an antiquity of diction that is no longer religious but metaphysical, no longer spatial but eternal, no longer cultural but cosmic, no longer political but mythic. Farrokhzad has let her camera loose to register the topography of a landscape she was at once privileged and condemned to see, and to show.[28]

I would suggest that the scenes of prayer and supplication should also be seen as part and parcel of the inextricable intermingling of suffering and joy throughout the documentary. Such scenes mark the continuities between life in and beyond the leper colony.

Farrokhzād's choices, both thematically and formally, move us close to the unbearable unsightliness of the disease and bring us back to an emotional register infused with scenes of children playing. The emphasis on play and playfulness is nowhere more emphatically emphasized as in a sequence when a young boy watches a little girl straddle a shovel and drag it along joyfully. Incited by her apparent pleasure, the young boy creates his own makeshift toy out of an older man's crutch. In the same frame we have a testimonial to the crippling effects of the disease and the resilience and desire to stand above the disease. Naturally these types of moments are more common among children. But even among the adults we observe a strong will to endure and to partake of normalcy. Play, be it in the form of a game of checkers played with pebbles and walnuts on a makeshift board drawn on the ground, or a sole man singing and dancing to his own tune, gives us a counter-example to the man pacing along a brick wall and counting the days of the week. We see a woman applying mascara to her eyelashes, despite the fact that her gnarled fingers cannot hold the tube with ease. The made-up face of the bride-to-be (like the dancing and singing accompanying the wedding) speaks to an existence that defies the disease and brings the abject into the realm of the object.

In relation to one of the six dimensions Michael Fischer attributes to Iranian cinema, Farrokhzad's film could be seen belonging to a style that 'one could call post-traumatic realism, drawing on earlier Italian neorealist and Eastern European absurdist-surrealist styles, which focuses on the everyday, on the problems and repair of society, and on the problematic cultural codes inherited from the past.'[29] The interweaving of the ethical and the aesthetic carves out a space in which Farrokhzād trains our gaze to see what we refused to see before, and to do so as a first step toward refocusing the nation's vision of itself and including its disfigured and disenfranchised.

The ways of seeing to which Farrokhzād introduces us resonate deeply with Sohrāb Sepehri's poetic re-envisioning of the verbal and the visual. As another member of Farrokhzād's cohort, in his long poem, 'Water's Footsteps', Sepehri also questions the aesthetic yardsticks by which beauty is encoded by culture:

> I do not know
> Why it is said that the horse is a noble creature, that the pigeon[30] is a
>   beautiful bird.
> I do not know why nobody keeps a vulture in a cage.
> I do not know why clover flowers are considered inferior to red tulips.
> Words should be washed
> Eyes should be washed to see things in a different way.
> To become the wind itself, the rain itself.[31]

It is interesting to note that Sepehri's long poem incorporates a double movement of giving the speaker a sense of home, 'I come from Kashan',[32] to only later subject it to radical homelessness:

> I come from Kashan
> But Kashan is no longer my town.
> My hometown has been lost.
> With feverish effort, I have built myself a house
>   on the other side of the night.[33]

The journey to the 'other side of the night' depicted by Sepehri captures the ultimate displacement of home and belonging which Farrokhzād also invites her viewers to experience. Like Sepehri, Farrokhzād asks us to perform a ritual ablution of the eyes and to enter a zone of instability in which the home and the nation need not banish the bodies which do not conform to their self-image. The lepers left behind the gates of the colony, the film reminds its spectators, might be out of sight, but, as their movement toward the closing gate of the colony at the end of the documentary suggests, the barriers separating them from the rest of the nation might well prove penetrable. The moving images that Farrokhzād asks her viewers to equate with their self-reflection trouble the sense of self, home and collective identity. The phrase, which becomes the title of the documentary, 'the house is black', composed in the schoolroom in the leper colony by one of the students who is asked to make a sentence with the word 'house', implicates not only *jozām-khāneh* but *khāneh* ('house' and 'home') in the utter darkness that envelopes both the subjects of the film and its viewers. It calls for a different house to be built 'on the other side of the night' of the soul in which the nation finds itself.

Chapter 10

The House is Black:
A Timeless Visual Essay

Maryam Ghorbankarimi

Perhaps this clear and long interaction of poetry with, and within, other art forms explains our implied acknowledgement that poetry exists independently of any one medium and that therefore film, too, can be poetry.[1]

Focusing on the editing and visual composition of Forugh Farrokhzād's documentary *The House is Black* (*Khāneh siyāh ast*), this essay will discuss how Farrokhzād's use of images to form a visual essay is comparable to her use of words in poetry. Farrokhzād has employed a formalist editing style by juxtaposing two different styles of editing throughout the film. *The House is Black* consists of two sections: the fast-cut montage of images of daily life in the leper colony set against the factual scenes in the hospital, which are classically edited with regard to time and space continuity. Her formalist approach is not only confined to the order in which the images follow one another, it is also evident in the composition of each frame. Following the discussion of the treatment of images, this essay will look at the purpose of the film-maker in employing such methods. In doing so, I will compare *The House is Black* with Luis Buñuel's *Land Without Bread* (*Las Hurdes*, 1933), a film with which *The House is Black* has often been compared.[2] For this research, I have consulted the VCD version of the film, published in Iran in 2002, under the title *The House is Black: The Original Version* (*Khāneh siyāh ast: noskheh-ye asli*).[3]

Farrokhzād's involvement in the art of film-making began with her joining the Golestān Film Unit (Sāzmān-e Film-e Golestān) in 1956. Ebrahim Golestān, a film-maker, writer and translator, launched the Golestān Film Unit in 1955 while he was working on six documentary shorts, under the title

Perspective (*cheshm-andāz*),[4] about the establishment of some oil companies in the south of Iran. He was the first film-maker in Iran at the time to have established his own film studio.[5] The main purpose of the Golestān Film Unit was to produce documentary films by providing the best available technical equipment while giving the film-makers complete artistic freedom in approaching the subject, and allowing for experimentation. By creating an ideal environment for talented young artists, the Golestān Film Unit, as Mohammad-Rezā Sharifi explains, became an educational institution, where some of the more prominent Iranian directors such as Nāser Taghvā'i and Forugh Farrokhzād started their film-making careers. At first, Farrokhzād joined the Golestān Film Unit as a typist; as time went by, she was given more significant tasks, leading to her working there as an editor, which, in turn, led to her directing *The House is Black*.[6]

The Society for Aid to Lepers (Anjoman-e Komak beh Jozāmiān) commissioned *The House is Black* from the Golestān Film Unit in 1962, and Farrokhzād was chosen to direct the piece. After a short research trip, in the summer of 1962, to the Bābādāghi leper colony near Tabriz, in northwest Iran, Farrokhzād went back in the fall of 1962, with five colleagues, to shoot the film.[7] She went there without any prior 'decoupage', script, shot list or shooting plan. She and her colleagues spent the first two days of the total twelve-day shoot familiarizing themselves with the environment and the people, letting their surroundings inspire them for the different parts of the film, or, as Farrokhzād puts it, they let the environment arouse their *she'r-e sinemā'i* or 'cinematic poetry'.[8] After the first couple of days, Farrokhzād found the direction she wanted her film to take, so they began shooting. Amir Karāri, the film's assistant cameraman, explains that she spent time with the people in the leper colony, gaining their trust and looking for key moments to capture, which, later in the editing process, would once again come to life, depending on how they were assembled.[9] Although The Society for Aid to Lepers commissioned the project, this did not take away from its artistic value. They gave Farrokhzād total freedom in terms of how the finished product should look. Also, as Farrokhzād herself states, an artist is an artist at all times; it is not something that can be switched on and off.[10] The outcome therefore had the potential to become a work of art, regardless of whether it was commissioned or not.

Although *The House is Black* is the only documentary that is fully credited to Farrokhzād as director and editor, this was not her first experience with cinema. She started working at the Golestān Film Unit a few years prior to the production of *The House is Black*, editing several documentaries and working as assistant director on a few projects. Farrokhzād's first practical experience in editing was in 1959 on *A Fire* (*Yek ātash*, 1961), a short documentary about the extinguishing of a fire at an oil refinery in Ahvāz.[11] This film was used as an educational tool for young film-makers in the Golestān Film Unit and took around two years to complete. As part of the editing process, Farrokhzād was sent to England for the summer to take an intensive editing course, specializing in documentary editing.[12]

The Golestān Film Unit subsequently took on the production of a miniseries commissioned by the Iranian Oil Company, but only the first six episodes were completed, as the studio gradually moved on to films that were not oil related. Farrokhzād was the editor for most of the completed episodes and was also the assistant director on several of them. It was during the making of these films that she showed her talent for both editing and directing. Her technique was to reduce the amount of descriptive narration in some of the episodes by turning the raw material into a coherent narrative that would not need further explanation.[13] For example, her dynamic editing turned one of these episodes, *Water and Fire* (*Āb va ātash*), into a lyrical film about the fire station in the Ābādān refinery. This film was not merely, as Hamid Naficy points out, 'a simple reportage of ordinary events and processes'.[14] In praise of her work on the same episode in the series, Hushang Kāvusi, an Iranian film critic and film-maker, states the following:

> This is a cinematic exploration. It is an elegant piece of work like a classical
> poem with modern meaning. All the aesthetics of cinema have been used in
> this film to create a deeper meaning than what is simply before us.[15]

By the time Farrokhzād made *The House is Black*, not only was she more familiar with the medium, but, as noted above, she had gained ample experience in film production. Moreover, her visits to Europe, whether for training courses or otherwise, no doubt introduced her to the works of contemporary European avant-garde film-makers.

Farrokhzād's untimely death at the age of 32 should be seen as the reason why this was her only major contribution as a film director and, therefore, *The House is Black* should not be devalued as a one-time success of a sentimental and inexperienced film-maker with a poetic nature – a view often taken by critics of the film.[16]

Although Farrokhzād's primary legacy is her poetry, which, as Farzaneh Milani asserts, introduced the feminine voice into Iranian literary works and challenged the dominant value systems of Iranian culture through this distinctive voice,[17] her film, *The House is Black* has similarly played an important role in the history of Iranian cinema. Hamid Dabashi describes *The House is*

Black as 'the brilliant film inaugurating contemporary Iranian cinema', and says that Farrokhzād proceeds and surpasses anything that happened in her time.[18] Agreeing with Dabashi, Jonathan Rosenbaum also looks at *The House is Black* as the predecessor to the works of Iranian New Wave directors such as Abbas Kiarostami. Rosenbaum claims, 'Farrokhzād, like later Iranian New Wave filmmakers working with non-professionals in relatively impoverished locations, created rather than simply found, conjuring up a potent blend of actuality and fiction'.[19] The blend of fiction and reality that Rosenbaum mentions led to debates on whether or not *The House is Black* could be considered a documentary. Although there are some parts of the film – most significantly the school scenes at the beginning and the end – that must have been staged, they do not necessarily preclude the film from being a documentary. Documentaries, as Stella Bruzzi argues, are inevitably created by the intrusion of the film-maker onto the subjects; as a result, 'the important truth any documentary captures is the performance in front of the camera'.[20] It is the fact that more is shown in this film than a mere depiction of reality that makes it a piece of art, distinguishing it from mere news reportage of the daily lives of the lepers within the colony.

A dual process, film-making is made up of two fundamental parts: the filming process and the selecting and assembling of the raw materials into a coherent piece. Depending on the type of film, one of these two processes can be more accentuated than the other. For example, often with documentary films, the story only comes to life during the editing stage, because of the lack of control during the shoot. Although several editing techniques exist (such as linear or narrative editing and montage), there is no single way to edit. It is a very fluid process, even within any one of the defined techniques. As with any other art form, the personal taste of the editor is also very important; the editor's role in the outcome of a film can therefore be quite significant. According to Podovkin, who values the editing stage very much, each shot only in conjunction with other shots, set in the frame of a complex form, is given life and reality.[21] In a film, such as *The House is Black*, it is significant that the director and the editor are the same person, because there will be far fewer thoughts lost in translation when the material is passed from the director to the editor. Karāri also mentions that Farrokhzād preferred long camera takes while shooting, allowing her to cut accordingly on the editing table.[22]

In defining the term 'editing' in cinema, the analogy of another art form, especially literature, has often been used. Podovkin explains, 'To the poet or writer separate words are as new material. They have the widest and most variable meanings, which only begin to become precise through their position in the sentence.'[23] This is also true about the raw footage in film-making: the meaning of the individual images becomes apparent only when those images are edited together in a sequence.

For Farrokhzād, taking up editing was a natural progression from writing poetry; instead of using words, she would write poems with images. Farrokhzād defines cinema as 'speaking through images', and she believed that in order to convey an idea through images, above all one needs to have something to say, an idea with some potential value.[24] In her opinion, as long as one has an idea, the medium that he or she employs is not important; the message is the key element. Confirming this, Farrokhzād says of her move to cinema: 'This is a way of expression; just because I have been writing poems that does not mean that poetry is the only medium I can employ to express my ideas. I like cinema.'[25]

The House is Black is often called a poetic documentary. Naficy states, 'The film eloquently and lyrically portrays the people of the colony, expressing the joy and humanity in their daily lives.'[26] In this lyrical documentary, Farrokhzād offers a poetic treatment of leprosy, allowing the film to move beyond the mere reality of the subjects and to enter the symbolic world. In a 1963 interview with the Italian writer and director Bernardo Bertolluci in Tehran, Farrokhzād, in regard to her approach to making *The House is Black*, says that it would have been easy to focus on the disease when making a film about leprosy, but she saw the leper colony as an example or a model of a world imprisoned by its illnesses, difficulties and poverty.[27] Through the combination of her insightful vision with the strong subject, Dabashi states, she 'detects and unveils the poetic souls hidden inside these ravaged bodies, and does so with a quiet elegance that has never been matched.'[28]

In comparing Farrokhzād's poetry to film editing, Ziā Movahhed, in an article entitled 'Farrokhzād in Relation with Images' ('Farrokhzād dar raftār bā tasvir'), explains the importance of the way she puts the words together in her poetry: '. . . in Farrokhzād's poetry, which is considered as visual poetry, the main artistic achievement is the art of relating the images, their order, and how they are edited together'.[29] Her sensibility towards words in her poetry resembles her choice of editing style in *The House is Black*, a film that can be argued to have been conceived mainly in the editing room.

Looking closely at *The House is Black*, it can be discerned that Farrokhzād employed two different styles of editing throughout the film. The film can be divided into two entities: the scenes in the hospital where doctors are treating the lepers, and the scenes representing daily life in the leper colony. In the hospital scenes, Farrokhzād has employed the narrative editing technique, creating a sense of continuity in a linear, sequential series of images; while in the other section, depicting daily life, she has employed the fast-paced montage technique. Montage, unlike the narrative editing technique, is not a thought constructed through a series of shots filmed one after another, but rather is an idea conveyed through the collision of two independent shots put together.[30] The scene that best illustrates this is the long take of a man walking back and forth along the side of a wall, intercut with static short shots of different people in the leper colony, while Farrokhzād's voice can be heard over it counting the days of the week and months of the year, thereby convey the repetitive pace and slow nature of life in the leper colony.

Farrokhzād has employed a formalist means of expression, using two different modes of editing in her short documentary. This method of construction is very similar to what the formalists employ in comparing the storytelling and the plot structure of films to the 'prose' and 'verse' structures in literary practices. *The House is Black* incorporates both of these elements. The factual hospital scene can be likened to prose work for its continuity, development and conclusion, and is more based on the story actions rather than on formal patterning, and this is also evident in this section's straight forward narration in Ebrahim Golestān's voice. On the other hand, the scenes of everyday life are more verse-like because of the formal oppositions, repetitions and parallelism, which is also evident in the poetic narration read in Farrokhzād's own voice.[31]

In comparing *The House is Black* to Luis Buñuel's 1933 film *Land without Bread*, many similarities and differences emerge. The films of this Spanish film-maker are famous for their surrealist imagery. His most famous film is *An Andalusian Dog* (*Un chien andalou*, 1929), which was made in collaboration with his friend and colleague, the painter Salvador Dalí. In his works, Buñuel usually attacks the bourgeoisie and the religious establishment. *Land without Bread* (1933) is a documentary that follows a narrative storytelling structure, mapping the film-maker's journey to Las Hurdes, a deprived village in northern Spain. Buñuel's film successfully depicts the horrifying and shocking lives of the Hurdanos, the people of Las Hurdes. The main difference between the two films is in the formalist style of editing in *The House is Black*. The startling short shots juxtaposed with longer, smoother clips in *The House is Black* prevent the viewer from becoming a passive observer, and therefore, while raising awareness, the film does not normalize the lepers' situation. This is not the case in *Land without Bread*. As Raymond Durgnat says, 'Buñuel begins by presenting a harrowing fact, shows the glimmer of hope, and then reduces that hope to something derisory.'[32] By midway into the film, the viewer becomes more or less used to the subject, and even though there are more horrid scenes to come, they are expected and less surprising.

The purpose of each of the films is also quite different. In *Land without Bread*, Buñuel's approach to the subject is quite analytical, even clinical,[33] while Farrokhzād's approach is a more compassionate report of the lives of the lepers. Another difference, which may at first be viewed as a similarity, is in the way that the two films have made use of the voice-over narration. The film-makers themselves read the majority of the narrations in both films. As Elisabeth H. Lyon explains, 'In *Land without Bread*, Buñuel recreates the essence of life in Las Hurdes through the dissociative processes, by the tension created between sound and image.'[34] In *Land without Bread*, the narration is disengaged and anaesthetized, and accompanied by the out-of-place Brahms's Fourth Symphony. In *The House is Black*, however, the narration in both sections of the film is on par with the imagery, complementing what is portrayed. One scene from *Land without Bread* that lends itself to a comparison with *The House is Black* is the scene of the fevered sufferers. As William Rothman explains, in the narrator's eye the victims are 'dwarves and morons'; they are 'so unaware that their existence is a horror, that they do not even suffer, or they suffer unawares.'[35] While the tone of narration in *Land without Bread* forces the viewer to see the horror of the lives of the Hurdanos, the narration in *The House is Black* softens the imagery and calls for sympathy towards the lepers. Despite the difference in narration, the images in *Land without Bread*, like those in *The House is Black*, 'reveal in a flash, vividly and intensely, the humanity of the people' being filmed.[36] Although in both films no one character is brought into focus and we never learn any of their names, their humanity comes through both Buñuel's and Farrokhzād's cameras, 'which enables us, indeed compels us, to recognize that they are human beings, just as we are.'[37]

Both films are considered to be analogies of their unhealthy contemporary societies. With regard to *The House is Black*, Naficy states, 'The government felt that Farrokhzād had presented a false and unnecessarily cruel picture and suppressed the film'.[38] The Spanish government, for very similar reasons, banned *Land without Bread*. The ironic juxtaposition of images of human degradation with the factual, insensitive narrations, along with Brahms's Fourth Symphony, as Raymond Durgnat argues, 'shrieks the hideous indifference of a society that, while priding itself on its elite culture, can find in all its finer feelings so little incentive to remedy degradation.'[39]

The formalist approach to editing in *The House is Black*, juxtaposing the reportage-like documentary style of the scenes in the hospital with a more poetic depiction of life in the leper colony, has been employed to raise awareness of the situation of the people in the leper colony, without normalizing their situation. Farrokhzād has employed this method of editing to keep the full attention of the viewer through to the end without the subject becoming ordinary for the audience. In comparisons of *The House is Black* to *Land without Bread*, Farrokhzād's formalist approach has been criticized as unnecessary: she did not need to use any technical shock effects, such as the fast-paced and jumpcut editing, as the audience was already psychologically predisposed to see such an upsetting subject.[40] However, Farrokhzād used the formalist technique that Victor Shklovsky coined as 'Defamiliarization' in order to change the existing ingrained perception and to try to make the audience see the world differently. In other words, as Robert Stam says, 'Defamiliarizing, or making strange is to denote the way that art heightens perception and short-circuits automatized responses.'[41] It is probably true that the audience knew in advance what the film was about; the same way they were probably also aware of the existence of the leper colony, but, as the narration at the beginning says, they have shut their eyes to it. If the film had been a mere visual report of the people in the leper colony, first, it would not have endured long enough for us to see and view it as a piece of art to this day, and second, the contemporary audiences would have seen it, perhaps been moved a little, but then simply carried on with their lives, just as we do all the time after watching the headline news on television. The film owes its long-lasting appeal to Farrokhzād's innovative treatment of the subject matter.

Farrokhzād has avoided the normalization of the subject by introducing the lepers in a new light. She portrays their human side while showing their horrifying appearance. Farrokhzād includes scenes of everyday life, things to which everyone can relate one way or another. In the film, people eat, pray, get married, fight, play, and so on. This normalcy helps introduce the humanity of these people, who live on the margins of society, to the audience. However, through her editing, Farrokhzād ensures that the minute the viewers become immersed in the normalcy of the lepers' lives, they are reminded that the film is about leprosy. Farrokhzād chooses to disrupt the shots depicting everyday life with close-up images of deformed faces or other parts of the body and, through this technique, alerts the viewers to the fact that although lepers have routines and monotonous lives like ordinary people, they also have to live and cope with leprosy. For example, in the scene where a man blows a whistle calling people to come and get their food, and people start to crowd around. In the few crowd shots, people pass before the camera and move up the line with their trays and bowls. Leprosy is not quite evident in these long shots – the scene is fluid and full of life and movement, and conveys the feeling that it could be anywhere, but then it suddenly cuts to a series of quick close-ups of the lepers eating. This juxtaposition is startling, and produces in us a sudden shock that allows us to see the reality. Throughout the film, Farrokhzād has not only managed to represent the underprivileged lives of the people in the leper colony and raise awareness of the state of leprosy, but she has also managed to avoid making their lives ordinary in the audience's eyes. She realizes that once something is normalized, it no longer holds enough weight to move people to change.

The majority of the shots in the film are under five seconds long and are mostly tight, detail shots of the lepers; the rest are under a minute, except for a couple of shots that run for a longer period of time, such as the shot towards the end of the film of a man approaching the camera on his crutches. This noticeable disparity in shot length is intended to maintain the audience's interest throughout the film. In response to the question of why the film has fast-paced editing, Farrokhzād explains, 'When first stepping into the leper colony, seeing everyone the first time is shocking, but after a while this will decrease, and in order to prevent the film from having a slow pace I have decided to adapt a fast-pace editing technique.'[42]

The film's formalist nature is not confined to its editing, however; it is also evident in the colour and visual composition throughout the film. Although high contrast is one of the characteristics of a black-and-white film, Farrokhzād has put this characteristic to use to better deliver her message. It is almost inconceivable that the film could ever have been shot in colour. Throughout the film there are several metaphorical references to white and black, light and dark, reflecting life within the leper colony. The film starts with the title handwritten in white chalk on a blackboard, then it cuts to black while the voice-over reads, 'There is no shortage of ugliness in the world. The world's ugliness would be more if the humans would close their eyes to it.' These two lines imply that it is in human nature to beautify, but it also implies that there is more beauty than ugliness to be seen in everything around us (with more careful observation, of course!). She uses the black screen, which is normally associated with the blank screen either before or after the film, as her first scene. The voice-over says there will be more ugliness if people shut their eyes to it: the film starts with the audience's eyes figuratively closed. Farrokhzād has put the title before this scene to clear any doubt in the viewer's mind that the film has yet to begin. The voice-over on the black screen concludes with the statement of the film-makers' intention: 'Finding an answer to their pain, helping cure their disease, and bringing aid to the ones infected has been the motivation and the aim of the filmmakers.' The next scene after the black slate opens the audience's eyes onto the reality and hardship of life with leprosy: a woman's face, deformed by leprosy, is shown staring into her own reflection. This shot of the woman is more likely to have been staged. The fact that the first shot after the black slate is not a candid shot shows that the woman who is in the frame is aware of being filmed. This shot, although it might not be read as the declaration of permission of the lepers to be shot, certainly conveys their willingness to be filmed, that is, to be seen by others.

What this film does best is to go against the conventional set definitions of beauty and ugliness. Farrokhzād, in this shot as well as in some later scenes, shows that the women in the colony have feelings, and do look at their faces in the mirror and put on make-up like anyone else, even though they may be suffering from leprosy. She shows that they do not hide their deformity, but that it is the rest of society who has forced them into exile – perhaps because they do not have the courage to face them.

Throughout the film, Farrokhzād plays with the concepts of beauty and ugliness. This can be seen especially in the scenes depicting the everyday lives of the people in the leper colony, in which she incorporates elements of beauty. In doing this, she goes against the commonly held prejudices, not just showing the darkness and horrifying reality of leprosy, but also looking past the ugliness to find the beauty, love, and hope for the future – everything that gives meaning to the lives of those afflicted. In response to the question of whether there were any records of suicide in the leper colony, Farrokhzād states:

> Disappointment has no meaning there. The lepers, when going to the colony, have passed the disappointment stage. They have accepted life as it is. I have seen more people there that are attached to life and love to live [than anywhere else].[43]

This love for life is depicted throughout the film in different ways, some of the more obvious scenes being the wedding scene, the shot of a woman breastfeeding a baby, the scene with a woman putting make-up on her face, and the shot of a woman combing her long black hair. One of the more significant sequences portraying hope for the future is the praying sequence in the mosque. This scene can be read in two different ways. One is that these people have not lost their faith and are still thankful to their God, even though they are afflicted by disease. The second is in reading this scene as an ironic juxtaposition. Michael Hillman asserts, '*The House is Black* depicts a leprous society in which the people trust in God and see a cure for their condition through prayer, whereas only science and surgery can affect a cure.'[44] This latter reading would make the film seem similar to what Buñuel depicted in *Land without Bread*, wherein he contrasts the luxurious church with the impoverished homes of the Hurdanos to question their blind belief. As Durgnat writes, 'The villages are so degraded as to have no folklore, *but* there is a church, bedecked with gold; in short, it has been a supplementary drain on their material resources, and its spiritual consolations have been of the usual obscurantist variety.'[45] I would argue that the first reading must have been the aim of the film-maker, because the film is trying to portray the fact that the lepers have not lost their hope. The main function of prayer is to thank God for all that He has given, and a faithful person would still be thankful even in the worst situations. The fact that they are still standing before their God raising their deformed hands up in worship demonstrates that they have not lost their faith, and therefore hope for life.

The beauty of life is not confined only to those shots mentioned above (the wedding scene, woman putting on make-up, and so on); beauty is evident in every shot where a person is occupied in an activity, whether it is lining up to get medicine or whether it is fighting; each shot in one way or another portrays an eagerness for life. Despite the fact that there is no bright future for them, as they are trapped within the walls of the leper colony, they have not stopped living, and this is one of the key messages that this film conveys.

Farrokhzād has almost book-ended the film with scenes of children in a classroom. The first scene following the zoom-in shot of the woman looking into her reflection is the school scene, and the film ends with a school scene, with a boy writing 'The House is Black' on the blackboard. But there is a difference between the early scene and the final scene. In the early scene, the students are reading from their books, thanking God for creating them, giving them kind parents, hands to work with, eyes to see with, and so on. But in the final scene, the teacher asks the students questions to see what they have learned. One of the questions the teacher asks is why one has to thank God for giving them a mother and a father. The boy questioned answers that he doesn't know, because he has neither. The teacher then asks a couple of students to name some beautiful things and some ugly things, to which they answer, 'moon, sun, flower, and play', and 'hand, foot, and head', respectively. Although these two scenes are probably among the most planned and staged scenes in the film, they carry a very important message: the students learn more from life and experience than they do from reading books. Even though the books have taught them that they have to thank God for giving them kind parents, the orphaned boy is hesitant simply to repeat what he has read. These two scenes, apart from their obvious interpretations, also illustrate the film-maker's criticisms of an educational system that presents profound subjects as facts without any further explanation, and how the students are expected to have one set answer to each question.

Closer to the end, the film makes more stark references to the fact that the people in the leper colony are imprisoned within its walls. The second to last shot includes an ironic image of all the lepers coming to the door of the colony while the camera is backing up and the gate doors are closed, leaving the audience outside. This shot is depicted as the imagination of the boy standing by the blackboard, thinking of how to write a sentence using the word 'house'. Finally, he writes, 'The House is Black', which is subsequently chosen as the title of the film. Coming full circle, the film begins by going into the leper colony, opening the audience's eyes to what they have previously closed their eyes to, and then it leaves them behind at the end. Throughout the film, the camera seems as though it has gradually become integrated into the subject, but the audience is reminded by the closing scene that it never really belonged there, because the camera – that is, the audience – can leave the prison, but the lepers cannot. Hence the allegory, 'the house is black'.

Despite the different aims and styles of *The House is Black* and *Land without Bread*, one of the important similarities is what the films represent today, now that they are both removed from the initial time and place in which they were shot. The films do not merely represent the physical place and people, but rather a larger scale of places and people. E. Rubinstein writes about Buñuel's *Land without Bread*, 'The film demonstrates the condition of the Hurdanos and thereby, at least by implication, the condition of all the forgotten and unwanted of the world, as the direct result of the injustices and stupidities of specific cultural and political circumstances.'[46] *The House is Black* is also a timeless film, not only because it is a report on life at a leper colony in north-west Iran, but also because it is based on a thought: life in the leper colony is a metaphor for life in general. As Ebrahim Golestān has stated, the director wished to convey a personal message in this film: to try to bring attention to life, pain and suffering in the world, and to try to portray this closed and secluded world and the people trapped in it. Farrokhzād believed that this kind of world is not necessarily found only in the leper colony.[47]

Farrokhzād was able to portray the lepers without morbidity, and she was capable of depicting beauty and ordinary life there. She created a work of art that can still be seen and read with relevance, despite its original time and place of production. *The House is Black* is not only a valuable artefact left behind by a legendary icon of Persian literature, but is also a valuable short film in its own right.

Chapter 11

Forugh Farrokhzād as Translator of Modern German Poetry: Observations About the Anthology *Marg-e man ruzi*

Nima Mina

In 2000, 33 years after Forugh Farrokhzād's death, an unknown translation work of hers was published under the title *Marg-e man ruzi* in Tehran.[1] The subtitle identifies this book as an anthology of 'German poets from the first half of the twentieth century'. In the bibliographical note on the cover, the name of Forugh Farrokhzād's older brother, Amir Mas'ud, is mentioned as cotranslator and editor. The sudden discovery of this book surprised Farrokhzād's aficionados as well as Farrokhzād specialists among modern literary scholars. Since Farrokhzād's passing, her books have been published in numerous editions by her 'home' publishing house, Amir Kabir. In 2002, the Iranian book company Nimā in Essen, Germany, published a two-volume edition of her collected works[2], in over a thousand pages, containing her poetry, scripts from her films (including *Khāneh siyāh ast*), her travelogues, a selection of her drawings and sketches, and a reprint of the translation from German.

The introductory notes to the anthology are written by Purān Farrokhzād, the older sister of Forugh and Amir Mas'ud, who lives in Tehran. Purān's introduction contains some revealing information about the pre-publication history of the translation. In the summer of 2007, I had the chance to interview Purān to obtain some additional details.

Upon divorce from her husband Parviz Shāpur and subsequent separation from her son Kāmyār, Farrokhzād published her first two collections of poetry, *Asir* and *Divār* in the years 1955 and 1956 and shortly thereafter became relatively well-known as a poet at around 21. In early 1956, Farrokhzād left Iran for a nine-month long study trip to Italy, from where she travelled to Germany where her brother, Amir Mas'ud, had just finished his medical studies at the Ludwig-Maximilians-Universität in Munich. In the following years, several more Farrokhzād siblings (namely Fereydun, Gloria, Mehrdād and Mehrān) also relocated to Munich to pursue higher education. Forugh Farrokhzād's connection to German language and literature that became evident through the publication of the anthology is understandable within the context of her family's links to Germany, and in particular, to the city of Munich.

Farrokhzād arrived in Munich in the winter months of 1956 and stayed in her brother's small apartment. As she was interested in painting, photography and film, she spent most of her time visiting museums, galleries, libraries and movie theatres in the city. At the same time she started studying German in a more systematic fashion with the help of her brother.

During her time in Rome, Farrokhzād studied Italian, in order to – as she put it – 'read the literature in the original tone of its creators'. Her fascination for the great works of world literature was accompanied by a strong interest in classical Persian literature. This is clearly reflected in her use of rhetorical and poetic features found in pre-modern Persian literature in her earliest poetry, that is, before her 'rebirth'.

According to Purān, who recounts the memories of her deceased brother Amir, Forugh came across a book of poetry in Amir's private library. In Purān's introductory notes to the anthology, the original book remains unidentified. Upon my inquiry, Purān confirmed that Amir, who was alive when the first and second editions of the anthology were published in Tehran, could no longer recall the original title. During the winter months of 1956, brother and sister sat together in the evenings, deciphered the original German texts, and Forugh wrote down her poetic version of the interlinear translations into a booklet. The translation work continued over several weeks, until Forugh finally left Germany for Italy, whence she returned to Tehran.

Later that same year, Farrokhzād published her third collection, *'Esyān*. In the same year, she began her collaboration and later her relationship with Ebrāhim Golestān, in whose film studios she had been initially hired as a secretary. In 1962, Farrokhzād produced the documentary *The House is Black*, for which she subsequently received the first prize at the Oberhausen documentary film festival. In 1963 her fourth collection, *Tavallodi digar* appeared, and during 1965 she wrote most of the texts that were published posthumously under the title *Imān biāvarim beh āghāz-e fasl-e sard*. It would appear that during the almost nine turbulent years between her first visit to Munich and her death on 14 February 1967, Farrokhzād showed no interest in publishing the translations she had jointly produced with Amir Mas'ud.

The booklet remained in Amir's possession. After living 20 years in Munich, Amir relocated back to Iran in the early 1970s with his German wife and three children. Amir and Purān were very close, and for a long period their places of work (his surgery and her publishing house) were located in the same building on Varzandeh Street. Shortly after his arrival in Tehran, Amir mentioned the booklet in conversations with Purān. Upon Purān's request, he promised to dig it out and bring it to her as soon as possible. In fact, this process took more than 28 years. The anthology appeared in print in Iran just a few months after Amir had surprised his sister with the booklet. At first glance, Purān was convinced that this was an unfinished work. Although the texts were more advanced and refined than simple draft versions, she felt they still required some editing. However, in the end, Purān decided to publish the texts as she had found them. Purān told me, that she was not sure how critics would react to the publication and whether the anthology would ever be acknowledged as part of her sister's literary legacy.

The booklet seems to have received several provisional titles while the translation work was in progress. All but the final title, *Bāl-hā-ye āyandeh* (*Wings of the Future*), had been crossed out by Forugh and Amir on the cover page. By the time of the anthology's publication in Tehran, neither Purān nor Amir could understand the reasoning behind the choice of *Bāl-hā-ye āyandeh* for the title and decided, for reasons I shall explain later, to publish the book under the title *Marg-e man ruzi*. As a comparatist, I was intrigued to try and find the original German anthology. Looking at the table of contents in the Persian edition, it was obvious that almost all of the listed 29 poets[3] were more or less well-known figures of the Germanic exile literatures of the 1930s and 1940s. Most of them fled the reign of the Nazis in 1933 because they were Jews and/or politically convinced anti-fascists. I surmised the anthology Forugh and Amir worked from must have been published some time between 1945, when the dissemination of works of exile literature became possible in post-war Germany and Austria, and before Forugh's trip to Munich in 1956. With these parameters, I managed to deduce the title of the original book, and I am grateful to Forugh Farrokhzād's adoptive son, Hossein Mansouri, who sent me a copy of the book from Munich. The book the Farrokhzād siblings worked from is an anthology of modern German poetry since 1910, edited by the

London-based exiled writer Eric Singer. It was published in 1955 in Munich.[4] So, when Farrokhzād visited Munich in the winter of 1956, the anthology would have had considerable novelty value. The Persian 'translation' is shorter than Singer's anthology by more than half.[5] In both books, the poems are arranged by author's surname in alphabetical order, and it is clear that Forugh and Amir consciously selected the poets and poems they wished to translate.

The selection criteria do not seem to be clear, as some historically important figures like the expressionist Franz Werfel, the 'inner exile' Erich Kästner and the later icon of world poetry Paul Celan[6] were left out in favour of a number of less significant poets. The Persian edition also contained a single poem by Rainer Maria Rilke, which does not appear in Eric Singer's anthology. Indeed, Eric Singer's anthology and the smaller selection by the Farrokhzād siblings are both collections of Germanic (and not simply German) poets, who were born in Austria, Germany, (including Schlesia, Pommern and Western Prussia), Switzerland, Prague, Lithuania, the Bucovina (in Romania), northern Italy, the Alsace region in France, and even Venezuela. As mentioned above, almost all of them left Nazi-controlled territories in 1933 and went into exile.

The Persian anthology (which was originally a private matter between Forugh and her brother, and as such was not addressed to any audience), presents texts in Persian that deal with the experience of exile, and the Holocaust. The short biographical sketches preceding the poems are based on the annotations in Eric Singer's anthology and clearly show that the Farrokhzād siblings were well aware of the political significance of the texts.

In my view, Forugh and Amir's choice of Singer's anthology was not a coincidence. It was also not a coincidence that the book was in Amir's possession in the first place. He had come to Germany one year before the military coup of August 1953; in the mid-1950s, the number of politicized Iranian students in the Munich area increased gradually, and Amir was one of them. Among his fellow students at the Medical Faculty of the Ludwig-Maximilians-Universität was Kurosh Lāshā'i, one of the later founders of the Maoist faction, Sāzmān-e Enqelābi-ye Hezb-e Tudeh-ye Irān (The revolutionary wing of the Iranian Communist Party), who also befriended Forugh during her stay in the city.[7] Later on, Lāshā'i left his German wife, children and job in Munich and became engaged in a clandestine effort to start an armed uprising against the Shah's regime through contacts with rebels in Kurdistan, and by mobilizing Iranian immigrant workers in the Persian Gulf emirates. He was ultimately arrested by the Shah's secret police (SAVAK), in the late 1960s, inside the country. In

1956, the soon-to-be Maoist commentator of Radio Beijing, Mehdi Khānbābā Tehrāni,[8] was released from prison in Iran and came to Munich to study law. He too became one of Amir's (and subsequently Forugh's) close friends in Germany. Mehdi Tehrāni was also incarcerated in the Stadelheim Prison in Munich shortly after the German Communist Party (KPD) was banned in 1956, thereby acquiring the reputation of being one of the first prisoners of conscience in the history of West Germany. Conversations with friends like Mehdi Khānbābā Tehrāni and Kurosh Lāshā'i left an everlasting impression on the mind of the young Forugh Farrokhzād. Mehdi Tehrāni claims that, the naïve narrator's messianic tone and choice of social revolutionary words in Farrokhzād's posthumously published poem 'Kasi ke mesl-e hichkas nist' ('Someone Who is Like No Other') echo the poet's interaction with him and their discussions about politics in Munich.[9]

This anthology was in fact not Amir and Forugh's only shared venture into German-Persian translation. In the mid-1950s, Mostafā and Mahin Osku'i (who had worked under 'Abdo'l-Hoseyn Nushin at Tehran's Ferdowsi Theatre) moved from Moscow to Munich. In Germany, they founded a small film synchronization studio, acquired mainly German films, dubbed them with the support of local Iranians, and sold them off to distributors and movie theatres in Iran. During a later trip to Germany, Forugh, Amir, Manizheh Nirumand, and Homā Zarrābi (who later became a close friend of Farah Pahlavi) were involved in synchronizing the feature film *Ohne Dich wird es Nacht* with Curd Jürgens and Eva Bartok.[10]

During those years, Amir was active in the Iranian National Front. Among the Munich-based Iranian students, Amir was considered particularly cultivated and well-read. Despite the general climate amongst his fellow expatriates in the aftermath of the 1953 coup, he was not exclusively obsessed with Iranian exilic politics,[11] although he did occasionally contribute articles on the subject to the journal *Irān-e Āzād*. He was very interested in German literature and modern German history, which explains his interest in Eric Singer's anthology.

Before his death in 2003, Amir shared some of his fragmented memories about the joint translation work on the German anthology with his sister Purān. One particular episode, recounted to me by Purān, is interesting in terms of what it tells us about the inspiration for some of Forugh Farrokhzād's own poetry. One evening, after the translation of the poem '*Wenn mich der Tod ereilt*' by Ossip Kalenter[12] had been completed, the poet's mood suddenly changed. She was overcome by deep sadness and decided to withdraw into her room. This mood continued until the following morning. At breakfast, she mentioned to her brother how Ossip Kalenter's text had moved her. She told her brother she had stayed up all night and written a poem about her own death. After she returned to Iran, this poem penned in Munich, entitled 'Ba'd-hā', was published the same year in her third collection, *'Esyān*.[13]

There are a number of similarities between the texts by Farrokhzād and Kalenter on various levels, especially in the choice and composition of motifs. In both texts, there is a narrator's voice (the lyrical 'I'), which can be assumed to be identical with the poet him- or herself. Toward the end of Kalenter's poem, the narrator addresses 'the reader'. In the sixteenth line from the bottom in Farrokhzād's poem, an unidentified 'you' (*to*) is addressed without its relationship to the narrator being specified. This 'you' could refer to a lover, a male or female friend, or even her son. Both pieces play with variations on the key motif of time: the time of the day, week, or the year. In Kalenter's poem these variations appear as 'neue Sommer', ('early summer'), 'Morgen und Abend' ('morning and evening'), 'Woche und Mond' ('week and month'), 'Herbstabend' ('autumn evening') and 'das 20. Jahrhundert' ('the twentieth century'). In Farrokhzād's text the variations are: *ruz* ('day' as in: *marg-e man ruzi*), *ruz-hā* ('days'), *ruzān-e degar* ('other days'), *diruz* ('yesterday'), *hafteh-hā* ('weeks'), *māh-hā* ('months'), *bahār* ('spring'), *zemestān* ('winter') and *khazān* ('autumn'). Both texts describe scenes and visions from the intimate personal space of the narrator in a future that s/he will not experience. Kalenter's text is narrated in simple and laconic language. His trademark of a silent, slightly depressed but humoristic style is clearly recognizable. Farrokhzād's poem, on the other hand, is tragic and bitter. This can no doubt be explained by the particular circumstances of her personal life at that time (divorced from her husband, and separated from her son). Large sections of Farrokhzād's poem resemble fragments of a motion picture, illustrating events that will occur after the narrator's death (lovers who will lay flowers on her grave, foreign gazes perusing the lines of her writings,[14] foreigners who enter her small private room). In the poem, Farrokhzād describes her soul moving away like a sailboat beyond the horizon, her eyes resembling dark labyrinths, and her cheeks feeling like cold marble. The language employed by Farrokhzād in this poem clearly belongs to the early phase of her poetry, where a slightly archaic literary register is predominant. Only in her fourth and fifth collections does the poet move away from this archaism, purposely using words and expressions which refer to everyday, domestic life.[15] The rather simple language used in the translation of Kalenter's poem (and in the anthology as a whole) could be seen as an anticipation of her later move toward a simpler, arguably more colloquial register of Persian.

The verse structure in 'Ba'd-hā' follows the traditional form of the *chahārpāreh*, best known from the poems of Farrokhzād's more senior contemporaries, such as Fereydun Tavallali. Only in her later period did Farrokhzād actually experiment with the amalgamation of two or more poetic metres. The rhyme structure in 'Ba'd-hā' on the whole follows the traditional rhyming system (*nur + dur + shur, mi-nahand + mi-ravand + mi-khazand, sard + dard*). Kalenter's poem consists of 11 strophes, each including three or four phrases or complete sentences, each pair of strophes being connected by an end rhyme. The rhythmical verse structure is irregular. In both texts the repetition of 'Wenn mich der Tod ereilt' (four times) or *marg-e man ruzi farā khvāhad resid* (twice), creates a certain parallelism.

Love, the ephemeral nature of life, and death itself are key subjects throughout Farrokhzād's lyrical oeuvre. This explains why Kalenter's poem, with its specific leitmotif immediately captured her interest. Farrokhzād's preoccupation with death (particularly her own death) is reflected in her entire oeuvre, from the beginning to the end. This can even be seen in the last two lines in Farrokhzād's very last poem 'Tanhā sedā-st ke mi-mānad' ('It's Only Sound That Remains') from her posthumously published collection.

Marg-e man ruzi ... is Farrokhzād's variation on her own translation of the title of Kalenter's poem, which was chosen as the title of the anthology by Purān and Amir. As mentioned before, Purān and Amir could not understand the connection between the booklet's original title (*Bāl-hā-ye āyandeh*; *Wings of the Future*) with the translated poems. In fact, *Bāl-hā-ye āyandeh* is a literal translation of the German idiomatic expression, 'der Zukunft Flügel verleihen' ('giving wings to the future'), which, out of its context and in literal Persian translation, almost sounds like a surrealistic metaphor.

'Wenn mich der Tod ereilt' and 'Bei Spezia'[16] were the first (and remain the only) texts by Ossip Kalenter published in Persian translation.[17] Through these translations, and moreover, via Farrokhzād's poetic response, a circle that Kalenter himself had started in the early 1920s by choosing a Persian-inspired penname for himself, was closed.[18]

Apart from Farrokhzād's poetic dialogue with Kalenter's text, her interest in translating the German anthology is also indicative of another important feature of her life and work: through the translation of poetry, Farrokhzād also transferred her personal approach to German language, literature and culture into the realm of poetry. This was in accordance with her often-expressed ambition to be a poet in all situations of life, to experience life as poetry, and to translate life into poetry.

بیوگرافی:

Ossip Kalenter

بیوگرافی:

در سال 1900 در درسدن متولد شد و حالا در زوریخ زندگی میکند. کتاب های شعر او به نام:
«گردش جدی»، «اشعار»، «استراحتگاه»، «سال پر قیافه»، «اشعار برای کودکان»
و کتاب دیگری به نام: «درسدن طلایی» تا به حال منتشر شده اند.

وقتی که مرگ من فرا میرسد ...

وقتی که مرگ من فرا میرسد، هنوز کتابهای زیادی در گنجهٔ من
خواهند بود، که من میخواستم آنها را بخوانم.
بعدها، شاید در روزهای بهتری،
وقتی که مرگ من فرا میرسد. هنوز داستانهای زیادی،
خواهند بود که من میخواستم آنها را بنویسم.
من هیچ وقت به آنها نرسیدم
تابستانهای تازه خواهند آمد و همه چیز ادامه خواهد یافت.
صبح و عصر، هفته و ماه، و سالهای سال،
این چه ارزشی دارد؟
بعد دیگر در دنیا هیچ کس نخواهد بود که من زمانی دوست داشتم.
هیچ کس که با او من جامم را به شادی خالی کردم،
دیگران به جای ما همین بازی را تکرار خواهند کرد. کلمات پر از
لطف و اعمال مملو از نفرت را در میان یکدیگر رد و بدل خواهند کرد.
دیگرانی که من نخواهم شناخت اما میترسم چهره ای مانند ما داشته باشند.
مردان رشید، زنان دوست داشته شده و پسران کتک خورده و بی رنگ.
وقتی که مرگ فرا میرسد، هنوز خیلی چیزها باقی خواهند بود که
من میخواستم ببینم و بشناسم.
دریا ها، منظره ها، دیوارهای تنها، و خودم.
زیرا در اطراف زندگی من آئینه های زیادی وجود نداشتند!
وقتی که مرگ من فرا می رسد، تصویری که در مغز من رسم
شده بود نابود میشود. دنیای من ...
خواننده، وقتی تو این را میخوانی، بعدها، سالهای بعد،
و شاد در آن تابستان که من دیگر ندیدم،
به من فکر کن. من این را در نیمه اول قرن بیستم مینویسم.
در یک عصر پائیز، در حدود ساعت 10.
از شراب طلایی Orvieto خورده ام که برای شب
و آرامش مفید است.
منزلی داشتم که در بالای آن ستاره ها می سوختند،
و روی هم رفته انسانی بودم مثل تو . . .

Farrokhzād, Forugh and Amir Mas'ud trans. and eds, *Marg-e man ruzi . . . Majmu'eh'i az nemuneh-hā-ye āsār-e sho'arā-ye ālmāni dar nimeh-ye avval-e qarn-e bistom* (Tehran, 2000): 84.

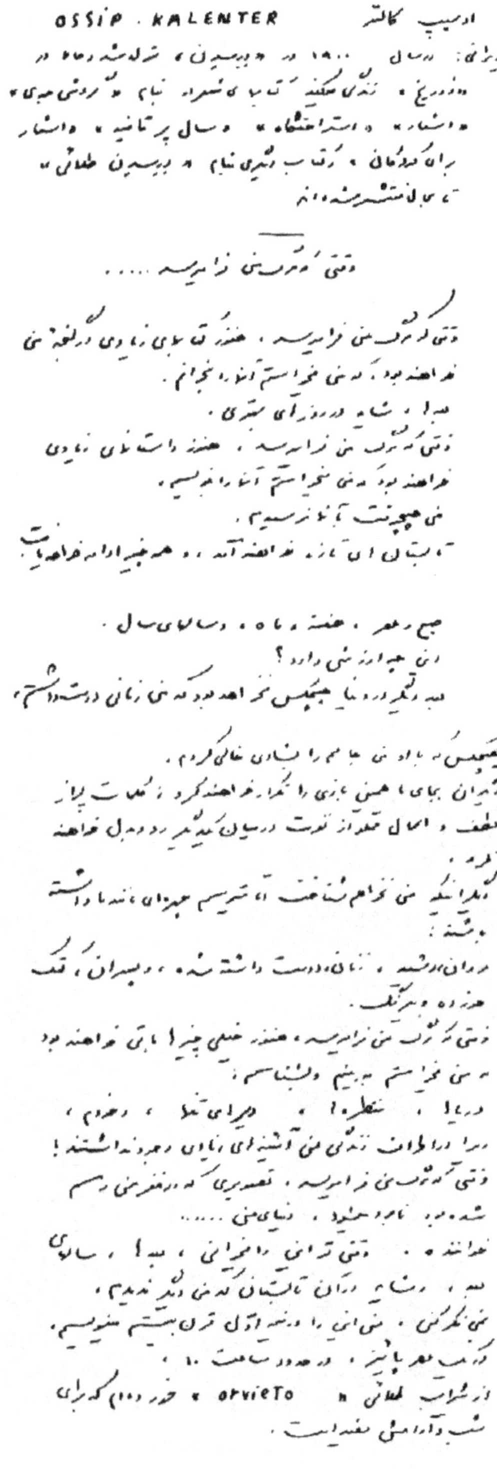

اوسیپ کالنتر OSSIP . KALENTER

شاعر آلمانی: در سال ۱۹۰۰ در «درسدن» متولد شده و حالا در
«زوریخ» زندگی میکند. کتابهای شعر او بنام «گردش مجدد»
«اشعار» «استراحتگاه» «سال [illegible]» «اشعار
برای دوستان» «کتاب دیگری بنام «درسدن طلائی»
تا حالا منتشر شده‌اند.

وقتی که مرگ من فرا برسد.....

وقتی که مرگ من فرا برسد، هنوز کتابهای زیادی در کتابخانه‌ی من
خواهند بود، که من میخواستم آنها را بخوانم.
همراه شاید در روزهای بهتری.
وقتی که مرگ من فرا برسد، هنوز داستانهای زیادی
خواهند بود که من میخواستم آنها را بنویسم.
من هیچوقت به آنها نرسیدم.
تابستانهای تازه خواهند آمد، و همه چیز ادامه خواهد یافت.

صبح و عصر، هفته و ماه، و سالهای سال.
این چه ارزشی دارد؟
به دیگر دنیا هیچکس نخواهد بود که من زمانی دوستش داشتم.

هیچکس به یاد نمی‌آورد که من جامم را شادمان خالی کردم.
دیگران بجای ما همین بازی را تکرار خواهند کرد، کلمات پر از
لطف و امیال متعدد از قدرت در میان یکدیگر رد و بدل خواهند
کرد.
کسانیکه من نخواهم شناخت، با ترسهای جوانی‌شان را داشته
باشند:
مردان رشید، زنان دوست داشته شده، و پسران کوچک
هرزه و زیرک.
وقتی که مرگ من فرا برسد، هنوز خیلی چیزها باقی خواهند بود
که من میخواستم ببینم و بشناسم:
دریا، منظره‌ها، ویرانی تمدن، و مردم،
زیرا در اطراف زندگی من آشنائی زیادی وجود نداشتند!
وقتی که مرگ من فرا برسد، تصویری که در مغز من رسم
شده بود نابود میشود، دنیای من.....
خواننده. وقتی تو این را میخوانی، بعدا، سالهای
بعد، و شاید در آن تابستان که من دیگر ندیدم،
فکر کن، من این را در شب اول ترن بهشتم مینویسم،
در شب عصر پائیز، در حدود ساعت ۱۰،
از شراب ایتالیائی «ORVIETO» خورده‌ام که برای
شب و آرامش مفید است.

OSSIP KALENTER

یا نیز

کمی پائیز میشود ، اگر زود غروب مشود .
را دیگر شعله سری آتش ، سهد .
کمک گیاهی رست .
محبت بلاغ کوچک ، آمیه .
کمی آتش لطفای .
درد آنشکده ، لعیا درآمد .

شاید کنار کاروان رناه نشسته .
بنا م اینقد خوشبختی بود ......

دیگر پائیز میشود و شب سردی آمده را
در تجتی تنهای ، درازمیکشه .

-) اینشعر باید به نظر شعر باوفی کوتین ایرانیا زادیسه ، خوب
شود ، چون ستی بینی شد ات

Persian translations of Osip Kalenter's poems in Forugh's handwriting
(Courrtesy of Purān Farrokhzād)

Amir Masʻud and Forugh Farrokhzād in Munich during the winter of 1956.
(Courtesy of Purān Farrokhzād)

Forugh Farrokhzād in a group picture with students and graduates of the Ludwig-Maximilians-Universität, as well as some exiled members of the Tudeh Party.

Front row from left to right: Aqabayāti, Dr. Mortezā Kiānuri, Farānak Shāhi, Mehrpuyān, Manizheh Nirumand and Dr. Nahāvandi.
Back row from left to right: Hoseyn Osku'i, Haratuniān, Dr. Vahāb Akbariyeh, Mostafā Osku'i, Māhedi, Mehdi Khānbābā Tehrāni, Forugh Farrokhzād, Changiz Mehrupuyān and Mahin Osku'i.

(Courtesy of Mehdi Khānbābā Tehrāni)

Ossip Kalenter
Wenn mich der Tod ereilt . . .

Wenn mich der Tod ereilt, werden noch viele / Bücher in meinen Regalen stehen, die ich lesen wollte, später in besseren Tagen vielleicht.

Wenn mich der Tod ereilt, werden noch viele / Geschichten sein, die ich schreiben wollte: ich habe sie nicht erreicht.

Neue Sommer werden kommen, und alles wird weitergehn: / Morgen und Abend, Woche und Mond und Jahr um Jahr – was hat es für Wertā

Dann ist niemand mehr in der Welt, den ich geliebt, / niemand, mit dem ich froh den Becher geleert.

Andere treiben an unserer Statt dasselbe Spiel, tauschen / Worte voll Huld und Taten voll Haß.

Andere, die ich nicht kennen werde, doch fürchte, / mit Anlitzen wie wir: Männer kühn, Frauen geliebt und Knaben / verschlagen und blaß.

Wenn mich der Tod ereilt, werden nicht viele / Dinge sein, die ich sehn und erkennen wollte: Meere, Landschaften, / einsame Klöster, mich selbst – denn mein Leben war von wenig / Spiegeln umstellt.

Wenn mich der Tod ereilt, bricht zusammen, die sich malte / in meinem Hirn, meine Welt . . .

Leser, wenn du dies liest, später, in Jahren einst / und in jenen Sommern vielleicht, die ich nicht mehr gesehn:

Denke an mich, ich schrieb dies in der ersten Hälfte / des 20. Jahrhunderts, an einem Herbtabend, es war gegen zehn;

Trank vom goldenen Wein aus Orvieto dabei, der gut / für die Nacht und die Ruh, Hatte ein haus, darüber die Sterne brannten, und war / alles in

allem ein Mensch wie du . . .

Source: Singer, Eric ed., *Spiegel des Unvergänglichen. Deutsche Lyrik seit 1919* (Munich, 1955): 60–61; 141.

روزی که مرگ من برسد

روزی که مرگ من برسد
در قفسه کتاب‌های زیادی هست که قصد داشتم بخوانم
در روزهای بهتری شاید.

روزی که مرگ من برسد
هنوز داستان‌های زیادی هست که خواستم بنویسم
اما فرصتی نیافتم.

تابستان‌هایی دیگر از راه می‌رسد و همه چیز می‌گذرد:
شب و روز، هفته و ماه و سال
اما دیگر چه ارزشی دارد؟

در دنیا دیگر هیچکس نیست
کسی که دوستش داشته
و با او جامی نوشیده باشم.

به جای ما کسانی دیگر هستند
که باز با رأفت حرف می‌زنند
و با نفرت عمل می‌کنند.

کسانی می‌آیند
که من نمی‌شناسم، اما از آنها وحشت دارم
کسانی درست به هیئت ما:
مردانی جسور، زنانی دلربا، کودکانی رنجور.

روزی که مرگ من برسد
برجا نیست آنهمه چیزها که خواستم ببینم و بشناسم:
دریاها و دشت‌ها
دیرهای تنها، و خودم ـ
زیرا از زندگانی من نقشی اندک باقی ماند.

روزی که مرگ من برسد
با من فرو می‌میرد دنیایی که در سر ساخته بودم

ای خواننده که این کتیبه را بعدها می‌خوانی
شاید در تابستان‌هایی که دیگر نخواهم دید

مرا به یاد آور
و بدان که این خط را در نیمه اول قرن بیستم نوشتم
در شبی پاییزی، حوالی ساعت ده،
در آن حال که جامی از شراب زرین اورویتو کنارم بود
باده‌ای نیکو برای شب و برای آرامش،
خانه‌ای داشتم که بر فراز آن

ستارگان می‌سوختند، و بر روی هم انسانی بودم مانند تو . . .

Unpublished translation, courtesy of 'Ali Amini Najafi.

فروغ فرخزاد

بعدها

مرگ من روزی فرا خواهد رسید:
در بهاری روشن از امواج نور
در زمستانی غبار آلود و دور
یا خزانی خالی از فریاد و شور

مرگ من روزی فرا خواهد رسید:
روزی از این تلخ و شیرین روزها
روز پوچی همچو روزان دگر
سایه ای ز امروزها، دیروزها!

دیدگانم همچو دالان‌های تار
گونه هایم همچو مرمرهای سرد
ناگهان خوابی مرا خواهد ربود
من تهی خواهم شد از فریاد درد

می خزند آرام رو ی دفترم
دستهای فارغ از افسون شعر
یاد می آرم که در دستان من
روزگاری شعله می زد خون شعر

خاک می خواند مرا هر دم به خویش
می رسند از ره که در خاکم نهند
آه شاید عاشقانم نیمه شب
گل بروی گور غمناکم نهند

بعد من ناگه به یکسو میروند
پرده های تیره دنیای من
چشمهای ناشناسی می خزند
روی کاغذها و دفترهای من

در اتاق کوچکم پا می نهد
بعد من، با یاد من بیگانه ای
در بر آئینه می ماند بجای
تارمویی، نقش دستی، شانه ای

می رهم از خویش و می مانم ز خویش
هرچه بر جا مانده ویران می شود

روح من چون بادبان قایقی
در افقها دور و پنهان می شود

می شتابد از پی هم بی شکیب
روزها و هفته ها و ماهها
چشم تو در انتظار نامه ای
خیره می ماند بچشم راه ها

لیک دیگر پیکر سرد مرا
می فشارد خاک دامنگیر خاک!
بی تو، دور از ضربه های قلب تو
قلب من می پوسد انجا زیر خاک

بعدها نام مرا باران و باد
نرم می شویند از رخسار سنگ
گور من گمنام می ماند به راه
فارغ از افسانه های نام و ننگ

Farrokhzād, *'Esyān* (Tehran, 1958): 127–130.

Forugh Farrokhzād
Aftertimes

Death shall come upon me one day,
In a spring brightened with waves of light,
In a winter foggy and far;
Or in an autumn void of howling and mirth!

Death shall come upon me one day,
On a day amidst these bitter-sweet days,
On an idle day much like other days;
A silhouette of the days of now and ere!

Mine eyes like Smokey lanes,
My cheeks like marbles – cold,
Engulfed in a slumber deep;
Empty I shall become of holler and pain!

Gently crawling upon my book,
My hands devoid of the spell of song,
I recall how from these hands in the past,
Surged someday the song's feral fane!

Dust beckons me down with every breath,
As they arrive to bury me in,
Ah, would that my lovers upon midnight
Bring flowers for my downcast grave!

Once I'm gone; apace to the side,
Haste away darksome shades of this life of mine,
As strangers' eyes ran their glance
Over the pages that remain mine!

Upon my modest room enters through,
A stranger with thoughts of me after I'm gone,
By the mirror remains in place
A hand print, a brush, or a strand of hair!

Fleeing myself, I sever from self,
As lay waste all that remains,
My soul like a vessel's sails
Fades off into the horizons' ways

Headlong, haste away one upon another,
The days and the weeks and even the months,

Your eyes eager for receipt of a letter
Stares into the roadways afar!

But alas my cold frame,
Crushed by the dust – the earth holding ever fast,
In want of you and far from the palpitations of your heart,
Mine own heart withers within the layers of earth abound!

My name shall the winds and the rain in the aftertime,
Gently wash away from over my grave,
My tomb endures nameless on its way;
Free of the tales of scandal and fame!

Unpublished translation, courtesy of Ms Gloria Shahzadeh.

Chapter 12

Alien Rebirths of 'Another Birth'

M. R. Ghanoonparvar

As native speakers of one language, more specifically, as educated native speakers of our mother tongue, we develop a sensitivity to the aesthetics of the language when it is manipulated by writers and poets with an intuitive talent to use it euphoniously and even cleverly. The euphonious and clever use of language, of course, could function both as a means to enhance meaning and facilitate the ideas that are to be communicated and, in some cases, as an appealing cover to hide the shallowness of the content or the failure of the communicator to present his or her ideas in a logically coherent and structurally communicative fashion. As native listeners/speakers/readers, more often than not, our emotional attachment to the language hinders our close reading of a literary text by one of our literary icons and our ability to detect the shortcomings of the author in the task of communication. In addition, our emotional attachment as native speakers of the language often impedes a thorough understanding of the works of great writers and poets which are masterpieces of literary success, both in terms of language use and innovative ideas. A case in point regarding the latter is the extraordinary popularity of Hāfez, the 14th-century Persian poet, among native speakers of Persian. Hāfez is widely quoted, even by the illiterate, and whenever there is an opportunity to listen to the recitation of a *ghazal* by Hāfez, virtually everyone is attentive, nodding his or her head as a sign of reflection and understanding of the poem, while the fact remains that at times not even many trained scholars are quite certain about the meaning of the poems.

I would like to suggest that the act of translating is a process through which the problems I have briefly outlined here can be remedied. In this process, the translator who strives to transmit the form and content – the music, if you will – or tone and imagery and the logic and structure of a work in the source language to a new cultural and linguistic environment is obliged to fully comprehend and in a sense ingest and digest every word, image, and notion as well as the overall structure and argument of the original text before he or she can produce, if not a replica, at least a semblance of that text in the target language. A common anxiety of translators is that they may be blamed not only for the inadequacies of the translation at hand but, generally, also the shortcomings of the original work. A translator, therefore, must strive to fully comprehend the logical progression of the text, in other words, the way words, images and ideas are strung in a linear form, to produce a translated text that will also unfold logically. It is in this process that a translator, in some ways, becomes more intimate with the text than any other reader, often even the creator of the original work. This degree of intimacy with a text, and attention to detail, in actuality facilitates a sort of critical scrutiny or a very close reading of a literary text that, I posit, would be perhaps nearly impossible in other critical approaches.[1]

Many critics agree that among the prominent twentieth-century Persian poets, Forugh Farrokhzād has a greater universal appeal than her contemporaries. We can postulate that in contrast to the works of other major modernist poets, including Nimā Yushij, Ahmad Shāmlu, Mehdi Akhavān-Sāles, Nāder Nāderpur and Sohrāb Sepehri, the universal appeal of Farrokhzād's poetry is evident in the number of graduate and undergraduate theses written about her in various countries and in different languages, the number of seminars and conferences about her life and work, the number of both journalistic and scholarly articles and books that deal with her poetry, the number of items on the Internet when her name is googled, and, of course, the number and volume of translations of her poetry into other languages.[2] Farrokhzād's relative popularity outside Iran may be due to the universality of the content and message of her poetry as well as the translatability of her language. In contrast to the poetry of Nimā Yushij, which seems somewhat enigmatic to many readers because of its rather idiosyncratic language, and the work of Mehdi Akhavān-Sāles, with his culturally and linguistically complex modes of expression, Farrokhzād's language, on the surface at least, seems to be characterized by such remarkable clarity that most readers feel they can relate to her poetry, while – perhaps for the same reason – experienced and amateur translators alike think they can easily render her poetry into another language. The problem, as we shall see, is that Farrokhzād's poetry, in spite of its linguistic clarity or seeming simplicity, is complex in terms of its imagery. Any translator who fails to fully grasp the web of her intertwined and carefully interwoven images that contribute to the logical progression of her ideas in a poem would also fail in rendering her work into another language. To demonstrate the complexity of the process of translating Farrokhzād's poetry and the pitfalls that translators face, I would like to examine and compare some of the translations of only a few stanzas of one poem, namely, 'Tavallodi digar'. Dozens of translations of 'Tavallodi digar' have appeared in English since the poem was published in a volume with the same title in 1964. Translators of the poem include professional translators, academics, literary scholars and critics, and even social scientists, as well as general Farrokhzād enthusiasts. There are translations by native speakers of either Persian or English, and even those whose mother tongue is neither. And, of course, inevitably, there are also collaborative renditions by teams of native speakers of both languages. I have selected only eight English translations of the poem and will focus, in particular, on a number of lines that seem to have undergone some odd rebirthing processes and appear rather alien to the original. I will identify each of the translations by a letter of the alphabet, from A to H.[3]

The title of the poem is rendered as 'Another Birth' in five of these eight translations, while the other three translations of the title appear as 'Born Again', 'Rebirth', and 'A Rebirth'. The translation of the title alone can affect the reader's comprehension of the entire poem. The version that was prepared by Karim Emāmi and Forugh Farrokhzād herself bears the title 'Another Birth', which is shared by four other translations and seems to be less problematic than the other versions. 'Born Again' has specific Christian religious connotations and 'Rebirth' would be accurate if the Persian title were something like 'Tavallod-e dobāreh' or 'Tavallod-e degarbār'.

The first stanza of the poem seems to have particularly presented the translators with several problems and challenges. Let us first look at the original Persian and then the eight renditions of this stanza into English:

همهٔ هستی من آیهٔ تاریکیست

که ترا در خود تکرارکنان

به سحرگاه شکفتن ها و رستن های ابدی خواهد برد

من در این آیه ترا آه کشیدم، آه

من در این آیه ترا

به درخت و آب و آتش پیوند زدم

A: My whole being is a dark chant
    which will carry you
    perpetuating you
    to the dawn of eternal growths and blossomings

in this chant I sighed you
in this chant
I grafted you to the tree to the water to the fire.

B: All my existence is a dark verse,
     which repeatedly within itself will take you
     to the dawn of eternal blooms and growths.
     In this verse I, alas, drew you, alas,
     in this verse
     I joined you to tree, water and fire.

C: My whole being is a dark verse
     repeating in itself
     that it will carry you to the dawn of eternal blossoming and growth

     Ah, I sighed to you in this verse;
     in this verse
     I grafted you to tree and water and fire.

D: All my being is a dark verse
     making you new in itself
     carrying you to the dawn
     of perpetual growth and budding.
     In this verse I have breathed you out, ah
     in this verse I have grafted you
     to the tree, to the water, to the fire.

E: All my existence is a dark verse
     which will take you within itself, repeating,
     to the dawn of eternal burstings and growings.
     In this verse I sighed to you . . . Ah,
     in this verse
     I grafted you to tree and water and fire.

F: All my existence is a dark verse
     which repeating you in itself will take you
     to the dawn of eternal blossoming and growth
     I have sighed to you in this verse, ah,
     in this verse I have grafted you to tree and water and fire.

G: One dark word is all I am
     uttering you again and again
     until you wake where you blossom forever

In this word I breathed you, breathed
and in this word bound you
to trees, water, flame.

H: All my existence is a dark sign a dark
                                    verse
that will take you by itself
again and again
through incantation of itself
over and over
to eternal dawn
                    bloomings and eternal growth
in this verse, in this sign
I sighed for you, sighed
in this verse, in this sign, I versified
you, I joined you
to tree and water and fire[4]

In the first line of the poem, the translators seem to be in disagreement about the translation of two words, namely *hasti* and *āyeh*. In three of the translations, *hasti* has been rendered as 'being'; in four, as 'existence'; and in one, the translators have opted for the present tense of 'to be'. In fact, the word *āyeh* seems to have posed even more problems. While the version by Karim Emāmi, who translated the poem in collaboration with the poet, renders it as 'chant', one team of translators translates it as 'word'; the majority of the others translate it as 'verse'; and one translator reveals his frustration in choosing among these terms and decides on the two words 'sign' and 'verse', thereby adding extra words to the line and rendering the opening line as 'all my existence is a dark sign a dark verse'. While the Arabic loan word literally means 'sign' and usually in Persian denotes a verse from the Koran, it also connotes 'chant' (which appears to be the poet's choice), in addition to 'word', and even 'miracle' (which none of the translators use). In this stanza, I mainly want to point out how the various connotations of this term change the meaning – and, of course, as it appears in the opening line of the poem, those connotations affect the entire poem. Questions such as: *Is verse more appropriate? What is a dark verse? and, Would 'chant' work better because of the word 'repeating' in the second line?* and the like might often escape the reader who is not attempting to translate the poem. By the way, there is also the problem in the fourth line in which the word *āyeh* is used once again, and which careless translators often miss.

The second and third lines of the opening stanza (which basically complete the full sentence that starts in the first line) present the translators with a new, albeit different, set of problems, and consequently different interpretations and renditions. Some translators try to stay closer to the original through more or less literal translations, while others try to base their renditions on their own interpretation of the poem.[5] Karim Emāmi's rendition, which, as he reports, is based on Farrokhzād's own interpretation, perhaps a year or so after she composed it, moves some distance away from the original in terms of both phrasing and number of lines:

> which will carry you
> perpetuating you
> to the dawn of eternal growths and blossomings

Interestingly (the questionable use of 'which' aside), in the rendition of the two words, *shekoftan-hā* and *rostan-hā* , Emāmi reverses the order of these words as they appear in the original and opts for such a literal translation that he is forced to fabricate a plural for the English gerund 'blossoming'.[6]

Other translators facing the dilemma of translating these two lines present the English-speaking world (sometimes in two or three and even in one instance six lines), with such varied, diverse and, occasionally, baffling versions as:

A: which will carry you/ perpetuating you/ to the dawn of eternal growths and blossoming

B: which repeatedly within itself will take you/ to the dawn of eternal blooms and growths

C: repeating in itself/ that it will carry you to the dawn of eternal blossoming and growth

D: making you new in itself/ carrying you to the dawn/ of perpetual growth and budding

E: which will take you within itself, repeating,/ to the dawn of eternal burstings and growings

F: which repeating you in itself will take you/ to the dawn of eternal blossoming and growth

G: uttering you again and again/until you wake where you blossom forever

H: that will take you by itself/ again and again/ through incantation of itself/ over and over to eternal dawn/ bloomings and eternal growth.

What seems to baffle most of these translators, who we should assume are not trying to utterly confuse the unsuspecting target-language reader, should actually be rather clear to readers of the Persian original, once they grasp the meaning of the first line. In the first line, the poet establishes an equation between her life and poetry. Both components of this equation – that is, poetry and life – function as the subject of the second and third lines. Through repetition, the speaker's poetry, as the subject, perpetuates and immortalizes the object 'you'.[7] It is the notion of poetry as a creative act (the act of creation) that continues in the fourth line, and also the perpetuating or immortalizing power of poetry that continues in the final two lines of the first stanza. The fourth line (*man dar in āyeh torā āh keshidam, āh*) is one of the most mistranslated lines, I would hazard to say, of virtually all modern poetry translated from Persian. The eight 'reborn' versions of the line in the sample translations I have selected are:

A: in this chant I sighed you, sighed
B: In this verse I, alas, drew you, alas
C: Ah, I sighed to you in this verse
D: In this verse I have breathed you out, ah
E: In this verse I sighed to you . . . Ah
F: I have sighed to you in this verse, ah
G: In this word I breathed you, breathed
H: in this verse, in this sign/ I sighed for you, sighed.

It should be quite clear that the mistranslations of this line are the result of the translators' failure to follow the logical progression of the poem or the logic of the poem as it unfolds. The poetic 'sigh' is indeed the creative act that creates the 'you'. The idiosyncratic, nonconformist use of the language and the poet's inventive use of an intransitive verb, *āh keshidan* (to sigh), as a transitive verb with the direct object 'you' is, in fact, the root cause of all the misreading, misinterpretations and mistranslations of this line.[8] Without comprehending this usage and the creative process that Farrokhzād explains so deliberately in the first four lines of the poem, our understanding of the next two and final lines of the opening stanza would be shallow at best. Having equated her whole being with poetry and having told us about the creative and immortalizing power of poetry, following the logic of her argument and her text, she reiterates so succinctly the ideas in the first four lines and displays her powers as a poet and a creator by grafting the 'you' of the poem to tree (symbolizing continual growth and evolution from birth to death), water (representing the eternal source of life) and fire (implying destruction and death). It is this cycle of birth, life and death that is explicated in the remainder of 'Tavallodi digar'.

For the sake of brevity, I will avoid comparing the eight translated versions of the entire poem and merely review a few more particularly problematic lines that seem to have been a cause of confusion and discord among the translators. A few stanzas later in the poem, after having established what her whole being is, the poet/speaker makes a series of observations about what life is, concluding with:

زندگی شاید آن لحظهٔ مسدودیست
که نگاه من، در نی نی چشمان تو خودرا ویران میسازد
و در این حسی است
که من آنرا با ادراک ماه و دریافت ظلمت خواهم آمیخت

With the collaboration of the poet, Emāmi translates these lines as follows:

A: Life is perhaps that enclosed moment
       when my gaze destroys itself in the pupil of your eyes
       and it is in the feeling
       which I will put into the Moon's impression
              and the Night's perception.

In an interview with Emāmi, when the poet was asked about what she had in mind in the last two lines of this stanza, Farrokhzād responds that our stay in this world is so brief that the truly important thing is what the more lasting elements, such as the moon and darkness, perceive of our lives, and not vice versa.[9]

The problem is that it makes little sense for the speaker of the poem to know what the moon can perceive and the darkness comprehend. For this reason, the translator who is conscious of the illogicality of the idea and the break in the logical progression of the narrative is at a loss and confesses that he does not think that his renditions of *edrāk-e māh* as 'moon's perception' and *daryāft-e zolmat* as 'night's impression' will make any sense to the reader of the English text, who in fact may infer the opposite notion. Aside from such lexical mistranslations as 'no' and 'no-no' for the Persian *ni-ni* (pupil; misread by some as *ney ney*) and the improper use of the singular, 'pupil', for the same noun in English, the same illogical miscomprehension of the segment quoted above persists and is reflected in several translations of these lines:

B: Perhaps life is that closed moment,
     when my look destroys itself in the 'no' of your eyes.

And in this is a feeling
I will mix with the perception of the moon and the reception of
    darkness.

C: Or perhaps life is that closed moment
   when my glance meets ruin in the pupils of your eyes:
   a feeling that I shall mingle
   with my visions of the moon and the darkness.

D: Life is perhaps that closed moment
   when my look destroys itself in the pupil of your eyes
   and in this lies a sense which I shall mingle
   with fathoming the moon
   with perceiving the dark.

E: Perhaps life is that closed-off moment
   when my look destroys itself in the pupil of your eyes:
   and in this is a sensation
   which I will mix with the perception of the moon and the reception
      of darkness.

F: Perhaps life is that thwarted moment
   when my gaze destroys itself in the pupil of your eyes
   And in this lies a sensation
   which I will mingle with the perception of the moon and the
      discovery of darkness
G: Life may be that sealed moment
   when my gaze disintegrates in the lens of your eyes
   and the moon
   senses itself in me and the darkness

H: Perhaps life is that stopped instant in which
   my gaze lays waste to itself,
   my gaze into the no-no of your eyes
   self-destructs
         and there is a sense in this
   which I shall mix in with
   comprehension of the moon
   and with perception of the pitch dark.

Following these general observations about life, the speaker of the poem then
focuses on her own life and childhood and memories of growing up, and as a

woman and an artist, and finally offers us her philosophical reflections on the meaning of life.

سفر حجمی در خط زمان
و به حجمی خط خشک زمان را آبستن کردن
حجمی از تصویری آگاه
که ز مهمانی یک آینه برمیگردد

The seemingly abstract and at the same time poetic language of these reflections once again become the source of various interpretations and misinterpretations by the translators:

A: The journey of a form along the line of time
    inseminating the line of time with the form
    a form conscious of an image
    coming back from a feast in a mirror.

B: The journey of a mass in the line of time
    and the mass making pregnant the dry line of time,
    a mass aware of an image
    which returns from visiting a mirror.

C: The journey of a mass along the line of time
    and the mass making pregnant the dry line of time,
    a mass aware of an image
    which a mirror brings back from a party

D: The journey of a mass through linear time
    and with a mass impregnating
    the barren line of time
    a mass of conscious images
    returning from the feast of a mirror.

E: The journey of a mass in the line of time
    making pregnant with a mass the dry line of time
    a mass of conscious image
    which returns from feasting with a mirror.

F: The journey of a form on the line of time
    and with a form, impregnating the dry line of time,

a form aware of an image
which returns from the party of a mirror.

G: A body travels the line of time
and a body makes that barren line conceive
a body that knows the image
returning from the feast of the mirror

H: The trip of a blob down the line of time
and said blob impregnating the dry line
of time
the blob of a conscious image which image
is reflected back from a party mirror

The ensuing three-line separate stanza, *bedinsān-ast/ keh kasi mi-mirad/ va kasi mi-mānad* (And thus it is/ that someone dies/ and someone remains), which concludes the poet's philosophical reflections in this segment of the poem, is in fact the logical progression of the narrative of the poem, Farrokhzād's narrative of her life as a poet and creative artist, and makes the seemingly abstract previous line quite clear. To the poet, the creative, artistic or poetic mind is a form conscious of an image (her 'whole being' represented by her reflection) that she has observed and studied in the 'mirror'. Without grasping this logical thought process, no translator would be able to transmit to readers in another language what the original conveys.

There are, of course, other examples in this poem, where generally native-speaker readers merely enjoy the 'music' of the language or a single image without trying to see its connection to what comes before and after and in the entire poem, and where the process of translating can shed light on the unfolding of meaning.

I have merely outlined some of the complexity of the ideas and the simplicity of the expression of the ideas in a few stanzas of Forugh Farrokhzād's 'Another Birth', and also how any reader or translator who fails to grasp how the words and images contribute to and advance the communication of the ideas and production of the meaning of the poem will also fail to comprehend and hence translate it. Let me also distinguish between casual readers and the translators of the poem and suggest that, despite all their failures, the translators are perhaps among the most fortunate readers of the poem, because they engage in an exercise that allows them the most intimate experience of Farrokhzād's poem Usually, the translators' efforts result in the transmission of a text from one culture into another. In a sense, the literary translator opens a window into the literary products of another culture, but often such efforts do not thoroughly accomplish the task that the translator ideally sets out to do. The side benefit of this process, that is, the act of translating, is that it opens to the translator and the recipients of his or her efforts a window to aspects of the literary text that would be otherwise overlooked by the monolingual reader.

Misreadings and misinterpretations aside, translators of poetry always face the dilemma of whether to sacrifice meaning for the music, rhythm, rhyme and form of the poem or to give preference first and foremost to the actual content and meaning. Poetry is music, many believe, especially given that in former times poets were often musicians, as well. The English word 'bard' conveys both meanings of 'musician' and 'poet'. Classical Persian poetry and classical Persian music were always interrelated in some way. The music of modern Persian poetry, however, is different. Modern poems, as the poetry of Forugh Farrokhzād shows us, are primarily dependent on imagery and, subsequently, meaning, every poem providing the reader with a new way of looking at the world. For this reason, accurately translating the imagery and the semantic content of a poem should be the priority in the task of the translator. With that in mind, and having benefited from both the errors and the successes of other translators of 'Tavallodi digar', I would like to offer that the following rather literal translation (much of it borrowed from other translators) renders the most essential components of the poem, its imagery and meaning, and is an attempt at yet another inherently flawed, alien rebirth of 'Another Birth':

My whole being is a dark verse
that, repeating you in itself
will carry you to the dawn of eternal blossoming and growth
I sighed you in this verse, ah
in this verse I
grafted you to tree, water, and fire

Life is perhaps
a long street through which a woman with a basket passes every day
Life is perhaps
a rope with which a man hangs himself from a branch
Life is perhaps a child returning from school

Life is perhaps lighting up a cigarette in the languid repose between two
    love-makings
or the confused passing of a passerby
who tips his hat
and with a meaningless smile says to another passerby 'Good morning'

Life is perhaps that closed moment
when my gaze destroys itself in the pupils of your eyes
and in this there is a feeling
that I will mingle with the perception of the moon and conception of
    darkness

In a room which is the size of one loneliness
my heart
which is the size of one love
looks at its simple pretexts for happiness
at the beautiful withering of flowers in the vase
at the sapling that you have planted in the garden of our house
and at the song of canaries
that sing the size of one window

Ah . . .
this is my lot
this is my lot
My lot
is a sky which the dropping of a curtain takes away from me
My lot is descending an abandoned stair
and joining something in decay and exile
My lot is a melancholy excursion in the garden of memories
and dying in the sorrow of a voice that tells me:

'I love
your hands'

I plant my hands in the garden
I will grow, I know, I know, I know
and swallows will lay eggs
in the hollows of my ink-stained fingers

I hang earrings on my two ears
made of two red twin cherries
and I stick dahlia petals on my nails
There is an alley where
boys who were in love with me, still
with the same disheveled hair and thin necks and boney legs
think of the innocent smiles of a little girl whom one night
the wind carried away

There is an alley which my heart
has stolen away from the neighborhoods of my childhood

The journey of a form on the line of time
and impregnating the dry line of time with a form
a form conscious of an image
that returns from the feast of a mirror

And thus it is
that someone dies
and someone remains

No hunter will find a pearl in a shallow stream that pours into a small ditch

I
know a sad little fairy
who lives in an ocean
and plays her heart on a wooden flute
softly, softly
a sad little fairy
who dies of a kiss at night
and is born of a kiss at dawn

Chapter 13

Re-Writing Forugh: Writers, Intellectuals, Artists and Farrokhzād's Legacy in the Iranian Diaspora

Persis M. Karim

Forty years after her death, Forugh Farrokhzād's legacy continues to influence and provide creative inspiration for countless writers, artists and poets, both inside and outside Iran. In light of all that has occurred in Iran since her tragic and premature death in 1967, it is not surprising that Farrokhzād's posthumous effect has grown rather than waned. Like many popular cultural icons who die young and at the height of their career, Farrokhzād's legacy has intensified with time; she has been remade, reinvented and re-imagined as an iconoclast, as well as a figure representing cultural transformation and the struggle for women's public presence in twentieth-century Iran. A number of Iranian diaspora writers have drawn on Farrokhzād's poetic voice and her life story to fuel their own, identifying with her plight as a frequently misunderstood and misrepresented cultural figure, and as an artist who broke new ground in poetry and visual arts. The remarkable power of her language, imagery, and the boldness with which she lived her own life, has compelled some diaspora artists to claim Farrokhzād as a kind of muse who embodies an exilic, post-migration sensibility and culture that is prevalent in Iranian diaspora communities in North America and Europe.

This essay traces some of the various forms that Farrokhzād's influence has exerted on the Iranian diaspora intellectual and writerly communities, and identifies some of the ways that the emerging literature of the Iranian diaspora has used her work as a touchstone for their own. Furthermore, I want to argue for understanding Forugh Farrokhzād as a transnational figure via which Iranians in the diaspora connect to their heritage in the midst of challenging political circumstances that inhibit stable associations with both Iran and those countries in which they reside.[1] These associations are, of course, mitigated by the differing identities and circumstances of immigration. For those writers who were born and schooled in Iran, and who left as young adults (often just before the Revolution), Farrokhzād represents something different than she does for those younger, hyphenated Iranians who discover her oeuvre through English translations for the first time. Regardless, these associations with Farrokhzād are often poetic, biographical and political, or some combination thereof. In the particular case of the USA, diaspora writers are often caught up in the fraught relationship between the USA and Iran that, since the 1978–1979 Revolution and the subsequent US hostage crisis, has been consistently hostile. To attempt to 'represent' Iran and Iranian culture in this climate is indeed challenging.

Farrokhzād's biography and her poetic oeuvre appeal to some of these writers because she is often viewed as a symbol of Iran's twentieth-century experience of modernity that many feel was interrupted by the Revolution and supplanted by a repressive, cleric-dominated regime of the Islamic Republic. Farrokhzād is also identified as a figure of resistance for some writers in Iran and in the diaspora because she often wrote against the conventional narratives of her gender and the prevailing poetic and artistic forms of her time. Farrokhzād also conveys a cosmopolitan sensibility that can be linked to the time she spent in Europe, and her explorations in visual arts (including film-making), make her appealing to a younger generation of writers, film-makers and artists who draw inspiration from inside and outside Iranian culture. For some diaspora writers, Farrokhzād embodies the energy and movement of those operating between cultures and between significant cultural moments.

To understand the literary and symbolic import of Forugh Farrokhzād, it is perhaps most useful to identify the Iranian diaspora's own complex sense of itself within the context of the USA. Although Iranians settled across the world in the aftermath of the Revolution and during the eight-year Iran-Iraq War, by the mid-1980s the USA had become host to the largest Iranian diaspora community. This was largely due to the USA's long-standing political and economic ties with Iran, as well as the significant number of US-educated Iranians who had historically resided in North America.[2] Iranian diaspora subjects, particularly after the Revolution and the 1979 hostage crisis, have typically gravitated towards more nostalgic representations of Iranian culture that fall outside current events and all-too-common, negative media depictions of Iran and Iranians. These nostalgic representations include notions of Persia (rather than Iran) that tended to focus on the arts and culture of pre-Islamic Iran, as well as 'Persian' symbols commonly associated with the country in the West, such as carpets.

The first generation of Iranian exiles and immigrant writers lacked what Hamid Naficy identifies as, 'direct relations with Iran', and thus created a relationship that was 'reconstructed and accounted for through memory and nostalgia.'[3] For Iranian diaspora writers, Farrokhzād exists outside the boundaries of the culture of the Islamic Republic, and her life and work express a bold, experimental sentiment that is connected to the best of Persian art and culture of the mid-twentieth century. Forugh Farrokhzād is identified with the period of Iran's rapid modernization and Westernization under Mohammad Rezā Shāh Pahlavi, when women pushed for more comprehensive civil rights. She is also associated with the modernist poetic tradition, initiated earlier by the poet Nimā Yushij.[4] This modernist poetry 'infused modern subjects, images, diction and perspectives into basically conventional forms.'[5] Other poets of the second generation included Mehdi Akhvān-Sāles, Ahmad Shāmlu, Sohrāb Sepehri, Simin Behbahāni and, of course, Farrokhzād herself. Farrokhzād's poetry openly expressed female sentiments, and pushed 'the boundaries of what could be said by an Iranian woman.'[6] For many Iranian diaspora writers and readers, Farrokhzād represents a particular moment in the history of modern Iran that for many first-generation immigrants has become frozen in time.

Forugh Farrokhzād as cultural icon

Farrokhzād's importance as a symbol of post-revolutionary diaspora culture was facilitated through Iranian-born exiles and émigrés who settled in large numbers in metropolitan areas of both the USA and Europe. Farrokhzād's poetry was regularly read and recited, and she became part of the landscape of exilic Iranian culture that expressed both longing for and alienation from Iran. Farrokhzād and her poetry became symbols of what Hamid Naficy articulates as the 'fetishism of exilic popular culture'.[7] The reading and recitation of Persian poetry (including that of Farrokhzād) enabled first-generation Iranian immigrants and their American-born children to engage in the 'formation and consolidation of exilic identity by circulating illusions that stand for the homeland but that either disavow the threat of, or invite nostalgia for, the homeland.'[8] For many Iranian-Americans (whether Iranian- or US-born), Farrokhzād is part of the catalogue of Iranian culture that has accompanied (and continues to accompany) Iranians on their journey to the West. Those who came from Iran brought Farrokhzād in their suitcases, recited her verses, held her story up as an icon of resistance, and reinterpreted the narrative of her life in both personal and national terms. Many second-generation Iranian-Americans have appropriated Farrokhzād as a means to reconstitute their vision of Iranian culture beyond Iran's borders.

Farrokhzād and memory in writing by US-based academics

Some of the most interesting and passionate cultural invocations of Forugh Farrokhzād have come from US-based Iranian academics who work in the cross-borders of various disciplines including literary, film and cultural studies. In his recent book, *Iran: A People Interrupted,* Hamid Dabashi provides one of the best examples of what Farrokhzād means to many Iranians who left Iran after the Revolution. In a chapter titled, 'On Nations Without Borders', Dabashi narrates an experience of his correspondence with a young, Iranian immigrant mother who is helping to prepare for her son's Bar Mitzvah in New York. The mother seeks Dabashi's help in finding an appropriate selection of poetry for the occasion, and asks for his expert advice because she has no access to Persian literature other than what she has brought with her from Iran: 'books of Forugh and a book of excerpts from the *Golestan* of Sa'di'.[9]

The emphasis on one of Iran's most celebrated classical poets, Sa'di, and its modernist icon, Forugh Farrokhzād, suggests something important about the role of poetry in the lives of Iranians: that like the Bible or the Koran, books of poetry are *sacred* to Iranians. Dabashi writes later in the chapter that it was not:

> surprising that she would have selections from the work of Sa'di at hand, but telling me that she had also brought Forugh Farrkokhzād along with her when she left Iran was a kind of message, a secret code though which she could create a bond with me even though we had never met.[10]

Dabashi's interpretation of the email from the young mother, and the larger cultural assumptions about what the work of Farrokhzād means in the lives of Iranians is clearly problematic. What kind of message or secret code does Farrokhzād exactly convey, and is it one that is necessarily political or critical if we assume that is what is meant by the 'secret code'? And, is the poet's biography also being alluded to in Dabashi's interpretation?

'Without having laid eyes on her', Dabashi goes on to write, he could *'locate her emotive topography (as she could mine) fairly accurately, just by that subordinate clause "except for books of Forough Farrokhzad and a book of excerpts from Golestan"'* [11] (emphasis mine). Dabashi suggests that the appeal of a poet like Forugh Farrokhzād, particularly in her poem 'O Bejeweled Land' ('Ey marz-e por-gohar'), is that she articulates some of what might be called 'Iranianness' – by pointing to and undermining the many ways that Iran has created what might seem an exaggerated image of itself as a nation based on an ancient history and authenticity. But Dabashi's mention of 'O Bejeweled Land', a poem that has been interpreted as a political commentary on Iran's condition in the mid-1960s, along with the young mother's email, confers on it (and on the poet's work) a singular and authoritative meaning that is highly problematic. It assumes a level of intentionality in the young mother's email that assigns a particular significance. It would appear Dabashi intended to suggest something about the kind of Iranian both he and she are.

Like Dabashi's reflections on the emotive quality of Farrokhzād and her oeuvre, Fatemeh Keshavarz's *Jasmine and Stars: Reading More than Lolita in Tehran* (2007), utilizes Farrokhzād as a tool in her critique of Azar Nafisi's highly acclaimed *Reading Lolita in Tehran: A Memoir in Books*. Criticism of Nafisi's omission of Iranian writers like Forugh Farrokhzād from her book is central to Keshavarz's critique of *Reading Lolita in Tehran*, which, she suggests, is a text that exemplifies a New Orientalist narrative. Keshavarz argues Nafisi displays in her book an essentializing tendency; for her it is a book that 'does not hide its clear preference for a western political and cultural takeover.' [12] Keshavarz's account of learning of Farrokhzād's tragic death from her beloved ninth grade teacher Mr. N., foregrounds the somewhat polemical enterprise that is *Jasmine and Stars*. Keshavarz's narration of the actual moment when she learned of the poet's death confers on her a kind of intimacy and authority with the poet that allows her to make a personal connection with Farrokhzād that facilitates her broader critique of Nafisi's book:

> Not only can you read a book such as RLT and not have any idea that a voice as feminine, strong, and articulate as Farrokhzad ever existed in Iran, you can come away thinking that contemporary Iranian culture denies any merit to literary works. [13]

Thus, the invocation of Farrokhzād's poetry and her biography becomes a tool with which Keshavarz challenges the central premise of Nafisi's book by undermining the assumption that Western literature is the most potent weapon to undercut the authority of the Islamic Republic and empower women readers.

By contrast, Keshavarz's identification with Farrokhzād legitimates the power and role of Iranian women in Iran's native literary tradition, and provides her with an emotional topos that challenges the pro-Western literary and aesthetic sensibilities that she believes govern Nafisi's *Reading Lolita in Tehran*.

Later, in the same chapter, Keshavarz describes her connection to her best friend, Zohreh, as having been channeled through the words of a poem by Farrokhzād which were written on the blackboard of her high school classroom. Having walked into the classroom, Keshavarz was arrested by the sight of a line (and its title) from one of Farrokhzād's most celebrated poems, 'Let Us Believe in the Dawn of the Cold Season'. The line, written on the board by her fellow ninth grade acquaintance, became the impetus for Keshavarz's bond with Zohreh; it was as if this single line of the poem connected her to a whole history of Iranian poetry, and further instilled in her a belief in the power of literature. These examples are not only profound in their literariness, but they also show the extent to which the poetry of Farrokhzād and, in particular, the meaning of her life and her death have become embedded in the experience of Iranians who now live outside Iran.

It is interesting to note that in her recently published memoir, *Things I've Been Silent About* (2008), Azar Nafisi makes a number of references to Forugh Farrokhzād. In one reference, Nafisi mentions Farrokhzād alongside Vis, the heroine of Gorgāni's eleventh-century epic romance, *Vis u Rāmin*. Nafisi says, as she continued to read Iranian poetry as a young woman, she 'was not surprised that almost a thousand years after Gorgani immortalized Vis . . . we have a woman called Forugh Farrokhzād who celebrates her lover in poems of unabashed sensuality and honesty.'[14]

When Nafisi leaves Iran for England to study at a high school in the dreary town of Lancaster, she appears to have taken two books with her, which were 'always by [her] bedside': the *divān* of the fourteenth-century poet Hāfez, and – as she phrases it – 'the poems of Forough Farrokhzad, the contemporary feminist poet'.[15] There is perhaps more than an echo here of the young immigrant mother preparing for her son's Bar Mitzvah in New York City.

These are not Nafisi's only references to Farrokhzād. In a chapter entitled, 'Women like that!' Nafisi discusses the poet's work and life in greater detail, and quotes from her controversial poem 'Gonāh' ('Sin').[16] Nafisi is keen to point out that her overbearing mother disapproved of Farrokhzād, and describes how she relished in reading books her mother did not think suitable for a young lady. Nafisi declares Farrokhzād to have been her 'favorite female poet' (presumably because of her rebellious streak in both her writing and her lifestyle). Nafisi is eager to stress how she saw Farrokhzād as integral to the history of a millennium of Persian literature, how she saw Farrokhzād's poems as 'embodiments of the potential' she had detected in the fictional characters she loved. She said she felt there was '[a]n invisible thread' linking Rudābeh (from Ferdowsi's *Shāhnāmeh*) to Forugh.[17] Like many young middle class women in Iran at the time, Azar Nafisi felt a connection to Farrokhzād. This showcasing of the poet's life and works in Nafisi's memoir, on one level at least, appears to be a response to some of the criticisms voiced by Fatemeh Keshavarz about *Reading Lolita in Tehran*.

For many Iranian immigrants and exiles, Farrokhzād stands as a cultural representative who refutes the often singularized narrative of women's oppression, and counteracts the plethora of negative media representations of contemporary Iranian life. Additionally, for those who lived during her life-time, and who first made contact with Farrokhzād when she published her first collection of poems in the mid-1950s and subsequently achieved notoriety both as a poet and as a figure of female rebellion, Farrokhzād has become, in a sense, a representation of their own literary awakening. It is this 'emotive topography' that makes Forugh Farrokhzād such an interesting subject for inquiry, as far as she and her poetry relate to Iranian diasporic writing. In looking at specific examples of this writing and several visual images that draw inspiration from and reinterpret the poet's work, we see how Farrokhzād provides for many an opening into Iranian culture, both from a female (or even feminist) perspective, and from the perspective of those who see her as a universal figure of liberation and transformation.

Translating Farrokhzād's poetry and life

In addition to the cultural transmission of poetry from Iranian immigrants and scholars, (such as the one described by Dabashi as discussed above), translations, whether in scholarly studies of her work documenting her significant role in modern Iranian letters, or else translations of individual poems published in literary journals, have brought Farrokhzād's work to a wider English-speaking audience.[18] For many young poets and writers of the Iranian diaspora, translations of Farrokhzād's poetry have provided them with an opportunity to appreciate and connect with her oeuvre, even if they do not read Persian. Translations of Farrokhzād's poetry have appeared in academic contexts such as Michael Hillmann's biographical and poetic study, *A Lonely Woman: Forugh Farrokhzad and Her Poetry*. There have been numerous collections of Farrokhzād's poetry published in English translation,

Sholeh Wolpé's 2007 *Sin: Selected Poems of Forugh Farrokhzad* being the most recent translation.

Several poems by Iranian-American poets have paid homage to Farrokhzād or else drawn on her life in their own poetry. Roger Sedarat, whose collection, *Dear Regime, Letters to the Islamic Republic* was selected as the winner of the Hollis Summers Poetry Prize and subsequently published by Ohio University Press in 2008, includes such a poem, entitled 'Farrokhzad's Paper Hat':

> Lines along which to cut out the crown
> Of Farrokhzad, anointed for an hour
> In the empty center of modernity's tragic circle
> Where meaning folds back
> Into itself. Beaks of nightingales
> To snip adjustable notches. Poetry's still
> The putting on of tradition,
> But as acknowledged play.
> Matches to a paper hat, ashes for staining
> Lyrics onto the skin: paper tattoos
> For a fantasy of permanence,
> We are running with scissors, cutting out words
> At random.[19]

While many American readers might completely miss the reference to Farrokhzād's biography in this poem, Sedarat's mere mention of her name in a collection that includes poems that are highly critical of the Islamic Republic, highlights her status as a figure of cultural and, more specifically, female resistance. But the resistance Farrokhzād represents to Sedarat functions in both the Iranian and American context. For Iran, she represents the idea of female agency and resistance to Islamic norms, and for the USA, she represents a different vision of Iranian womanhood. Interestingly, the poet refers to her by her last name, whereas among many Iranians she is affectionately referred to simply as 'Forugh'. Perhaps this is Sedarat's desire to make the poet's biography more accessible to the Western audience by making it possible for readers to look her up on the Internet, which is now home to many English-speaking websites now dedicated to her life and work. Whatever the case, Farrokhzād's position in the poem as an 'anointed' figure, one who is conferred with divine status, is as illusive as the paper crown she wears. Like the poet he writes, Sedarat, conveys the 'fantasy of permanence' that poets and poetry convey about their society. Much like Keshavarz's invocation of Farrokhzād as a response to the New Orientalist writing which she critiques,[20]

Sedarat finds in Farrokhzād a figure that transcends New Orientalist thinking about Iran:

> When I wrote that poem, I really was going for some kind of underground/ trespass motif, yet I wanted more of an assertion of identity in relation to the feminine as opposed to the mere *behind the veil* exoticism. To a point, I feel like the allusion to Forugh thwarts the Orientalist perspective.[21]

Depictions in the US media of Iran have often included singularized images of Iranian women in long, black veils. Farrokhzād's life and poetry has become more significant today, since she embodies a potent symbol of the agency of Iranian women, of literary boldness, and of the need to refute and challenge stereotypically negative ideas about Iran and images of Iranians.

Sholeh Wolpé, like many contemporary Iranian diaspora writers, sees Farrokhzād as embodying the defiance of prevailing cultural norms in mid-twentieth-century Iran. For Wolpé, Farrokhzād is someone who took great personal and artistic risks and produced poetry that both challenged not just cultural but also aesthetic conventions. Wolpé's poem, 'That Desire Called Sin', evokes the title of one of Farrokhzād's most famous poems, 'Sin'. She writes the poem as a kind of homage to the Iranian poet:

> Naked, you climb the boulder with a flashlight and mother's
> Painted bowl brimming with cherries.
> You whisper to the moon, I must be mad.
> You've come to wash away your sins, but the creek giggles,
> Runs watery hands on your thighs as Venus stares, spreads
> Her molten blue beams on your hair.
> The cherries explode red in your mouth and you spit out the seeds
> As if each is a planet crusted with guilt, swallow the soft flesh
> Mumuring, *nothing's more delectable than sin.*[22]

The poem draws on some of the erotic images from Farrokhzād's poem 'Bathing' ('Āb-tani'), from Farrokhzād's second collection, *Divār* (*The* Wall), in which the speaker describes the sensations of bathing naked in spring waters that lap against her thighs, and also ends with the image of sinning – a reference to the poem 'Sin'.[23] Both Farrokhzād's poem and that of Wolpé engage with the idea of sin – as woman's enjoyment of her sexuality, of pleasure in her body; as well as guilt for the 'sin'. However, Wolpé's poem moves beyond the subversion of Farrokhzād's poem, as if to answer for her sins, not in guilt or shame, but rather in a kind of resounding pleasure in the committing of the sin itself. Wolpé's poem performs a kind of diasporic Iranian female subjectivity that connects Farrokhzād's life and oeuvre with her own 'sin', thereby writing her Iranian female subjectivity completely free of the judgements and scrutiny of her society.

Another example of the re-articulation of what might be called Farrokhzād's feminist sensibility is evident in the work of New York-based film-maker and visual artist, Shirin Neshat. One of the most widely circulated depictions of Farrokhzād's work in the West is a photograph by Neshat, in her 'Women of Allah', a series of photographs and calligraphic montages that captivated the art world when it first appeared in the late 1990s.[24] These photographs garnered international media attention because in them Neshat plays with the juxtaposition of femininity and violence, as well as silence and defiance. To communicate this, Neshat draws on a series of widely circulated images broadcast during the Iranian Revolution – veiled women bearing weapons, scenes of segregation between women and men, and so on. One (untitled) image in the series features a woman whose face is mostly cut out of the frame (from just above the mouth) and whose tattooed hand is the focal point of the photograph. Her hand rests squarely in the centre of her lower lip. The hand (which recalls the Indian *mehndi*, a tattoo of elaborate, usually floral designs drawn in henna) is imprinted with a series of quotations from Farrokhzād, upon which is inscribed, in a much larger hand, the Shi'i invocation for Imām Hoseyn's loyal half-brother, al-'Abbās b. 'Ali, *Yā qamar-e Bani Hāshem* ('O Moon of the Hashemites'). On the five fingers of the woman's hand are inscribed jumbled lines (in a rather unrefined hand) from the opening stanzas of Farrokhzād's long, posthumously published poem, 'I Feel Sorry for the Garden' ('Delam barā-ye bāghcheh mi-suzad'):[25]

> No one is thinking about the flowers
> No one is thinking about the fish
> No one wants to believe the garden is dying
> That the garden's heart has swollen under the sun
> That the garden is slowly forgetting its green moments[26]

This poem has often been interpreted as a political allegory for the corruption and individualism of 1960s Iran. In the poem, the speaker sets up a series of characters whose behavior and actions point to what Michael Hillmann identifies as 'the individual self-centeredness, superficiality, and phoniness common among members of her [Farrokhzād's] upper middle class Tehran.'[27] The garden is a metaphor for Iranian society as a whole, and critics have suggested it shows Farrokhzād's insight into Iran's social malaise during the

1960s. In this poem, Farrokhzād expresses a metaphoric and poetic forecasting of the social unrest that would take place more than a decade later during the 1978–1979 Revolution. Neshat's use of the first six lines from 'I Feel Sorry for the Garden', as well as her use of visual images similar to those circulated around the world during the Revolution – those of veiled, weapon-bearing, stern-faced women – echo a kind of rebelliousness in her own work that captures the 'aesthetic nature of women's resistance'.[28]

The superimposition of lines from Farrokhzād's poem written in a poor hand is subversive in itself. But the image of the middle finger pressed against the lower lip implies a number of possible meanings: that of speech and silence, utterance vs. non-utterance, and also the possibility that the woman whose face is not visible and is partially erased is also recentred by the text of a defiant Iranian female poet. Milani identifies Neshat's work thus:

> Concentrating on the complex textual relations between body and veil, she transcribes Persian calligraphic script, often exquisitely rebellious poetry by pioneering women poets on the exposed faces, hand, and feet in her photographs. Giving voice to the body and body to the voice, she memorialized Iranian women's defiance at the same time as she launched her own artistic career.[29]

In answer to the 'the uselessness of all these hands' (*bi-hudegi-ye in-hameh dast*), a phrase that appears toward the end of the poem in question, Neshat makes a visual 'extension of her own hands as they inscribe the original Persian poem onto her subject's hand.'[30] Farrokhzād's legacy is thus borne on the body, signifying not silence, but instead self-expression. Neshat's work rewrites Farrokhzād's own narrative journey through acts of poetic resistance; Neshat reconnects her visual work with Farrokhzād's attempt at articulating a 'female voice that challenges the dominant value systems of her culture.'[31]

The act of memorializing Farrokhzād's life and work is also expressed in Maryam Habibian's play, 'Forugh's Reflecting Pool', which was first staged in New York in November 2002 against the backdrop of the events of 11 September 2001. The play incorporates poetry, dance and music; the multimedia aspect of the play expressing the 'nuances that inevitably get lost in another language'.[32] The play opens with a solitary silhouette and features both translations of Farrokhzād's poems, as well as speech drawn from interviews she gave. The play functions both as a retelling of the poet's bold and often troubled life, but also as a means through which to communicate the specificity of Farrokhzād's poetry in the Iranian context, as well as in its appeal to a wider section of humanity. Interspersed with monologues by Farrokhzād, the central character in the play, there is also dialogue imagined by Habibian between Farrokhzād the poet and Farrokhzād, the figure of exile. Habibian posits Farrokhzād's 'exile' as a kind of alienation and foreignness in her own country during her lifetime, and as a woman poet who has been exiled from history within the context of the Islamic Republic of Iran.

The poems and poetic fragments in the play are mostly made up of biographical information and poetry from the latter part of Farrokhzād's life, when her work took on a more overtly political character. In addition to giving voice to Farrokhzād's poetry in an American context and locating her poetry within the political context of pre-revolutionary Iran, the play also situates the poet in a more 'real', less idolized frame, resurrecting her not merely as an icon of Iran's recent past, but also imbuing her with a present-day relevance – not simply for Iranians of the diaspora, but for all those who appreciate how poetry can cut across cultural and national lines. In addition to long passages of poetic recitation, or even whole poems such as 'Imān biāvarim beh āghāz-e fasl-e sard' ('Let Us Believe in the Dawn of the Cold Season'), Habibian imagines the poet talking to the audience about her life. In one part before the recitation of the poem 'She'ri barā-ye to' ('A Poem for You', which was dedicated to her young son), Farrokhzād explicity talks of the conflict she entertains as a woman and poet:

> Then came my foolish love and marriage at 16. Well, it's hard for me to talk about my husband, but I was too young and stupid to get married. Besides, he never understood me. And then came my baby boy. I was torn between being a mother and a poet. As much as I loved my child, I could not be satisfied leading a purely domestic life. Poetry, that blood-thirsty goddess, would not give up her hold on me. To deny her would have meant denying myself.[33]

While this monologue is quite direct (and perhaps even a little out of place in 1960s Iran), it lends something to the performance of Farrokhzād as both a character and a national symbol. Habibian imbues her Farrokhzād with the 'unveiled' vocabulary of a Western feminist. While some critics see Farrokhzād as a public symbol of Iran's nascent feminist movement of the 1950s and 1960s, the poet's candour was an aspect of her life and work that exposed her to vehement criticism and judgement, both inside and outside literary circles.[34] For a writer like Habibian, Farrokhzād's life and poetry is recirculating in an American context, where she is celebrated as a figure of Iranian female liberation at a time when Iranian women are often viewed and depicted in images which are both homogenous and repetitive.

Other works by Iranian diaspora writers draw much less on the feminist aspects of Farrokhzād's biography, and more directly on the sensibility of foreignness and otherness expressed in many of her poems. Among the younger diaspora writers, one can trace elements of Farrokhzād's work and even detect traces of something which resembles her language and tone in their poems written in English. 'Tales Left Untold', by Désirée Aphrodite Navab, is a long poem told in a series of seven 'tale' stanzas (including a prologue and epilogue). This poem has a tone somewhat reminiscent of that in 'I Feel Sorry for the Garden', although the context is multicultural, rather than mono-cultural, given the poet's mixed Iranian-Greek-American heritage. In 'Tales Left Untold', Navab enunciates some of the complexities of claiming her heritage at a time when Iran has become a pariah nation through events such as the Iranian Revolution, the hostage crisis, and the Iran-Iraq War. Navab's voice and poetic style reminds us of Farrokhzād; her use of rhyme and meter similarly builds on more conventional poetic devices, but the poem in its entirety is a kind of manifesto against conventionality and normative notions of national and cultural identity. In tale #1, we see Navab wrestling with her multicultural identity against a sense of her outspoken criticism of the USA, where she is located:

> The flag of each nation
> In me, stirs little sensation
> No nationalism shouts loud in me
> Even after living in all three
> To see one flag burned
> In the other country
> There's no going back for me
>
> My people held my other people hostage
> The weight of this I carry in my luggage
> A criminal in reverse
> Hypocritical
> Perverse
> Even a blaming finger
> Becomes a hollow gesture
> Pointing at them
> Yet right back at me
> Because them
> Is me
> I am all three
> Both the beauty and blood they've shed
> All three[35]

The tone of this poem, both in its confidence and also its vulnerability echoes the voice of Farrokhzād and her criticism of contemporary Iran. Whereas Farrokhzād's poetry engaged with some of the struggles associated with gender and female identity in the Iranian context, Navab's speaker is much more directly engaged with cultural and national assumptions that surround her in the US context. The poem's imagery and the attention to rhyme (which is not easy to do in English without sounding overly facile) draw a lineage to Farrokhzād's poetry. While one cannot say definitively that Navab has sought to mimic Farrokhzād in English, it is interesting to note the synthesis of the personal and the political in this poem, something that is evident in a large number of Farrokhzād's poems.

Laleh Khalili, another diaspora poet, this time Iranian-American-British,[36] similarly invokes a tone and exilic sensibility reminiscent of what we find in Farrokhzād's poetry. Khalili's language is direct and critical, and it engages the reader of Iranian descent with their fate as post-1979 immigrants to the West. Khalili's use of the Persian word *'azizam* ('my dear') in a poem written in English, without providing a translation, creates two powerful effects: (1) it forces the reader to confront an experience of foreignness and otherness communicated in the poem (and thus in the speaker's perspective) and (2) it links the Iranian diaspora reader more intimately to the emotion expressed in the poem, which, at the time the poem was written, would have been felt deeply by many Iranian immigrants. By using *'azizam* (a term of endearment), alongside the strong statement 'I denied you', the reader is made culpable and cannot turn away, and thus cannot deny. This same intimacy and directness of Khalili's readerly address is found in many of Farrokhzād's poems. In Khalili's poem, one finds an address to Iran or Iranian society in much the same way as the 'you' in Farrokhzād's poetry is often intended – as an address, not to an individual, but rather to a collective reader. Khalili's synthesis of politics in the aftermath of the Revolution and the alienation of being an exile in America invoke the tone and spirit of Farrokhzād. In her poem, In Exile', Khalili recounts the ways that Iranians have denied their heritage in the face of prejudice and hostility in the context of what appears to be North America, or perhaps simply the West, in a more general sense:

> *'Azizam*, shamefaced I am, just shamefaced.
> The other day, you know,
> I denied being yours
> I denied being you
> I denied it all

the other day
I had to learn to unlearn you
the other day

'Azizam, how does one recount a story
In a language no one seems to understand?

there are times when you want to be a profusion of myths
When you know that
dormant histories lie unassumingly in the forgotten subcutaneous
region of your rib cage
There are times that you JUST want to declare yourself
in joy
in joy
in pride, even
and you can't.[37]

One can also read Khalili's direct address to the reader, 'you', and her own disclosure of 'I' as a kind of Farrokhzādian perspective, in which the poet draws the reader into the contradictory emotions of shame and joy, something that seems apparent in Forugh Farrokhzād's much-discussed poem, 'Sin'. Khalili's title, 'In Exile', suggests the poet not only seeks to examine physical exile beyond geographic and national boundaries, but also the exile of narrating one's self, of one's unique individuality against 'a profusion of myths'. The poem's use of the preposition 'in' suggests Khalili does not wish the poem to be read as specific to exile in any particular context, but rather as a comment on exile as a state of being; a condition made all the more pronounced because of the exile's inability to speak, to be heard or to be understood. Khalili's poem has a definite Iranian resonance, like much of Farrokhzād's poetry, but it has tinges of a more transcendent experience of exile than we find in the poetry of Farrokhzād, as well as in classical Persian poetry.

Forugh Farrokhzād as cultural map

Farrokhzād's poetry has inspired many writers and artists both inside and outside Iran. The works of translators, playwrights and poets who have drawn inspiration from Farrokhzād's poetry and her life have generated fresh interest in the poet and a critical eye on her contribution to Persian letters in particular, and, on a wider level, to world literature. The fact that her documentary,

The House is Black,[38] is now readily available to viewers outside Iran has greatly enhanced Farrokhzād's visibility in North America and Europe. In the last few years, Farrokhzād's life and poetry have been more widely celebrated and disseminated through websites, symposia, and conferences, reflecting a growing interest in her significance as a poet and film-maker. Farrokhzād has, on the one hand, been recast as a manifestation of Iranian feminist sensibilities, and on the other hand she serves to counter New Orientalist writing, which seeks to deny the existence of nonconventional models of Iranian femininity in pre-revolutionary Iran.

Farrokhzād's poetry – like her life – is infused with mystery, controversy and a unique vision. As one of a handful of bold contemporary women poets, she helped transform the landscape of modern Persian poetry, giving voice to a unique female subjectivity. Her poetic oeuvre and her fascinating life story is claimed and celebrated by many artists and writers who draw inspiration from her life and her poetry. Farrokhzād's oeuvre has served as a kind of cultural touchstone for many Iranian diaspora intellectuals and writers, both because of her aesthetics and the subversive nature of her writing. The writers and artists discussed in this essay consciously draw on Farrokhzād's voice, style and eroticism to suggest something about their own emerging subjectivity. They explore her work and biography in search of their own artistic identity, producing in turn a cross-cultural synthesis. For them, Farrokhzād functions as a visionary poet who moved beyond her culture's expectations and who dared to experiment with form, language and socio-cultural taboos. Some of these writers utilize and draw on her legacy directly, while others only hint at a connection to Farrokhzād. The artists discussed in this essay are almost all based in the USA, but there are many other writers and artists elsewhere who have engaged with Farrokhzād's imagery and her life narrative in their paintings, photographs and fiction. The mythic qualities of Farrokhzād's persona, combined with her powerful poetic oeuvre, suggest she will continue to attract new readers beyond Iran's borders. The synthesis of Farrokhzād's life with the lives of artists living now and in the future will continue to reshape and reimagine her as a poet, feminist and film-maker, enabling Farrokhzād to transcend her original Iranian context and, by association, engendering a collective re-visioning of Iran and its heritage in the diaspora.

Chapter 14

Cargo, Chickpeas, and Cobblestones: The Textures of Memory in Forugh Farrokhzād's Travelogue *Dar diyāri digar*[1]

Marie Ostby

Forugh Farrokhzād is perhaps the twentieth-century Iranian poet most closely linked to freedom of movement. Themes of mobility and captivity that permeate her poetry – by way of birds, flying, cages, and similar motifs – have been thoroughly and thoughtfully examined in existing scholarship, especially by Farzaneh Milani.[2] But Farrokhzād's 1956 travelogue, *Dar diyāri digar* ('In another land'), the most direct firsthand account of her own mobility, remains underexamined. Farrokhzād was two collections into her career when it was written, and it marks a shift in the scope, tone, and ambition of her work. Farrokzhād confides in the reader as she looks back on her pre-travelogue self: 'In those days, I was like a faraway flying bird that had extended its wings in the dark, limited, and empty space and reached the peak'.[3,4] The desperation Farrokhzād felt because her 'wings grew weary'[5] led her not only to travel, not only to write, but to deeply examine the possibilities of writing about travel. Ultimately, her cross-cultural and even transhistorical encounters revealed to her both the inherent vulnerable solitude of the traveling writer and their profound interconnectedness with strangers. The liminal, flexible travelogue genre helped her express both halves of this paradox.

The travelogue is a slippery genre. Travel itself is rarely as rejuvenating as we imagine it to be. As Vita Sackville-West wrote in her 1926 travelogue *Passenger to Teheran*: 'Travel is in sad case. It is uncomfortable, it is expensive; it is a source of annoyance to our friends, and of loneliness to ourselves.'[6] One might wonder how travel writing ever developed into a whole literary genre. On the other hand, travel is perhaps the sole most important source of inspiration for so many writers. How does travel, perhaps not inspiring in its own right, become psychological and internal? How are cross-cultural spaces produced by the traveler's imagination? Before Farrokhzād, notable Persianate travelogues from the nineteenth and twentieth centuries expanded their scope beyond early works in the *safarnāmeh* and *hajjnāmeh* genres. Scholars including Roberta Micallef, Sunil Sharma, and Thomas Wide have theorized that, in this period, travelogues became 'testament to wider patterns of interaction and integration between parts of the world that were formerly distinct,'[7] 'employ[ed] subversive strategies in their comments on masculine values in various cultures to express their emotions within the boundaries of what was deemed proper in narratives by women,'[8] incorporated 'substantial autobiographical content,'[9] and existed as works 'demonstrably tempered by [their] point of origin' that revealed more about the traveler's home culture than their destination. Farrokhzād's travelogue shares these qualities of connectedness, subversion, and autobiography, but also differs from other Persianate travelogues in the period immediately preceding hers, replacing what Sharma identifies as 'exaggerated wonder' and 'hyperbolic descriptions of modern and different ways of life'[10] with a materially grounded realism.

Nineteenth-century Persian travelogues from Europe, Naghmeh Sohrabi writes, lived in multiple sites and multiple genres: they described how 'both the origins and destinations were moving targets,' reflecting rapidly changing geopolitical landscapes both at home and abroad, and 'the lines between travelogues, geographies, histories, and memoirs remained blurred even as they took on new forms and meanings.'[11] Farrokhzād's straightforward syntax and personal diction follows developments of simple style (*sādeh-nevisi*), which Sohrabi argues started in the Qajar period, citing other scholars who attribute this style to 'the influence of translation from European languages in this period.'[12] The conversation between travelers' impressions and their evolving styles, in other words, had advanced quite far by the time of Farrokhzād's trip.

Dar diyāri digar is an example of what Louise Marlow has called a 'medi[um]' for exploring differing constructions of self and identity, home and community, gender and generation, in the course of the planned and unplanned encounters thrown up by their travels.'[13] As Mana Kia writes, Persianate travelogues in the early nineteenth century exemplify how 'social interaction . . . has a direct impact on perceptions of place, transforming the proximity and thus identity of place itself.'[14] Farrokhzād, a profoundly solitary traveler, seems mostly unaffected by her brief social interactions with those she encounters in Italy – if anything, these interactions present a mild annoyance. Hers is the record of a cultural immersion driven mostly by setting, not characters. It more closely aligns with Thomas Wide's description of the 'conceptual impact of. . . travels: how transformations in travel brought about new conceptions of the world, particularly changed notions of time and space, which had concomitant effects on conceptions of history and geography.'[15] Sohrabi argues that politically, Qajar-era travelogues are often anticolonial in spirit; they 'problematized the use of travelogues as purely depositories of knowledge about Europe and brought to light the ambiguities that lay at the heart of encounters with the West.'[16] Farrokhzād's travelogue does not explicitly challenge power by providing 'multiple narratives' as Sohrabi suggests many of the political Qajar texts do, but her intensely personal point of view subverts perspectival norms of gender, class, and mobility by focusing on materiality and personal horizons in order to expand the travelogue genre itself.

An Iranian woman traveled to Rome as early as the 1600s, when Teresa Sampsonia – the Circassian wife of Robert Shirley, lifelong envoy to Persia, who grew up at the Safavid court – retired to Rome in 1628 after Shirley's death and lived the last forty years of her life there.[17] But despite the breadth and depth of the Persianate-European travelogue circuit that existed by the time of Farrokhzād's trip, records of Persianate women's traveling voices were still relatively rare. Very few Iranian women traveled to Europe until the early twentieth century, and by the mid-1950s Farrokhzād was part of a growing trend, largely started by wives accompanying their husbands and women seeking medical treatment or higher education. One of the closest analogies to Farrokhzād's trip is that of Sadiqeh Dowlatābādi, who traveled to Switzerland, France, and Germany in 1923–1927 and produced an account thoughtfully historicized by Jasmin Khosravie. Like Farrokhzād, Dowlatābādi was a divorcée and an adoptive mother; she fostered her two younger half-sisters after their father's death. Both their fathers were powerful men: while Colonel Farrokhzād was a career military officer, Dowlatābādi's father was a religious leader of the Iranian Azali community. Unlike Farrokhzād, whose work was often interpreted politically but stayed away from politics herself, Dowlatābādi was 'actively involved in the nationalist fight for a constitution and a parliamentary system of power in Iran around the turn of the century and thereafter' through 'the networks of several Tehrani women's societies.'[18] She established two girls' schools and a women's textile cooperative, and published the feminist newspaper *Zabān-e zanān* ['women's voice'][19] in

1919-1922, prior to her trip. She was central to Reza Shah's *Nehzat-e bānovān* ['women's awakening project'], as thoroughly examined by Camron Michael Amin.[20]

For Dowlatābādi, Europe was a place of recovery as she suffered from chronic fatigue. But Khosravie suggests that she used medical therapy as an excuse for a long-awaited extended journey to Europe, twice postponed when she was younger due to her father's death and her sisters' youth. In her forties, Dowlatābādi gained a teacher's diploma at the Sorbonne. 'Metaphorically speaking, Europe not only offered her a cure for her physical ailments but also of a cure for her mind by acquiring a university degree she would not have been able to get back home.'[21] The earnest voice in Farrokhzād's travelogue is similar to Dowlatābādi's in that she 'remained the person she was and did not – as it was the case with many other female travelers – try to become someone who she hadn't been back home or to take on a different role.'[22] But a key difference between them lies, once again, in politics: despite her independence, Dowlatābādi's text still bears traces of the travelogue genre's early diplomatic function as she strives for a broader social critique, while Farrokhzād's cross-cultural judgments arise from personal encounters and do not suggest a political agenda.

Presciently and characteristically, Farrokhzād stretches the form of the travelogue to include poetic phrases, reflecting the multiple factors that restrict her freedom of movement through the several genres she employs to elude those restrictions. While one might rightfully extrapolate from the 'corrections' made by the metaleptic censor character named '*Aqā-ye Mosahheh*' ['Mr. Proofreader'], who enters the narrative at a late stage, that Farrokhzād's creative work in Iran was stifled, the narrator originally insists that her impetus to travel 'was not the desire to see new things or to touch other lives, happinesses, or colorful pleasures'.[23] Farrokhzād's implication that her travel is emancipatory – personally, politically, and artistically – rather than escapist or recreational (or simply ethnographic) is particularly vulnerable to the censoring authority's pen.

Sohrabi points out the flaws in treating the authors of earlier (nineteenth-century) Persian travelogues as 'anthropologists and Europologists.' While an ethnographic positioning, developed by Mohamad Tavakoli-Targhi and others, crucially 'imbues the travel writer with agency,' she argues that it 'operates on two problematic assumptions':

> First, by picking and choosing information about Europe (Europology), this approach necessitates discarding or ignoring the rest of these travelogues that treated more 'familiar territory' – inside Iran, for example

– with the same descriptive eye. Second, by designating these travel writers as anthropologists and ethnographers, it elevates experiential knowledge at the cost of other forms of knowledge that were as valid at the time as 'seeing with one's own eyes.'[24]

Farrokhzād's travelogue exemplifies an alternative to 'Europological' texts in both of these ways: her style is thoroughly comparativist; her epistemology stretches far beyond the visual into the tactile sensorium, and is ultimately most faithful to the historical.

An easy generalization about travel is that it makes the author more cosmopolitan in the etymological sense of the term – more committed to one's duties as a world citizen than to one's local or national affiliations. Bruce Robbins describes the accusations often levied against cosmopolitanism as a state of 'privileged and irresponsible detachment':

What is assumed is in fact a chain of successive *detachments*: *from true feeling*, hence from the responsibility that engages a whole person, not a sometime spectator; *from responsibility*, hence from the constituency to which one would be responsible; *from constituency*, hence from significant political action. The cosmopolitan is held to be incapable of participating in the making of history, doomed to the mere aesthetic spectatorship that he or she is also held secretly to prefer.[25]

Through linking key moments in *Dar diyāri digar*, in which material textures serve as both mnemonic devices and markers of class and mobility, I argue in what follows that Farrokhzād's trip to Italy developed in her a cosmopolitan sensibility that is grounded not in the accumulation of new sights and cross-cultural experiences, but in the contrapuntal, intimate connections she forges between her sensory experiences of past and present, home and abroad.

With Iran's socio-cultural reforms under the Pahlavis (1925-1979), restrictions on women's freedom of movement were relaxed and the veil was banned outright from 1936 to 1941. Still, a feminist literary expression was not available or acceptable to Farrokhzād because of social norms and attitudes, even in Tehran among the upper classes. Moralistic judgment and painful legal barriers still remained for women in Iran, as they do today. Farrokhzād first faced this kind of stigma when she was just nineteen years old and published the poem 'Gonāh' ['sin'], whose speaker makes a joyful confession of extra-marital sex. This scandalous poem led to widespread defamation, divorce from her husband, and loss of custody of her son. It was largely this personal tragedy that drove her abroad: twenty-one years old, having published two successful poetry collections (*Asir* ['captive'], 1955, and *Divār* ['the wall'], 1956) but also suffered a nervous breakdown and institutionalization, she embarked on a fourteen-month trip to Europe to escape a pressure-cooker environment that did not accept the kind of sexual agency for women for which her poems yearned.

In 1956, then, the composition of *Dar diyāri digar* marks a shift from the more personal, even confessional poetry of her early career. Traveling in Italy and Germany for a year and two months, she concurrently wrote several of the increasingly intertextual and historical-political poems in her third volume *'Esyān* ["rebellion"] (1958). Farrokhzād referred to this third collection, which would mark the midpoint of her short career, as "the hopeless thrashing of arms and legs between two stages of life; the final gasps for breath before a sort of release."[26]

The travelogue begins with anxiety. A clear hesitation to even approach the genre weighs down her opening lines:

> As I put pen to paper to jot down my recollections of the fourteen months I spent in Europe, I can say I'm a bit disheartened. I have to rely solely on what I can remember, and I confess I am rather weak when it comes to remembering. Or perhaps the problem is that I suspect my memories are not clear or prominent enough for the dust of oblivion not to have settled on them.[27]

Wistful at the outset, there is a materiality to the dread that quickly weighs down these opening thoughts. The 'dust of oblivion' (*ghobār-e farāmushi*) goes from affecting her vision (precluding 'clarity') to prohibiting movement (as she is too much of a 'weak person' (*ādam-e za'if*) to shake it off). Dust is, in fact, a recurring image in the poems of *'Esyān*:

عاقبت خط جاده پایان یافت / من رسیدم ز ره غبار آلود

The line of the road ended at last / Covered with dust, I arrived from the way

خانه ها رنگ دیگری بودند/ گرد آلوده، تیره و دلگیر

The houses had donned a different hue / Dusty, dark, and depressing[28]

The image of dust, or ambiguity (*ghobār*) (sometimes alternated or combined with 'polluted' or 'contaminated' [*ālud/eh*]), transcends the formal container Farrokhzād uses in each case, as it becomes both the subject of memories and the figure for what obscures them. The weightiness of her return matches the struggle with which she lifts herself out of a heavy, foggy confusion to frame her own travel narrative. The 'dust' is distracting, or prohibitive, enough that the narrator muses for several paragraphs on the nature of perspective and relativity before diving in to relate the experiences themselves: 'Something that brings me joy can provoke indifference in someone else whose tastes are other than mine, whose feelings are different, who has a dissimilar mind',[29] she writes, but soon concludes that evoking the experience itself is paramount for cross-cultural understanding: 'In either case, the moment we both encountered remains stable and real. And so, I believe, this could provide an example for life.'[30]

A different kind of materially based dissociation occurs when the narrator describes her last glimpse of Iran: 'A bunch of waving hands, like the branches of a tree in the wind, and a cluster of colorful handkerchiefs fluttering back and forth in the air'.[31] The mournful synecdoche that turns family members and friends into material traces here suggests the lens of memory that filters the experience, gathering snatches of color and gesture that will recur in her reverie after she has boarded the flight, and that she will compare to similar sensory impressions in Europe to tie together her present and past. One sees this pre-emptive mnemonic imagism in a more literal way through her view from the airplane window: 'From up there, the plains looked like pieces of colored paper, and the trees blots of ink that had dripped onto a sheet of paper from the tip of a pen'.[32] This is quintessentially a writer's journey, figured through the tools of a writer's trade – a voyage that will bloom into a lyrically mediated comparison between cultures, but here begins with a desire to gain some narrative perspective on her shattered life.

Absent any sense of adventure or excitement that might typically characterize a twenty-one-year-old's first trip overseas, the narrator's tone and captivity metaphors make clear that the trip was a desperate emotional measure.

> The pressures of life and the stress of the environment added to the chains cuffing my hands and feet. With all my power, I was trying to face them. It made me tired and distressed . . . I had simply run out of energy and strength, from all the fighting. So in order to find new energy and the strength to laugh again, I decided, quite abruptly, to leave this environment.[33]

This emotional weight translates quite physically into where Farrokhzād is situated in her travels. She flies from Tehran to Rome (with an overnight stop in Beirut) on a cargo plane, which raises eyebrows among her peers. She shrugs off their judgment and embraces the rudimentary nature of the journey:

My friend was embarrassed to come bid me farewell at the airport. She didn't know that I have never in my life valued people who seek glamorous appearances. For me, traveling in a cargo plane was a little pleasurable, since the purpose of this journey was not to show off to others about the price of the ticket or the glamour of the plane.[34]

'Commercial flights,' Micallef and Sharma point out, 'changed the patterns and routes of travelers, ushering in a new era of travel writing'[35] – while decades earlier, the advent of the steamship had 'created a whole new set of classification systems, and even class relations.'[36] Farrokhzād travels not on a consumerist passenger plane but via cargo, suggesting an earlier era in which travel was not associated with 'happinesses, or colorful pleasures' but with conquest, warfare, conversion, or trade. Once on board, she is literally seated alongside heavy baggage, as the cargo plane does not have enough seats for all the passengers and she is left perched on top of crates. The haphazard layout of people and things on the plane prefigures a trip that will not be touristically guided or mediated – the plane, she explains, has no flight attendant or consistent passenger announcements. Resourceful and intrepid, the narrator manages to avoid conversation with a pesky older American man who insists that she speak to him using her English phrasebook, by requesting a blanket from the pilot and laying herself out on top of the crates to seek a primal sort of comfort: 'The motion of the plane at takeoff and landing resembled mothers' hands rocking a cradle',[37] she reflects. Turning herself into cargo, Farrokhzād literalizes the heaviness and clunkiness of travel as well as the disempowerment she feels due to her gender, language barrier, cultural difference, economic precarity, and solitude.

Upon arrival in Beirut (and Rome soon thereafter), Farrokhzād's impressions are continually filtered through two lenses: her transnational comparisons to sensory impressions she remembers from home (for example, she immediately compares the humid air in Beirut to her childhood experience of Khuzestan), and her wish to connect with her new environment. Before she even leaves the airport terminal: 'My feet imbibed the delightful, cool humidity of the earth.'[38] She is particularly entranced by the beach on her first night in Beirut, and wishes to sleep on the beach rather than in her hotel: 'There, I could be free. There, I could shout and sing and run anywhere . . . I felt that to have to stay in one of these ostentatious palaces, even for a short while, would be like entering a prison'.[39] Each detail of the physical landscape affects her ecstatically:

I was walking happily, and something in the air made me dizzy as I walked. The streets were deserted and our shadows on the asphalt looked wet in the

CARGO, CHICKPEAS, AND COBBLESTONES 203

humid air. They were drawn to each other at every moment. That night I played with my own shadow as I walked along. I invented wild shapes and forms with my hands and feet, and I was laughing at seeing my shadow self mimicking all my moves . . . then I lay down on the sand, and became one with the sea.[40]

But while the sights and sounds of these new landscapes take her breath away, the narrator at first has little affection to spare for fellow tourists and Europeans she meets – from the man on the plane to American soldiers 'who were likely drunk' disturbing the peace outside her window in Beirut, to the Italians she encounters in Rome: aristocrats that were 'vacuous and snobbish,' a policeman who was even more distracted than the policemen back home, and an untrustworthy landlady laughing 'angrily,' whom she imagines would prefer to charge her for every cubic centimeter of air she breathed.[41]

Taken together, the people she encounters, almost all men, fail to fill any guiding or explicating role, and this solidifies her independence as a traveler – she says of the policeman: 'The way he treated me, and the lack of care and attention in his behavior, made me think I should not ask for help from the police again, and should rely on myself.'[42] By comparison, the male failure she identifies in Europe finds its parallel in the character of Mr. Proofreader, who enters the story when Farrokhzād catches herself for breaking too many diegetic levels and needs to course-correct.

Wryly, she wrests herself away from a moment of childhood reverie and back to the central temporality in Italy by doubling down on the value of detours:

Indeed, it is not bad if one sometimes needs to visit the plane of Karbala[43], and there is no opportunity more appropriate than the moment in which we can detach from the principal current, and in this environment, we can deal with more important issues. Sometimes one needs to digress and there are occasions when digression opens up great opportunities for it is precisely when we wander off the main topic that we notice more important matters. So, here's my complaint about Mr. Proofreader who, incidentally, has no connections with either Italy or my memories.[44]

This idea that 'we [can] detach from the principal current' (*az jaryān-e asli jodā mishim*) blurs the lines, as Farrokhzād often does in the text, between physical and mental acts of wandering (whether through memory, nostalgia, escapism, fantasy, or ideological departure). In the earlier airport passage, for example, she refers to *mosāferat* (travel or journey) when discussing the purpose of her trip. For the latter category, travels of the mind, Farrkohzād usually refers to her travelogue as *khāterāt*: memories, memoirs, or recollections. Both types of travel, of course, comprise the text itself and its chosen genre, overlapping and intersecting. In the context of modern Persian travelogues, this fluidity is reminiscent of Sohrabi's distinction between earlier terms for travel, *safar* and *siyāhat*, that can connote 'pilgrimage or journey,' and a growing use of *gardesh*, which suggests 'wandering and vagrancy,' in later travelogues.[45] As for her blundering censor-figure, Farrokhzād places him in Khorramshahr with knowledge of neither her Tehran environs nor her new European surroundings. As a character in the travelogue, the chief adjustment he makes is to Farrokhzād's aforementioned statement of insistence that travelogue is not a tale of leisure: 'My goal in going to Europe was not the desire to see new things or to touch other lives, happinesses, or colorful pleasures'[46] into:

...و یا لمس لذت ها، شادیها، و زندگی های رنگین تری <u>می نمود</u>!

'. . . it *seems it was* the desire to see new things or to touch other lives, happinesses, or colorful pleasures'.[47]

One must keep in mind, when reading this portrait of censorship, that the Farrokhzād who left Tehran in 1956 was a young, shunned divorcée who had been depicted in Tehran media as choosing sexual freedom and art over family and social propriety. Mr. Proofreader's correction is unmistakable: he wishes to depict her as carefree and irresponsible, and her travel as a frivolous luxury. As previously argued, however, the assertion that she did not go in search of 'lives, happinesses, or colorful pleasures' (*lezzat-hā, shādi-hā, va zendegi-hā-ye rangin*) is central to her positionality. The woman who stepped onto the plane was sorrowful, vulnerable, and traumatized, and it is through open-mindedness and the act of writing that she cast off that weight not only to heal, but to clearly see counterpoints between cultures using the narrative itself. In many little acts of rebellion, physical and textual – from dancing with her shadow in the streets and lying flat on the beach by night, to forcefully rejecting the association of travel with leisure – Farrokhzād's travelogue enacts a kind of feminist nomadic countermemory, a concept developed by Rosi Braidotti:

> Nomadic consciousness is akin to what Foucault called countermemory; it is a form of resisting assimilation or homologation into dominant ways of representing the self. Feminists – or other critical intellectuals as nomadic

subject ... their memory is activated against the stream; they enact a rebellion of subjugated knowledges.[48]

Farrokhzād's travelogue is written in the spirit of feminist nomadism, and in the tradition of what Nasrin Rahimieh terms an 'encounter narrative,' defined by 'instances of intense curiosity about the other, desire to discard one identity for another, attempts to renegotiate Persian cultural identity, and self-conscious enactments of newly adopted models.'[49] With often brutal honesty, the narrator constantly seeks positive and negative sources of comparison between Iranians and Italians once she has found her footing in Rome: 'From the moment I set foot on Italian soil, I recognized that many similarities existed in the mentalities of Iranians and Italians, and in their way of thinking.'[50] Among other qualities, she identifies a shared 'laziness'[51], a 'brilliant history of ancient art and civilization,' and shared 'superstitions.'[52] The balance between positives and negatives keeps this comparativism from having a discernible political agenda. It thus differs from, for instance, Hajji Sahhafbashi's indictment of Iranian 'laziness' in his nineteenth-century travelogue, which uses, as Sohrabi writes, 'his criticism of Europe as a way of criticizing Iranian "national culture."'[53] Instead of focusing on difference, as travelogues often do, Farrokhzād seeks parallels and echoes: 'Everything that was there reminded me of Iran,'[54] she writes. Dowlatābādi was also a comparativist, writes Khosravie: 'Besides exploring the foreign destinations along her route, she seems to have been particularly interested in observing the Iranian representatives' performances.'[55] Farrokhzād, on the other hand, has no political affiliation and no official representational role – she has no interest in speaking for Iranian women at large. She writes from a doubly subaltern position, vulnerable both at home and abroad, and more personal and impressionistic as a result.

It is language that ultimately makes Forugh develop a real intimacy with her foreign host country. After some time in Rome, she writes, she committed to learning Italian and 'things slowly began to take some order':

Listening to radio programs, talking to people in public parks, going to the movies, and most importantly, my interest in learning the language all helped me. I was able to learn enough to meet my needs sooner than I had imagined. After that, my life took an entirely different course and I could meet my needs independently. Gradually, the discomfort and sorrow that arose from being away from my family and the familiar environment in which I had been raised began to dissipate and I was able to habituate myself to my new life in this fresh environment.[56]

Farrokhzād only stayed in Italy for a little more than a year, but equipped with the Italian language, she immersed herself in Roman culture, from opera to sculpture – though her journey remains a solitary one; she does not describe connecting with a community of Iranian tourists or scholars of Italian art, architecture, or art history, though there were quite a few in this period. The travelogue describes the work of Raphael and Michelangelo in extensive detail. The following passage suggests that she ultimately grew attached to Rome gradually, through developing an appreciation for *small* things – everyday objects. She came to understand and value tourism not through the praise of another's national monuments or the camaraderie of fellow travelers, but through everyday textures of memory, the insistence on walking slower and observe more carefully in order to pause and remember the strange, small objects that always make up the past. The aforementioned flashback to her childhood, which reminds her of Mr. Proofreader's presence, develops as follows:

Often, in the vast and modern streets of Rome, I saw uneven, cobbled sections of the road fenced off by iron railings. In the uniform context of the asphalt streets, this seemed, at first sight, to be an unbecoming blemish, a mismatched patchwork, annoying to the eye. there occasionally objected to these demonstrations, believing they were meant to attract the attention of foreign tourists. As far as I was concerned, however, it was the cobblestones which mattered. In spite of their unassuming ordinariness, they seemed to conjure up a world of their own. I found myself inspired to move beyond their cold, rough surfaces to a world of beauty that shone through the grey fog of Rome.

Perhaps the reason for my love for these stones was my outsized imagination. My friends praised the Italians for their historical and artistic works, but objected to these overindulgences and considered them trickery and pretension. But I was never able to persuade myself that they were telling the truth.

Although I have passed the age of childhood and even youth (at least psychologically) and though I have been depleted of the kind of sentiments that people believe are caused by immaturity and childhood, there are many things that, in spite of seeming laughable, still greatly shock me. Even today, when my mother pulls out her children's old winter clothes from the trunk at the beginning of autumn, in order to 'give them the sun,' as it is called to expose them to the sun for the purposes of sanitation, the sight creates the strangest sensation in me. When I search in the pockets of my old clothes, to which my mother is greatly attached, and find a chick pea or a rotten raisin at the bottom, I suddenly find myself as a child again, small, innocent, carefree, and thoughtless. A few grains of wheat, a handful of hemp seeds mixed with the fluff at the bottom of a pocket, are enough take me to my distant past and awaken in me the most tender and joyous sentiments of childhood.[57]

Here, synecdoche reappears as a way in which Farrokzhād figures cross-cultural acceptance and even understanding. While she first finds Rome and the people she meets there obnoxious and overwhelming – drunk American tourists, snobbish aristocrats, and hostile policemen – in this passage, she describes her love of the cobblestones on the streets of Rome through a sense of developing an appreciation for small things – everyday objects. Khosravie characterizes Dowlatābādi's travelogue in terms of flexibility: 'In contrast to a formally composed travelogue or diary, this heterogeneous source material includes discursive dimensions otherwise likely to disappear.'[58] But Dowlatābādi's focus on conversation and representation echoes her political purposes, Farrokhzād's delicate observations of materiality reshapes the travelogue genre in her hands into an intimate psychological portrait. She comes to understand and value tourism not through the praise of Italy's national monuments, but through everyday textures of memory, the insistence on walking slower on the small, bumpy stones of cobblestone roads in order to pause and remember the material traces that make memories 'sticky' – like a chickpea or a rotten raisin in a child's coat pocket.

Towards the end of the travelogue, another metaleptic moment sounds the call to open-mindedness most directly. The lapse, however, interestingly has nothing to do with her Italy trip, but disrupts that narrative to tell a brief anecdote from 'a few days ago,' back in Tehran, about a conversation she has just had with an older male relative:

A few days ago, I was talking to a man who is one of our family acquaintances. I don't know how our conversation turned to poets and poetry. He said he was opposed to the New Poetry because he did not understand anything from it.

'When I read the poetry collection of Shater 'Abbas-e Sabuhi – let alone the poetry of Hafez and Sa'di! – his words are beautiful and recognizable to me, and his pain is tangible. But, how can you say, for example, that this Nima . . .?'

I interrupted and asked: 'Excuse me, but have you ever read any poems by Nima?'

He mumbled a moment and finally said: 'No. But I have read others.'

I then named a few other poets with none of whom he was familiar. And if he did know their names, he had not read any of their works. So I fetched Nima's *Māneli* which had only recently been published and asked him to please read it before giving himself permission to pass judgment.

But he retorted, 'Poetry is only poetry when even the grocer on the street corner can understand it.'

I was by then beginning to regret and feel sorry that I had given him the book and tried turning the conversation in such a round in order to take it back. At which point, he said, 'Whether I read the book or not my opinion remains the same: the New poetry is essentially nonsense.'

A short stanza from this same *Māneli* collection spontaneously came to my mind:

> *Let this suffice and be enough for you:*
> *that not everybody knows your grief.*
> I made no further effort to convince the gentleman.

As a general rule, the root of prejudice is ignorance. Were this not the case, we would never limit our tastes or imprison our minds in outdated definition of truth and beauty. It is impossible to do this in a world where nothing remains constant, everything evolves, and horizons expand daily before our very eyes.[59]

Like the interjection of Mr. Proofreader, this tangential conversation nominally has nothing to do with her travelogue, but it reminds her of the tipping point in her life when she replaced her horizon of judgment with an approach driven by comparison and wonder. Her interlocutor dismisses Nima Yushij and his fellow poets in *she'r-e no*, the new imagistic, impressionistic free verse poetry movement one might call 'modernist' – a huge departure from Iranian classical poetic traditions – without even deigning to read any of Yushij's poems. Rahimieh points out that 'the evolution of the genre of travel literature in the West is closely linked with the emergence of the novel.'[60] In Farrokhzād's case, the Iranian context instead shows an inter-generic conversation take place between travelogue and poetry. Her work would align itself more explicitly with *she'r-e no* several years later, with the publication of *Tavallodi digar* ('another birth') in 1964.

To further consider the context of Farrokhzād's conversations with two of the most judgmental men in this text, Mr. Proofreader and this gentleman, one might consider Braidotti's notion of a feminist nomadic countermemory alongside Hans-Georg Gadamer's metaphor, in *Truth and Method*, of the *horizon* as central to the practice of hermeneutics. 'We think we understand,' Gadamer writes:

> when we see the past from a historical standpoint – i.e., transpose ourselves into the historical situation and try to reconstruct the historical horizon. In fact, however, we have given up the claim to find in the past any truth that is valid and intelligible for ourselves. Acknowledging the otherness of the other in this way, making him the object of objective knowledge, involves the fundamental suspension of his claim to truth.[61]

To restore agency to the (historical or cultural) Other, Gadamer counters, we must not only expand our own horizons, but first recognize as equal, and then merge our perspective with, the equally subjectified horizons of others: 'In the process of understanding, a real fusing of horizons occurs – which means that as the historical horizon is projected, it is simultaneously superseded. To bring about this fusion in a regulated way is the task of what we called historically effected consciousness.'[62] The horizon between land and sea is what fascinated Farrokhzād on the shores of the Mediterranean Sea that first night abroad in Beirut. And the figurative 'horizon' (*ofoq*) where cultures and histories meet ultimately finds its formal expression in the range of registers and narrative modes she includes within the inherent openness of the travelogue genre – a horizon of forms.

It is striking that at the end of a text that fully embraces the travelogue genre (and self-consciously indicts itself for doing so), the final conversation Farrokhzād chooses to relay, as an illustration of prejudice and open-mindedness, is not about other cultures but *about other literary forms* – specifically, the advent of *she 'r-e no*. It is as if traveling to Italy and slowly but surely embracing its people through its language expressed itself at home not through encouraging fellow Iranians to embrace Italian culture specifically or European ways of life in general, but through prefiguring the location of her own space within the Iranian literary tradition – a desire to innovate, and through pushing the boundaries of genres, both poetry and travelogue, to 'find new energy and the strength to laugh again.' To bring in another term through which Sohrabi opens up for the expansion of the travelogue genre starting in the late nineteenth century, here Farrokhzād even reflects echoes of 'the Sufi genre of travelogue as a path for self-discovery'[63], in predecessors such as Hajji Pirzadeh and Hajji Sahhafbashi.

Jan Assmann foregrounds the role of memory in 'self-image' making: 'In the sphere of material objects, the memory function becomes manifest in a *will to form* or formative intention, which informs the productions of human activity so as to make them share a set of distinctive features or acquire a kind of family resemblance.'[64] A reading of Farrokhzād's travelogue in terms of its 'will to form' suggests that the more experimental, hybridizing, or playful the work is with its genre, the more conscious the author is of that genre's cultural 'baggage': its history, audience, associations, and limitations. That work is, in turn, less likely to carry stereotype and reinforce xenophobia – and more likely to shift historical horizons.

The final site Farrokhzād visits in the travelogue moves beyond the Iranian-Italian comparisons that characterize most of the text. She writes with wonder: 'In the Egyptian art museum, one sinks deep into a magical world.'[65] Daunted by the 'terrifying faces', the 'arrogance' in their smiles, and the 'anger and condescension'[66] she sees in the statues of ancient Egyptian deities, she again finds comfort in the small everyday objects that surround them: mummified pets, textiles, books, and jewelry.

Wandering through the Accademia d'Egitto in Rome, Farrokhzād was perhaps reminded that Iran-Egypt relations had recently turned rancorous following Gamal Abdel Nasser's rise to power in the 1952 Egyptian Revolution and the 1953 coup in Iran that unseated democratically elected prime minister Mohammad Mosaddeq and returned Shah Mohammed Reza Pahlavi to power. Equally present in her mind as she surveyed the remains of ancient kings and queens, however, may have been the recently failed unification of Iran and Egypt's thrones. *Dar diyāri digar* is written a decade after the failed marriage of Mohammad Reza Shah to Fawzia Fuad, part of the penultimate monarchic generation in Egypt.[67] For Fuad, suffering in an unhappy marriage, the suitcases she brought with her to Iran may well have resembled coffins, modern equivalents of the sarcophagus that arrests Farrokhzād's attention in the museum:

In one of the boxes, a woman is sound sleep. Her hair still maintains its reddish hue and when one gazes at her hands which are folded on top of one another on her chest, one is overwhelmed with sadness because there is still the remains of the paint she had obviously used as a cosmetic on her fingernails. Her dried body has taken on the color of coal. One's heart gives the illusion that if one were to extend one's hand and touch it lightly with the movement of the tip of a finger, she would crumble. Next to her lies a necklace and precious stones and brightly colored threads and all kinds of cosmetics; when one looks at her face one's heart is shaken by an ominous sense of death and nothingness, which involuntarily pulls one back towards life.[68]

In this blason of sorts, the glory of the age of kings is replaced by another form of awe, one of cross-cultural and trans-historical identification between women no longer trapped within their own lives. Despite the imperial plundering that brought this woman's remains to Rome, and the patriarchy that has broken the young Farrokhzād's heart, what she finds in the Accademia is a reflection of the fragility of perfection, and the vulnerability of beauty: 'if one were to extend one's hand and touch [the body] lightly with the movement of the tip of the finger, she would crumble'. Despite this ephemerality, the description is both a defense of the Egyptian woman's timelessness – her hair 'still retains its reddish hue' – and a wistful testament to her evisceration by time: 'an ominous sense of death.'

The intergeneric mix of memoir, personal essay, academic argument, dialogue, and poetry that has made up the travelogue so far ends on this sobering reflection on mortality, a mnemonic counterpoint to the travelogue's vitality but also a bookend to the film of dust under which it began. In 'Esyān, the poem 'Ba'd-hā' ('afterwards') brings this full narrative circle into a single couplet, this time using the same word for earth or land (khāk) to evoke both dust in motion and the dirt of the grave:

خاک میخواند مرا هر دم به خویش / میرسند از راه که در خاکم نهند

Dust calls me every moment to itself, / They come and pause to place me in my grave.[69]

For Farrokhzād, in both narrative and verse, this Egyptian female mummy becomes a vessel for a trans-historical, nomadic feminist fusing of historical horizons through the material traces of memory. From crates on a cargo plane, to shriveled chickpeas in a child's pockets, to bare feet on blemished cobblestones, Farrokhzād's travelogue from Italy winds its way through the materiality of memory as it compares cultures on a textual/textural path filled with tangents. It is precisely in such tangential moments, when her narrator rejects clearly defined and reified identity categories and instead chooses to occupy less cross-culturally judgmental positions, that her text expands its own historical horizons.

Chapter 15

Mourning the Death of Tulips: Love, War, and Despair in the Poetry of Laila Sarahat Rowshani (1958–2004)

Wali Ahmadi

Women's poetry from Afghanistan needs raise no eyebrows. As one observer maintains, 'poetry is an art that women of what is today Afghanistan were already pursuing at the dawn of recorded Persian literature in the tenth century. The love of poetry runs deep in the veins of anyone brought up on the rich traditions of the region – whether male or female, literate or non-literate, rich or poor, a speaker of Persian, Pashto, or any of the dozens of languages of Afghanistan.'[1]

It is true that, until quite recent times, Afghan women's voices, as expressed in their poetry, were marginalized, or simply ignored, within the larger literary-critical institutional establishment in the country.[2] Nevertheless, Persian literary production by women has been thriving in contemporary Afghanistan and is gradually gaining its due attention. Afghan women poets have strived, at times with an intense degree of defiance, to realize their creative spirit. Their corpus of writing, perhaps modest in size, has proven significant. More of their collections of poetry are being published and circulated, their contributions to the literary scene are acknowledged, and their works are increasingly becoming subjects of critical analyses and evaluations.[3]

The discovery of the pioneering modernist-feminist poetry of Forugh Farrokhzad by Afghan women poets undoubtedly helped them express their emotions more openly and vividly, articulate their feminine voices more boldly, and assert their message, *as women*, more assertively and evocatively.[4] Not only Forugh Farrokhzad's feminist poetics but also her innovative, yet measured, experimentations with new poetic forms hugely appealed to younger generation of Afghan poets since the 1960s. Her five collections of poetry, as well as various editions of her selected poems, would become no less than required readings for emergent new poets. It is worth mentioning that Forugh's poems would be recited in literary programs in Kabul radio, reprinted in the literary pages of newspapers and magazines, and in some occasions made into popular songs by a new wave of musicians. Within this context, the work of Laila Sarahat Rowshani (1958–2004), perhaps the most accomplished female voice in contemporary Afghan poetry, best exemplifies the extent and immediacy of the reception of Forugh's poetry in Afghanistan.[5] Above all, Laila Sarahat Rowshani's sincerity of expression and urgency of purpose recall Forugh Farrokhzad to the minds of her readers. Equally importantly – again, not unlike Forugh Farrokhzad who wrote during the formative period of 'new poetry' (*she'r-e no*) in Iran – Laila Sarahat Rowshani helped to enhance the institutional legitimization and propagation of modernist poetics in Afghanistan, at a time when adherents of the rules and conventions of classical poetry were less than accommodating of anything perceived to undermine the long revered Persian literary heritage. Laila successfully experimented with *she'r-e no* (pioneered principally by Nima Yushij), while simultaneously selectively drawing from classical forms and styles.[6] Thus, she became a major voice for new poetry in Afghanistan without necessarily discounting the poetic tradition or questioning its values, let alone its validity, in contemporary cultural and aesthetic spheres. A collection of critical essays on and about Forugh Farrokhzad, therefore, is an apposite venue to discuss the work of an outstanding representative of the poetry of women in Afghanistan and one of Forugh's rightful poetic progenies within the larger Persianate literary world.

Though not personally actively involved in politics per se, Forugh Farrokhzad's poetry nonetheless could be intensely political, though not necessarily strictly ideological.[7] Just like Forugh, the Afghan poet, Laila Sarahat Rowshani, was not, strictly speaking, ideologically committed, or perhaps even ideologically inclined; yet she produced a range of vocal poems that were at once highly personal and boldly political. Writing as a woman, she maintained a determinedly feminine voice throughout her work; she did so without being neglectful of momentous events of significant consequence taking place in the society around her. But for Laila the *sine qua non* of poetry is to remain responsive to the inner voice of the poet – a woman poet, to be exact – in conjunction with engaging productively with the socio-historical demands of her times. The circumstances leading Laila to this conclusion were many and complex. During her rather short life, Laila consistently remained an acute and sensitive observer of her surroundings, an astute student of history and society, and a visionary moving back and forth between romantic utopianism and sober realism bordering on despair. Throughout her poetic production, without losing sight of the universal, she concentrated on the particular, often writing about the momentous experiences she endured personally. The reflection of historical events in her poetry, expressed through her masterful use of language and poetic diction, remains a distinctive aspect of her poetry. She recalls Forugh Farrokhzad to our minds as a poet with unique sincerity – perhaps bluntness – of expression, distinguished candor, and urgency of purpose. Yet, while a reading of Laila Sarahat Rowshani's poetry clearly indicates the impact of Forugh's pioneering feminist poetics, the former succeeded in carving out an approach all of her own. Nevertheless, in the same way that Forugh's poetry was responsive to the larger political events of transformative significance in Iran, Laila's poetry, too, is distinguished by a comprehensive worldview, a worldview that is profoundly impressed by the poet's understanding of her own historical situatedness in contemporary Afghan society.

Through engaging with the work of Laila Sarahat Rowshani, this essay attempts, in part, to show how an Afghan woman poet is asserting her female subjectivity, her aspirations, her emotions and desires, and her sensual yearning with evident directness and, at times, via strikingly erotic diction and imagery. This essay further engages with how Laila addresses the perils and challenges she encounters while reclaiming her own authentic voice and inserting her power of agency as a *woman*. Finally, it looks into how she responds to, reflects upon, and negotiates through her dynamic presence as a member of a collectivity – a nation, a people – experiencing a volatile period of its history, a period characterized by protracted wars, repeated invasions, mass migrations, and (continuing) foreign occupations. The latter point is especially important because Laila Sarahat Rowshani came of age, literally as a woman and as a poet, at a time when Afghanistan was fast descending into chaos, experiencing a nightmarish period in its modern history. She was a personal witness to the violent 'Communist' coup (1978), the subsequent Soviet invasion (1979), the US-backed Mujahideen rebellions throughout the 1980s, the unceremonious fall of the 'Communist' regime (1992), the inter-Mujahideen most uncivil 'Civil War' (1992–96), the Taliban brutal reign of terror (1996–2001), and the US-imposed 'democratic' rule since 2002.[8]

I

Love has been an inexhaustible theme in Persian literature, whether classical or modern. It is also prevalent in the poetry of Laila Sarahat Rowshani, although its conceptualization, articulation, and poetic expressiveness in her case seems unique, for her poems are not cluttered by commonplace imagery and attitudes. She has a cluster of poems where love is central. In one of the first instances in the poetry of women in Afghanistan, the feminine is no longer a fleeting voice at the margins of poetry. For Laila, love maintains its vivid presence, and she openly and often provocatively expresses feminine feelings as a *total* subject. Furthermore, love is an ecstatic experience that is neither solely spiritual (as in its Sufi variations, for instance) nor simply sensual. It seems to fluctuate and vacillate between deeply felt physical sensations rooted in a romantic impulse and yearning for union with the lover, a kind of union that, in a sense, transcends spiritual union and physical proximity all at once. In the following lines, whose subversiveness is no less than obvious, the poet (as the narrator) reminisces how the touch of love is felt in physical sensations, leading to an unprecedented exhilaration, a remarkable moment of burning passion.

وقتی نسیم گرم نفس هایت
از لابلای گردن و موهایم
در رگه های نازک احساس جسم من
جاری شد
سرتا سر تنم را
پر ساخت از نوازش خورشید صبحگاه
پر ساخت از طراوت باران
پر ساخت از بهار.

When the warm breeze of your breath
Streamed down
through my neck and hair,
Into my sensitive veins,
It filled me
with the soothing rays of the morning sun,
the freshness of the rain,
and the spring.[9]

Although, on the surface, there may appear a dash of conventionality about her poetry when she writes about love, reading Laila's poetry more closely indicates that, for her, love is above and beyond the immediate gratification of desires. Without elevating, or reducing, love to the level of pure spiritual affair or pure physical union of lovers, she cherishes it as a transcendental 'mystery' and a 'magical treasure of secrets.' In a poem that is otherwise highly sensuous and romantic, she appeals to the lover thus:

اگر می توانستی
دوستم بداری
فراتر از تنم
هدیه ات می کردم
تمامی آن گنجینه جادویی راز را
که ویرانهٔ جانم در خویش دارد
فراتر از تنم
– اگر می توانستی
دوستم بداری.

If you could love me
Farther than my body,
I would offer you
The entire spell-bound treasure of secrets
That my worn-out soul holds.
If you could only love me
Beyond my body.[10]

Only when the core being of two lovers merge to complement each other and transcend into a new essence will there emerge a genuine union. More tranquil than her other love poems, 'Yegāneh-ye yegāneh,' contains a subtle touch of ambiguity where love becomes a 'mysterious,' yet transformative, affair that is conceived to be neither illusory nor unattainable (in a purely Sufi, mystical manner); neither confined to, or manifested in, purely sensual nor in carnal satisfaction. In the poem, 'Barā-ye dast-hā-ye to,' on the other hand, love becomes a synthetic convergence of authentic overcoming, at once ecstatic and emancipatory. The lover is supposed to give refuge, to hold on to the hands of the beloved, and not let go. In the absence of 'the warm nest of the lover's hands,' the poet expresses with fright, lies 'the desert of the night that smells of death.' Precisely for this reason, the poet appeals to her lover:

دو دست من
کبوتران کوچک شکسته پر
ز زمهریر سال های دور درد
– سال های انجماد دوستی و انجماد مهر –
به آشیان گرم دست های تو
پناه می برد . . .

—

تو ای عزیز همدلم

مباد!

این پرندگان خسته را

ز آشیان گرم شان جدا کنی

و در میان دشت شب

که بوی مرگ می دهد

ز دست خود رها کنی!

My two hands,
– after long years of frigid desire and frozen love –
Like small broken-feathered pigeons
Find refuge inside the warm nest of your hands . . .

–

O my intimate companion
May you not repel these wounded birds
From their warm home
May you not let them wander
Into the desert of the night
– that smells of death![11]

In her love poems, the poet deftly uses metaphors and symbols drawn from nature, with the effect of transforming love into an overwhelming, all consuming, and justifiably fulfilling, subject, without losing her admirable economic use of words. In these poems, where imagery of nature drawn from the spring (*bahār*) is prevalent, she appears jubilant over her relationship with her lover, whose presence in her is vast, vital, and vitalizing:

در من

حضور تو

آیینه یی است

به وسعت هستی

به باصفایی بهار

چشم هایم را در آیینه می کارم

تا آیتی روید

جاودانگی بهار را.

Your presence in me
Is like a mirror,
Vast like the expanse of being
Pristine like the spring.
I sow my eyes in the mirror

So a miracle may appear
A sign for the eternity of the spring.[12]

Or, as in the poem 'Ramz-e pā'iz,' it is spring that reverberates in the form of life, love, and light:

در بهار احساس کردم زندگی را
لمس کردم معنی تابندگی را
در بهاران عشق را آموختم من . . .
عاشقم من عاشق نور و بهاران
عاشق راز شکوه سبزه زاران . . .

In the spring
I felt life,
I sensed the meaning of radiance
I learned love in the spring . . .
I am in love with light and spring
I love the mystery of majestic meadows.[13]

The hopes of the poet, however, are dashed when the arrival of the long-expected spring produces not life and vegetation but death and decay. Did an unexpected, horrific event – a calamity of grand proportions – strike that the season of jubilance is now less than joyous? Spring seems wounded and the 'restless' birds of joy (*chelcheleh*) are singing the mournful melody for the demise of the 'tulip gardens.' In a poem written in the nontraditional *ghazal-masnavi* form – a form that has received much attention by Persian poets in Iran as well in Afghanistan in the past couple of decades – the arrival of the metamorphosed spring indicates a travesty is the making. Strictly speaking, while *ghazal* is traditionally associated with the lover's quest to achieve union with the beloved (either in worldly realm of human desires or in the Sufi mystical longing for union with the Divine), in the form of *ghazal-masnavi*, it embodies something ominous: the termination of the efflorescence of the spring, the season of renewal and joy. Some couplets of this poem are worth mentioning here:

وه چه خاموش آمده است بهار
زخم بر دوش آمده است بهار

. . .

قامت سبز باغ سوخته است
لب ز لبخند شاد دوخته است

. . .

چلچله باز بی قرار شده است

مرثیه خوان لاله زار شده است

Spring has arrived:

How silent, wounded . . .

The green figure of garden has burned

It has sewn its lips from smiling with joy . . .

The swallow is turning restless again

As she is singing an elegy for tulip fields . . .[14]

With the spring falling far short of what it is expected of it, love, too, remains not immune from the calamity that has overwhelmed all. Love is imprisoned, with its hands chained:

عشق، ای عشق

بر دست های نازنینت

زنجیری

با حلقه هایش

نیرنگ،

کین،

نفرت در پیچیده اند.

O love,

They have enveloped your delicate hands

in a chain,

With rings of deceit,

Malice,

And aversion.

Referring back to the image of spring, as in the poem 'Nowheh' the poet increasingly assumes an elegiac, mournful tone. Addressing the birds – the symbol of freedom and flight – she pleads that they witness how trees of the garden now blossom only 'branches of tears':

ببین

ببین

تو ای پرنده،

ای بهار

ای نسیم

که از درخت های باغ

فقط نهال اشک ها شکوفه کرده است.

The bird,
The spring,
The breeze,
Beware:
From trees of the garden
Blossom only branches of tears.[15]

And addressing the cypress tree – a symbol of pride and majesty – she asks:

ای سرو،

ای غرور بلند سبز

آیا شکوه قامت سبزت را

دست کدام فاجعه بشکست

کاینسان عزا گرفته و لرزانی

مصلوب لحظه های زمستانی؟

O cypress tree,
– The high, ever green shoot of pride –
The hand of what disaster
Cut your majestic green stature
That you are now mourning and trembling
That you are now crucified in the dark moments of winter?[16]

Why is the idyllic garden transformed into a place of executions, gallows, murder, and mayhem? What calamity (*fāje'eh*) must have struck the garden? Could it not be that the garden is a metaphor for the poet's homeland, which is now turned into a huge, well-fortified prison, and its inhabitants no more than hapless prisoners?

If the poet cannot afford to stay lethargic in the face of events of historical significance taking place around her, and if she is to remain engaged vigorously and meaningfully with history, what particular event, or series of events, then, could have led Laila's poetry to increasingly assume such an air of melancholy, despondence, and despair? Why did Laila choose to turn her poetry into a lament, a painful song of mourning; a tragedy? Here, it would be best to read Laila's poetry in conjunction with, and in the light of, significant historical events taking place around her.

II

Just days after the April 27, 1978 (7 Sawr 1357) *coup d'état*, which brought the 'Communist' People's Democratic Party of Afghanistan to power, Sarshar

Rowshani, the editor-in-chief of Kabul's widely circulating daily paper, *Anis*, was taken into custody by the new regime authorities, never to be seen again. He was either summarily executed or, like so many intellectuals and literati of the time, was incarcerated and tortured, and eventually perished in prison. The coup marked the beginning of a nightmarish period in the history of the ancient nation.

Sarshar Rowshani was Laila's father and her primary literary mentor. For Laila, therefore, the national descent into chaos in the wake of the Sawr Revolution meant not only a collective trauma but also a deeply personal tragedy. This tragedy was further magnified when, following the coup and the ensuing Soviet invasion of Afghanistan in December 1979, some members of Laila's own family, like countless other Afghans, fled their homeland for exile. In two separate, but strikingly similar, incidents, Laila's sister, her brother-in-law, and one of her nieces drowned in a beach in Australia in late 1990s. Laila wrote some extremely moving eulogies for her sister and her family, clearly expressing how these events had a devastating effect on her.[17] In Laila's poetry, therefore, there is an astonishing linkage between such deeply private and personal losses and tragic events of public manifestations taking place around her, in her beloved city of Kabul, and in Afghanistan at large. While from the publication of her first collection of poetry, *Tolu'-e Sabz* (1986) the young poet proved herself keenly aware of, and affected by, the consequential political events surrounding her, her later poems – as we shall discuss below – were especially consciously defined by such events.

As the twentieth century drew to a close, and as Afghanistan descended further and further into a horrific period in its history, the literary gaze seemed to turn backward ever more frequently; and in this backward look, memory figured most prominently. The subtle shift to memory in the writings of recent Afghan literati, including Laila Sarahat Rowshani, represented a trenchant critique of the historicism that dominated Afghan discourse of politics and development after the Sawr Revolution of 1978, when the diametrically opposing views of the so-called 'Communist' regime in Kabul and those propagated by the emergent, primarily US-backed 'Islamist' opposition to the regime (the Mujahideen) started to violently clash. As what follows attempts to show, by using the image of the Āsmāyi in several of her poems, Laila engages with an ancient tale to highlight the critical reality of her own time, especially as it relates to the destruction of her beloved city of Kabul.

A range of two mountains divides the western quarter of the city of Kabul into two, with Kabul River running serpentine in the middle. Since ancient times, the mountains – known as Āsmāyi and Shirdarvāzeh – were revered in folktales, myths, and common lore. They epitomized calm resolve, steadfastness, and resilience of the ancient city in the face of momentous, and often calamitous, historical incidents, invasions, wars – offering resistance against encroaching alien forces intent on overwhelming the city. If and when all defensive walls are demolished and barriers smashed, Āsmāyi (and Shirdarvāzeh) would stand tall, wounded and aggrieved but never subdued.

Laila Sarahat Rowshani, in a poem from 1992, calls Asmāyi 'the towering epic of history,' (she'r-e boland-qāmat-e tārikh) and 'a silent witness' to many crimes in history (shāhed-e khāmush-e jenāyat) – a diligent recorder of wars and pillages, a faithful scriber of agony and despair.

ای آسه مایی
ای به نفس های سنگی ات
روح هزار شعله خاموش
ای سنگ،
ای صبور
ای قامتت صلابت ایمان
شعر بلند قامت تاریخ.

ای سنگ
ای صبور
ای شاهد خموش جنایت

O you, Āsmāyi
The souls of a thousand silent flames
Are kept in your stone breath.
You are a patient stone
Your size is as commanding as your power of conviction
You are the lengthy poem of history.

O you,
The patient stone,
The silent witness of crimes.

But even the mightiest of mountains, the most patient of stones, possesses no inexhaustible degree of forbearance when facing a challenge of intense magnitude. It will eventually and inevitably burst into open, spilling out the anguish hidden at its core. It should come to little surprise then that the Āsmāyi mountain, as the rumor spread, 'cracked' on Nowruz 1370 (21 March, 1992). This cracking of Āsmāyi was perceived to be no less than the tearing apart of Kabul itself; it brought to the open the enormous sorrow that the devastated city and its inhabitants had endured, and were expecting to endure

further, as no end to the calamity engulfing them and relentlessly piercing
through their very being could be found. The poet asks Āsmāyi directly:

در سنگ‌های دل خونینت

آیا کدام درد

آماس کرده بود

کاین گونه پاره شد دلت

ای سنگ،

ای صبور؟

> In the bleeding stone of your heart
> What kind of pain
> Was swelling
> That your heart finally tore up?
> O you, the stone –
> the patient stone.[18]

The cracking of Āsmāyi, as explosive as it was, however, left Kabul to
continue to fall into the grips of horrific 'owls.' The brilliant sun illumining
the city of Kabul from the top of Āsmāyi disappears, and darkness overwhelms
the city. According to legends, the summit of Āsmāyi is the abode of the sun,
the throne upon which the sun rests. In one of the later poems of Laila, the
calamity is amplified as owls steal the brilliant crown of the sun, an act whose
news reverberates through the entire city of Kabul, ushering further destruction:

وقتی که

تاج خورشید را جغدان

از فرق آسمایی

ربودند

شب سنگ شد و ماند

کابل،

تمام آیینه هایش

شکست

و ریخت.

> When owls snatched
> The crown of the sun
> From the forehead of Āsmāyi
> The night petrified and remained.
> All the mirrors of Kabul
> Broke into pieces and
> fell to the ground.[19]

Thus, the poet, feeling desperate as she witnesses the destruction of the city and its descent into chaos, leaves her homeland for exile. The following lines are fairly representative of what prompted the poet to choose exile. After all, in her beloved city of Kabul, seeds of thorns are sewn, and gallows are on the rise:

اینجا
پرنده اگر بخواند
دارش می زنند
و ستاره اگر بتابد
بر دیدگان خارش می زنند.

In this land,
If a bird sings,
They will execute her,
If a star shines,
The will insert thistles into her eyes.[20]

Diasporic life (in Leiden, the Netherlands, where the poet lived from 1998 to her death in 2004) may have provided Laila the physical safety that she lacked once Kabul became the battleground for murderous forces engaged in a protracted conflict. Yet, in exile, too, she remains constantly weary, longing for reunion with her Kabul. The themes of separation and loneliness, which were present in Laila's love poems, take on a somewhat new meaning when they center on the poet's life in exile. They become essential in the writing of a poetry that is increasingly one of longing, melancholy, and gloom. In the following lines of a poem (in the *ghazal* form) written during the period the poet spent in exile, Laila invokes Āsmāyi again, as she longs for her beloved city of Kabul, now suffering alone, scared and scarred. Feeling like a 'broken feathered, encaged, and tied-winged' bird, she laments her separation from the Āsmāyi:

دلم گرفته شهر من برای آسه مایی ات
ببین تنوره می کشد ز دل غم جدایی ات
چه زخم هاست بر تنت چه قصه هاست بی منت
چه داغ هاست بر دلم ز درد بی دوایی ات
اگرچه پر شکسته ام اسیر و بال بسته ام
به بال ناله می رسم برای همصدایی ات

My city, my heart is yearning for your Āsmāyi
The pain of separation from you enflames my heart.
In my absence, how did you tend to your wounds, recount to me

How scarred my heart is, knowing of your incurable affliction.
Though I am broken-feathered, encaged,
I still yearn to come to you, using my wings.[21]

Yet, this is not a poetry that is simply expressive of the poet's feelings of despair and despondency, of anguish and dejection. It is also strongly woven with feelings of deep bitterness and rebellious anger. While in her earlier poems, it is the presence of the lover, as expansive as it can be, that the poet grows to witness the 'eternity of the spring,' her more recent work, written in exile, contained little sign of such a growth. The story of Āsmāyi, as poignantly seen through the lens of Laila's poetry, is not much different from the historical experience Afghanistan itself has endured in its recent past: the protracted reign of the night, the appearance of false dawns, the anxieties and traumas of exile, and the recurrence of a resurrected, ever darker night. As unfreedom reigns, emancipation remains as distant as ever. In such circumstances, the coming of spring turns into a mere illusion, an ever-tragic tale of devastation and defeat. Is despair, therefore, the end of history? A reading of Laila's poetry shows that, in spite of a sense of defiance in some of her poems, her response to such a question remains ambiguous at best, for history is, ironically, shrouded in a cloak of mystery. Despair, therefore, can be both universal and inevitable.

بنگر ! شکسته باورم، شوری شکسته در سرم
دست شررزای فنا پیچیده دور پیکرم
دریای من مرداب شد، بی باوری همبسترم
رویای دریاوارگی رفته ز یاد باورم . . .

See, my faith is no more,
Anxiety has struck my head.
I am entrapped in the wicked hand of fate
My sea has turned into a lagoon,
Faithlessness is now my bedmate
The hope of turning into a sea
Is gone from the memory of my belief.[22]

Notes

Introduction

1 Farzaneh Milani, 'Forugh Farrokhzad' in *Persian Literature*, (ed.) Ehsan Yarshater (New York, 1988): 367.

2 See Michael Hillmann's discussion in *A Lonely Woman: Forugh Farrokhzad and Her Poetry* (Washington, DC, 1987): 146–47.

3 Farzaneh Milani, 'Farrokzād, Forūg-Zamān', in Ehsan Yarshater (ed.), *Encyclopaedia Iranica*, IX (New York, 1999): 325.

4 Hillmann, *A Lonely Woman*: 24.

5 Quoted in Hillmann, *A Lonely Woman*: 37.

6 Hélène Cixous, and Catherine Clément, *The Newly Born Woman*, trans. Betsy Wing (Minneapolis, 1991): 90.

7 Cixous and Clément, *The Newly Born Woman*: 92.

8 Farzaneh Milani, *Veils and Words: The Emerging Voices of Iranian Women Writers* (Syracuse, 1992): 137.

9 Ibid.

Chapter 1

1 Farrokhzād, *Divār* (Tehran, 1956): 13. For a somewhat different translation which makes the poem look more elegant in English, see Zjaleh Hajibashi, 'Redefining "Sin"', in Michael C. Hillmann (ed.), *Forugh Farrokhzad, A Quarter Century Later* (Literature East and West, Austin, TX, 1987) 24: 68. Another translation may be found in *Another Birth, Selected Poems of Forugh Farrokhzad*, trans, Hasan Javadi and Susan Sallée (Emeryville, 1981): 11.

2 *Gonah kardam gonāhi por ze lezzat / Dar āghushi keh garm o ātashin bud.* Here the word *garm* is completely redundant and has been used to make up the metre. See Farrokzād, *Divār*: 13.

3 Farrokhzād, *Asir* (Tehran, 1955): 29. For a somewhat different rendering see *Bride of Acacias, Selected Poems of Forugh Farrokhzad*, trans, Jascha Kessler with Amin Banani (Delamar, NY, 1982): 125.

4 Farrokhzād, *Divār*: 15

5   Farrokhzād, 'Nā-āshnā,' *Asir*: 39.
6   Farrokhzād, "Harjā'," *Asir* 29.
7   Farrokhzād, "Div-e shab," *Asir*: 69–72. Kāmi is short for Kāmyār, the name of the poet's son.
8   Farrokhzād, "Dar barābar-e khodā," *Asir*: 141–4.
9   See for example, Eric Heller, *Kafka* (London, 1974).
10 See, Behruz Jalāli ed., *Dar ghorubi abadi, majmu'eh-ye āsār-e mansur-e Forugh Farrokhzād* (Tehran, 1997): 108. This particular letter (alongside a few to others) has also been published in Hamid Siyāhpush ed., *Zani tanhā, Yādnāmeh-ye Forugh Farrokhzād* (Tehran, 1997): 210–14.
11 Jalāli, *Dar ghorubi abadi*: 110.
12 Jalāli, *Dar ghorubi abadi*: 112.
13 Ibid.
14 Jalāli, *Dar ghorubi abadi*: 113. This earlier letter is also published in Siyāhpush, *Zani tanhā* : 209–210.
15 Jalāli, *Dar ghorubi abadi*: 109.
16 Jalāli, *Dar ghorubi abadi*: 115–122.
17 Jalāli, *Dar ghorubi abadi*: 119.
18 Jalāli, *Dar ghorubi abadi*: 113 and Siyāhpush, *Zani tanhā* : 210.
19 See further Homa Katouzian, *Sadeq Hedayat, The Life and Legend of an Iranian Writer* (London and New York, 2002); 'The wondrous world of Sadeq Hedayat', in Homa Katouzian (ed.), *Sadeq Hedayat, His Work and His Wondrous World* (London and New York, 2008); Heller, *Kafka*; J. P. Stern (ed.), *The World of Franz Kafka* (London, 1980); Ernst Pawel, *The Nightmare of Reason: A life of Franz Kafka* (London, 1988).
20 Jalāli, *Dar ghorubi abadi*: 116–17.
21 Jalāli, *Dar ghorubi abadi*: 118–19.
22 Jalāli, *Dar ghorubi abadi*: 119–120.
23 See Amir Esmā'ili and Abo'l-qāsem Sedārat, *Jāvdāneh Forugh* (Tehran, 1968): 14.
24 Ibid.
25 Ibid.
26 Ibid.
27 Esmā'ili and Sedārat, *Jāvdāneh Forugh,*: 15.
28 Esmā'ili and Sedārat, *Jāvdāneh Forugh*: 16.
29 See Farrokhzād, "Kasi keh mesl-e hich kas nist," *Imān biāvarim beh āghāz-e fasl-e sard* (Tehran, 1974): 64–72. I have benefitted from the following English translation, but the rendering in the text is my own. See 'One Like No Other,' in *Bride of Acacias*, trans. Kessler with Banani: 112–15.
30 See Farrokhzād, 'Dar Khiyābān-hā-ya Sard-e Shab', *Tavallodi digar* (Tehran, 1964): 83–6. I have benefitted from the three following English translations, but the rendering in the text is my own. See 'In Night's Cold Street', in *Bride of Acacias*, trans, Kessler with Banani: 49–50; 'In the Cold Streets of Night', in *A Rebirth, Poems by Foroogh Farrokhzad*, trans. David Martin (Lexington, 1985): 43–6. 'In the Cold Streets of Night,' in *Another Birth,* trans., Javadi and Sallée: 42–3.

31 Farrokhzād, 'Imān biāvarim beh āghāz-e fasl-e sard', *Imān biāvarim beh āghā z-e fasl-e sard*: 11–37. I have benefitted from the three following English translations, but the rendering in the text is my own. See 'Let Us Believe in the Oncoming Season of Cold', in *Bride of Acacias*, trans. Kessler with Banani: 95–102; 'Let's Bring Faith to the Onset of the Cold Season', in *A Rebirth*, trans. Martin: 113–122; and "Let Us Believe in the Beginning of a Cold Season," in *Another Birth*, trans. Javadi and Sallée: 65–76.

Chapter 2

1 Farrokhzād quoted in Rivanne Sandler, 'Change up to a point: Iranian Women's poetry to the 1950s', in *Forugh Farrokhzad: A Quarter Century Later*, 24 (ed.) Michael C. Hillmann (*Literature East and West*, Austin, TX, 1987): 39.

2 Hamid Dabashi, 'Forugh Farrokhzad and formative forces in Iranian culture', in Hillmann, *Forugh Farrokhzad: A Quarter Century Later*, Vol. 7.

3 See Farzaneh Milani, *Veils and Words: The Emerging Voices of Iranian Women Writers* (Syracuse, 1992): 127.

4 Milani, *Veils and Words*: 127–8.

5 Michael C. Hillmann, 'Forugh Farrokhzad: A chronology', in Hillmann, *Forugh Farrokhzad: A Quarter Century Later*: 3–6.

6 Farrokhzād, 'Goftegu bā Forugh' with M. Ā zād, in (ed.) Behruz Jalāli, *Forugh Farrokhzād: Jāvdāneh zistan, dar owj māndan* 2nd ed. (Tehran, 1996): 197. Farrokhzād's statement of regret is also quoted in Amin Banani, 'Introduction', in *Bride of Acacias: Selected Poems of Forugh Farrokhzad*, trans. Jascha Kessler with Amin Banani (Delmar, 1982): 5; and in Hamid Zarrinkub, 'Darun-māyeh-hā-ye she'r-e Forugh', in Jalāli, *Forugh Farrokhzād: Jāvdāneh zistan*: 313.

7 Michael C. Hillmann, *A Lonely Woman: Forugh Farrokhzad and Her Poetry* (Washington, 1987).

8 Zarrinkub, 'Darun-māyeh-hā': 313–16.

9 Farzaneh Milani, 'Forugh Farrokhzad: A feminist perspective', in trans. Kessler and Banani, *Bride of Acacias*: 142–5.

10 Ebrāhim Malakān, 'Forughi digar dar *Tavallodi digar*', in (ed.) Behruz Jalāli, *Forugh Farrokhzād: Jāvdāneh zistan*: 427–8.

11 Milani, *Veils and Words*: 127.

12 Farrokhzād, 'Shab o havas', *Asir* (Tehran, 1955): 11–14.

13 Farrokhzād, 'Shab o havas', *Asir*: 12.

14 Farrokhzād, 'Shab o havas', *Asir*: 12.

15 Farrokhzād, 'Shab o havas', *Asir*: 13.

16 Farrokhzād, 'Shab o havas', *Asir*: 13.

17 A similar 'parity of the sexes' in a reprise on a mythical theme is found in the poem 'Daryā' ('Of the Sea'), which closes the collection. Here, alone on the seashore, the woman looses herself in the embrace of her lover who has assumed the shape of a sea- god, or of the sea itself. In this passionate interlude his outstretched arms are likened to 'endless currents', and

Forugh Farrokhzād, Poet of Modern Iran

his lips 'crash' (*virān gashtan*) on her lips, evoking the image of waves crashing on a shore in the meeting of land and sea. The woman's reverie ends as the waves draw the lovers apart. Farrokhzād, *Asir*: 171–4.

18 Farrokhzād, 'Sho'leh-ye ramideh', *Asir*: 15–17.

19 Farrokhzād, *Asir*: 16. In some poems (such as 'Buseh' ['A Kiss']), it is the man who seduces the woman and is the source of sinfulness, but there is neither censure nor remorse associated with it. The responsibility is still placed on her 'inarticulate needs'. Farrokhzād, *Asir*: 37–8.

20 Farrokhzād, 'Harjā'i' , *Asir*: 29–31.

21 Farrokhzād, 'Harjā'i', *Asir*: 29.

22 Farrokhzād, 'Harjā'i', *Asir*: 30. The irony of this statement is heightened by the fact that rain is traditionally equated with God's mercy to humankind, for it ensures the earth's fertility.

23 See *Zand-Akash: Iranian or Greater Bundahishn*, Ch. 4, 'As regards the adversary's approach to the creation', http://www.avesta.org/mp/grb1.htm#chap4 [accessed December 2008].

24 On the emergence of feminist literature in Iran after the Revolution of 1978–79, see Kamran Talattof, *The Politics of Writing in Iran: A History of Modern Persian Literature* (Syracuse, 2000): 135–140.

25 Farrokhzād, 'Nā-āshnā', *Asir*: 39–41.

26 Farrokhzād, 'Nā-āshnā', *Asir*: 39–40.

27 Farrokhzād, 'Nā-āshnā', *Asir*: 41

28 Leonardo P. Alishan, 'Forugh Farrokhzad and the forsaken earth', in (ed.) Hillmann, *Forugh Farrokhzad: A Quarter Century Later*: 121.

29 See e.g., Farrokhzād, 'Asir', *Asir*: 33–5.

30 See e.g., Farrokhzād, 'Asir', *Asir*: 33 and, "Esyān", *Asir*: 74–5.

31 Farrokhzād, 'Div-e shab', *Asir*: 69–72

32 Farrokhzād, 'Yādi az gozashteh', *Asir*: 47–9.

33 See e.g. Farrokhzād, 'Asir', *Asir*: 33–5.

34 The two poems were written in close succession: 'Asir' is dated Mordād 1333/ July-August 1954 and 'Yādi az gozashteh', Shahrivar 1333 / August-September 1954.

35 Farrokhzād, 'Yādi az gozashteh', *Asir*: 48.

36 Farrokhzād, 'Yādi az gozashteh', *Asir*: 48.

37 Farrokhzād, 'Bimār', *Asir*: 119.

38 In idiomatic compounds like *pāk-dāman* (lit. 'clean-skirted'), 'skirt' stands for 'honour', while *dar āb rafteh* (lit. 'fallen in the water') means 'lost', 'forfeited'.

39 Another possible exception is the poem 'Ro'yā' ('Dream', *Asir*: 25–28), a lament for a love lost, which the *dramatis persona* has sent to its grave with her thoughtless and cruel behavior.

40 Farrokhzād, 'Vedā'', *Asir*: 53–4.

41 Farrokhzād, 'Goriz o dard', *Asir*: 62.

42 Farrokhzād, 'Vedā'', *Asir*: 54.

43 Farrokhzād, 'Goriz o dard', *Asir*: 61.

44 Farrokhzād, 'Goriz o dard', *Asir*: 62.

45 Farrokhzād, 'Asir', *Asir*: 35.

46 See Milani, *Veils and Words*: 145.

47 See Farrokhzād, "Esyān', 'Bāz-gasht', and 'Khāneh-ye matruk', *Asir*: 73–6, 111–13, and 133–5. respectively.

48 Farrokhzād, ''Esyān', *Asir*: 73–6.

49 Farrokhzād, ''Esyān', *Asir*: 74.

50 See, e.g. the opening stanza of 'Asir': 'You are the sky, bright and clear/ I – in this cage – am a captive bird'.

51 Farrokhzād, afterword to *Asir*, 1956, quoted in Hillmann, *A Lonely Woman*: 28–29.

52 Farrokhzād, ''Esyān', *Asir*: 75.

53 Farrokhzād, ''Esyān', *Asir*: 76.

54 Farrokhzād, 'Bāz gasht', *Asir*: 111–13.

55 Farrokhzād, 'Bāz gasht', *Asir*: 111.

56 Farrokhzād, 'Bāz gasht', *Asir*: 113.

57 Farrokhzād, 'Khāneh-ye matruk', *Asir:* 133–5.

58 E.g. 'Tonight, from the sky of your eyes/ stars rain upon my poem / My fingers sow sparks/ in the white silence of the pages'. Farrokhzād, 'Az dust dāshtan', *Asir*: 161.

59 Farrokhzād, 'Naqsh-e penhān', *Asir*: 115–7.

60 Farrokhzād, 'Naqsh-e penhān', *Asir*: 116.

61 Farrokhzād, 'Khāneh-ye matruk', *Asir:* 135.

62 Farrokhzād, 'Didār-e talkh', *Asir*: 83.

Chapter 3

1 Michael Hillmann, 'An autobiographical voice: Forugh Farrokhzad', in Afsaneh Najmabadi (ed.), *Women's Autobiographies in Contemporary Iran* (Cambridge, MA, 1990: 45) stresses the importance of not confusing or over-identifying the poetic voice in Farrokhzād's poetry with the poet herself: 'Although in her poetry Farrokhzad rejects or discards the veils that her society and culture wove for her and refuses to use the sort of mask that serves to hide personality from view, her poetic voice is a persona or mask and not the actual person of Farrokhzad'. Nasrin Rahimieh ('Beneath the veil: The Revolution in Iranian women's writing', in Anthony Purdy (ed.), *Literature and the Body* (Atlanta, 1992: 102) notes that critics and readers began to equate the speaker with the poet herself, some believing that her distinct achievement was her ability to reveal herself in her poems. Rahimieh observes: 'By making her body and her sexuality the subject of her poems, she became further entrapped in the very discourse she wanted to subvert'.

2 Discussing the contribution of some of the most influential women writers of 20th-century Iran, Farzaneh Milani (*Veils and Words: The Emerging Voices of Iranian Women Writers*, Syracuse, 1992: 127) says: 'These writers created, to varying degrees, a sense of self divorced from the conventional definition of womanhood in Iran, a self that is

all the more vulnerable in a society where walls and veils have been customary and censored communication the order of the day . . .'

3   More specifically, the voice of an Iranian woman. Hillmann (*A Lonely Woman: Forugh Farrokhzad and Her Poetry* (Washington D.C., 1987: 29) sees a greater Iranianisation in Farrokhzād's subsequent collection, *Divar*, whose poems: 'seem very Iranian in their moods and reflective of emotional states natural for an Iranian woman in the poet's circumstances.'

4   On the frequency of words such as *panjareh* ('window') and *daricheh* ('shutter') in Farrokhzād's later poetry, see Ruhangiz Karāchi, *Forugh Farrokhzād* (Shiraz, 2004): 102.

5   On the shocking boldness with which Farrokhzād openly talks about love and female sexuality in some of her early poems, see Kamran Talattof, 'Iranian women's literture: from pre-Revolutionary social discourse to post-Revolutionary feminism', *International Journal of Middle East Studies,* 29.4 (November 1997): 538. Rahimieh ('Beneath the veil': 101) notes: 'Both in her writing and in her life Farrokhzad shattered the myth of the obedient and modest woman. Although her personal life became a legend in its own right . . . it was her poetry that made her so highly controversial. Much of the controversy centred around her "unconventional" depiction of carnal pleasures'.

6   Farrokhzād, 'Jom'eh', *Tavallodi digar* (Tehran, 1964): 69–70.

7   All translations from Farrokhzād's poetry in this essay are my own.

8   On the centrality of sexuality in this poem, see Hillmann, *A Lonely Woman*: 79.

9   As Milani has noted ('Voyeurs, nannies, winds, and gypsies in Persian literature', *Critique: Critical Middle Eastern Studies* 8:14, Spring 1999, 107) traditionally, the virtuous Iranian woman was expected to maintain a secluded existence, apart from the outside world: 'She covered her body, guarded her honor, controlled her desires, measured her words, and unfailing remained in her "proper place". Codes of ideal femininity, masculinity, and honour demanded the exclusion of women from the public sphere'.

10   See Hillmann, 'Sexuality in the verse of Forugh Farrokhzad and the structuralist view', *Edebiyat* 3.ii (1979): 196. Farrokhzād herself sought to escape her own stifling adolescence through marrying Parviz Shāpur at the tender age of sixteen. Milani ('Voyeurs, nannies, winds, and gypsies': 109) notes one of the most compelling justifications for seclusion of women in traditional Iranian society is their sexual conduct: 'An old Persian saying compares the free mingling of men and women to the exposure of cotton to fire. To assure their sexual integrity, to keep the fire from consuming the cotton, women are secluded and immobilized'. Rahimieh ('Beneath the veil': 99) makes a similar observation: 'The justification for the spatial confinement of women (including the imposition of the veil) is rooted in what Mernissi calls women's destructive element. In Shi'ism this view of women rests upon the assumption that they are closer to "nature" and are therefore much more in touch with their sexuality'.

11   One of these major events was the forced unveiling of Iranian women in the second half of the 1930s. See H.E. Chehabi, 'The banning of the veil and its consequences', in

Stephanie Cronin (ed.), *The Making of Modern Iran: State and Society under Riza Shah, 1921–1941* (London, 2003): 193–210.

12 Rahimieh, 'Beneath the veil': 101.

13 Farrokhzād, 'Deyr', *'Esyān* (Tehran, 1958): 69–72.

14 Farrokhzād, "Arusak-e kuki', *Tavallodi digar*: 71–5.

15 According to Hillmann (*A Lonely Woman:* 81), Farrokhzād acts as a more explicitly feminist spokesperson in this poem, cautioning Iranian women 'against acquiescing in the submissive roles for which society destines them'.

16 Karāchi (*Forugh Farrokhzād*: 41) argues here Farrokhzād is saying the ability to think has been taken away from the women of her era.

17 Farrokhzād, 'Khāneh-ye matruk', *Asir* (Tehran, 1955): 133–5.

18 John Zubizaretta ('The woman who sings No, No, No: Love, freedom, and rebellion in the poetry of Forugh Farrokhzad', *World Literature Today* 66.3, Summer, 1992: 423) notes: 'The awful dilemmas experienced by Farrokhzad in her personal life and revealed through her art express her strong desire not to be captive to the old ways and her inability often not to remain caught within the walls of established definitions of her gender and her art form'.

19 On a purely linguistic level, it appears that there is a relatively high instance of words denoting confinement (such as *zendān* ['prison'] and *qafas* ['cage']) in Farrokhzād's first three collections, see Mohammad Hoquqi, *She'r-e zamān-e mā, 4: Forugh Farrokhzād* (Tehran, 1994): 13. For Tikku ('Furūgh-i Farrukhzād: A new direction in Persian poetry', *Studia Islamica* 26 (1967): 153) the titles of Farrokhzād's first four collections are themselves significant and, 'show a gradual psychological change taking place in her'.

20 Milani, 'Love and sexuality in the poetry of Forough Farrokhzad: A reconsideration', *Iranian Studies* 15 (1982): 120. Milani ('Forugh Farrokhzād', in Ehsan Yarshater (ed.), *Persian Literature* (Albany, NY, 1988): 372) notes in her earlier poetry Farrokhzād, 'is attracted to women's independence and intellectual growth, but she cannot abandon the traditional virtues expected of a woman: purity expressed by chastity, devotion expressed by commitment to domestic concerns .. [S]he voices the painful tension between independence and conversely, domestic security and traditional women's roles'. Talattof ('Iranian women's literature': 537) believes Farrokhzād, 'genuinely divulges her feminine sensibilities' in her early poems.

21 See Hillmann, An autobiographical voice': 48–9.

22 See Milani, 'Farrokzād, Forüg-Zamān', in Ehsan Yarshater (ed.), *Encyclopaedia Iranica*, IX (New York, 1999): 324.

23 Farrokhzād, 'Ā n ruz-hā', *Tavallodi digar*: 9–16.

24 See Hillmann, *A Lonely Woman*: 10.

25 On the garden as locus of the praise for the ruler in medieval Persian panegyric poetry, see Jerome W. Clinton, *The Divan of Manūchihrī Dāmghānī: A Critical Study* (Minneapolis, 1972): 101–106.

26 See Dominic Parviz Brookshaw, 'Palaces, pavilions, and pleasure-gardens: The context and setting of the medieval *Majlis*', *Middle Eastern Literatures*, 6.2 (2003): 199–223

on the medieval Persian *majles* and the garden as setting for poetry performance, wine-drinking, and associated pleasure-taking.

27 In Farrokhzād's poem 'Gol-i sorkh' ('Rose') there is a description of a sexual liaison in a garden which echoes the bawdier side of medieval Persian poetry; see Alishan 1988: 119.

28 Farrokhzād, 'Bolur-e ro'yā', *'Esyān*: 81–3.

29 Farrokhzād, 'Jonun', *'Esyān*: 121–124.

30 See Clinton, *The Divan of Manūchihrī Dāmghānī*: 76–8 and 107–8.

31 Farrokhzād, 'Zendegi', *'Esyān*: 133–6.

32 Farrokhzād, 'Fath-e bāgh', *Tavallodi digar*: 125–9.

33 For Milani ('Nakedness regained: Farrokhzad's Garden of Eden', in Hillmann, Michael C.(ed.), *Forugh Farrokhzad, A Quarter Century Later, Literature East and West,* Vol. 24, 1987: 101) this garden is not as idyllic as one might gather from a first reading: 'The oasis of harmony between the lovers and nature is not a place of comfort. Intruders – real or imagined – haunt it and give an anguished depth to the plight of the narrator'.

34 Hāfez, *Divān*, Qāsem Ghani and Mohammad Qazvini eds (Tehran, 1999): 301, *ghazal* 393.

35 Milani *Veils and Words*: 151.

36 Milani ('Nakedness regained': 101) detects an underlying fear of the other in this poem; a fear of the inhabitants of the town – of broader society – and their reaction to the lovers' union.

37 In her poetry Farrokhzād uses windows to enable her protagonists to gaze on the outside world. The window allows this gaze to penetrate the walls of the confined space, be it a house, a prison or a cage.

38 It is within the paradisiacal garden setting that the poet chose to depict what Milani ('Nakedness regained': 91) calls one of her, 'most fervent celebrations of male companionship'.

39 For Milani *(Veils and Words:* 150), one of the most significant aspects of Farrokhzād's reworking of the story of Adam and Eve is that, in her garden, 'the woman neither speaks for the devil nor assists Satan . . . If Eve seems to be a captive of the identity imposed upon her, if in her sins as in her virtues she proves to be unchanging and unchangeable, the woman in this poem is on a journey of her own. Her body, stretched to new experiences, refuses to return to its original dimension. Her mind, exposed to new horizons, refuses confinement'.

40 Milani, 'Nakedness regained': 96.

41 In Farrokhzād's third collection, *'Esyān*, Hillmann (*A Lonely Woman:* 34) says the addition of Biblical, Qur'anic and Persian literary imagery creates a new 'poetic texture' in Farrokhzād's writing.

42 According to Ardavan Davaran ('"The Conquest of the Garden": A significant instance of the poetic development of Forugh Farrokhzad', in *Another Birth: Selected Poems of Forugh Farrokhzad*, trans. Hasan Javadi and Susan Sallee (Emeryville, 1981): 119) the water, mirror and light mentioned here relate to traditional Iranian marriage rites.

For Davaran (ibid., 120) the union celebrated here is 'a matter of real emotional and sensual communication'.

43 Milani ('Nakedness regained': 97) argues 'the intellectual, emotional and sexual reciprocity of such a relationship is rarely conceptualized in Persian literature'. This is almost uniformly the case for the Persian *ghazal*, but I would argue strong elements of amorous and sexual reciprocity are to be found in some of the Persian romance *mathnavi*s.

44 Milani, 'Forugh Farrokhzād': 377.

45 For Milani ('Nakedness regained': 99) the construction of this new Eden inevitably means the destruction of the marital home: 'In Farrokhzad's paradise . . . Walls are demolished, curtains pulled, veils cast aside. Here bodies, like feelings, don't need a cover. Nakedness, both in its literal and figurative sense, is sought and valued'.

46 For Leonardo P. Alishan ('Forugh Farrokhzād and the forsaken earth', in *Forugh Farrokhzād: A Quarter Century Later* (ed.) Michael C. Hillmann, Austin, 1987: 118) this poem is 'Forugh's most powerful statement on Nature as the proper source and context for love'. Hillmann (*A Lonely Woman*: 98) argues that in Farrokhzād's eyes the lovers' guiltlessness as depicted in 'Fath-e bāgh' stems from their perfect harmony with nature.

47 Rahimieh (Beneath the veil': 102) sees a similarly mystical bent to Farrokhzād's much earlier poem, 'Gonāh': 'Deliberately alluding to the traditions of Persian mysticism, Farrokhzad paints a picture of bliss which would normally be equated with Divine ecstasy. Through the poem, ["Gonāh"] she evokes the language of the Persian mystics and raises the readers' expectation of the final spiritual illumination'.

48 Shamisa (*Negāhi beh Forugh*, Tehran, 1993: 106) says for Farrokhzād, the meadow symbolises a space filled with life, tranquillity and happiness.

49 See Davaran, 'The Conquest of the Garden': 122.

50 Farrokhzād, 'Delam barā-ye bāghcheh mi-suzad', *Imān biāvarim beh āghāz-e fasl-e sard* (Tehran, 1974): 51–60.

51 See Hillmann, *A Lonely Woman*: 6: the Farrokhzād family home was a 'comfortable house in the central Tehran Amiriyeh neighbourhood'.

52 Hillmann (Hillmann, *A Lonely Woman*: 103–4) argues that in her poem '*Vahm-e sabz*' ('Green Delusion'), Farrokhzād recognises 'that nature can no longer be a comforting idyllic force in her life, that she is far beyond being able to seek refuge in comfortable maternal and domestic female roles . . .'

53 As noted by Milani ('Nakedness regained': 102), the bliss enjoyed by the lovers in the garden proves to be short-lived.

54 Hillmann, *A Lonely Woman*: 119.

55 Rahimieh ('Beneath the veil': 103) notes a similarly satirical tone vis-à-vis what she calls, 'the Pahlavi monarchy's obsession with a glorious Iranian past', in the poem, 'Ey marz-e por-gohar' ('O' Bejewelled Realm'), *Tavallodi digar*: 148–157.

56 This could also be seen as Farrokhzād prophecying the pomp and extravagance of Mohammad Reza Shah Pahlavi's coronation ceremony in October 1967.

57 Farrokhzād, 'Kasi keh mesl-e hich-kas nist', *Imān biāvarim beh āghā z-e fasl-e sard*: 64–72.

58 The description of the sister in 'I Feel Sorry for the Garden' reminds the reader of passages from Jalāl Al-e Ahmad's *Gharbzadegi* ('Westoxication'), published in 1962. Talattof ('Iranian women's literature': 534) notes: 'Jalal Al-i Ahmad in his book . . . links both consumerism and women's emancipation to what he perceives as the sub-versive, colonial, Western influence on the pure, indigenous Iranian culture.'

59 See Hillmann *A Lonely Woman*: 122.

60 This adoption of a broader vision on Farrokhzād's part does not imply that she felt more at ease with her society at this point in her life. As Amin Banani ('Introduction', in *Bride of Acacias: Selected Poems of Forugh Farrokhzād*, trans. Jascha Kessler with Amin Banani, Delmar, 1982: 9) has noted, Farrokhzād's 'self' is a reflection of her society. Banani sees these two 'selves' (the personal 'self' and the societal 'self') as ultimately inseparable, and observes: 'What bonds them together is the theme of alienation, from the self and society, arising from helplessness of the individual to influence her society and personal life, and her struggle to achieve integration on both levels'.

61 As Milani ('Forugh Farrokhzād': 376) notes, 'In her later poems, there is further transformation, as her personal rage, suppressed emotions, and social frustrations become integrated with a more public perspective. Identifications between the poet and other women are replaced by a move toward larger human concerns and preoccupations'.

62 Zubizaretta ('The woman who sings no, no, no': 425) says, in her later poems Farrokhzād shifts, 'from private warfare upon her predominantly masculine Persian world to a consideration of greater issues of general human isolation, universal order, and spiritual rebirth from a more truly feminist perspective, in that she arrives at a more inclusive rather than exclusive understanding of the human condition'. For Hillmann (*A Lonely Woman*: 99) the speaker in Farrokhzād's later poems voices an 'anti-patriarchal clarion call that knows no gender'.

63 See for example Talattof, 'Iranian women's literature': 539.

Chapter 4

1 In this study 'muse' is used in the sense of one who assists in the creation of a poetic work.

2 Barbara Garlick (ed.), *Tradition and the Poetics of Self in Nineteenth-Century Women's Poetry* (New York, 2002): viii.

3 Farrokhzād, 'Goftegu bā Forugh no. 5', in Behruz Jalāli (ed.), *Jāvdāneh zistan, dar owj māndan* (Tehran, 1993): 202–3.

4 Behruz Jalāli, *Dar ghorubi abadi* (Tehran, 1997): 172–3.

5 Farrokhzād, *Imān biāvarim beh āghāz-e fasl-e sard* (Tehran, 1974): 59–65.

6 Jalāli, *Dar ghorubi abadi*: 172–3.

7 Farrokhzād, *Tavallodi digar* (Tehran, 1964): 55–60.

8 Farrokhzād, *Bargozideh-ye ash'ār-e Forugh Farrokhzād* (Tehran, 1978): 7.

9   Farrokhzād, 'The Voice Alone Is Left', in Jascha Kessler with Amin Banani trans., *Bride of Acacias: Selected Poems of Forugh Farrokhzad* (Delmar, NY, 1982): 116–17.

10 Jalāli, *Dar ghorubi abadi*: cover page. This untitled poem is taken from Behruz Jalāli ed., *Divān-e ash'ār-e Forugh Farrokhzād* (Tehran, 1995): 350.

11 Jalāli, *Dar ghorubi abadi*: 63.

12 Farrokhzād, 'Khāneh-ye matruk', *Asir*, (Tehran, 1955), 133–5.

13 Farrokhzād, 'Ma'shuq-e man', *Tavallodi digar*: 78–82.

14 Farrokhzād, 'Goftegu bā Forugh no. 5': 202.

15 Banani, *Bride of Acacias*: 7.

16 Girdhari Tikku with Alireza Anushirvani, *A Conversation with Modern Persian Poets* (Costa Mesa, 2004), English text: 38.

17 Tikku, *A Conversation*, English text: 15.

18 Tikku, *A Conversation*, English text: 16.

19 Tikku, *A Conversation*, English text: 41.

20 Tikku, *A Conversation*, English text: 23.

21 Tikku, *A Conversation*, English text: 23.

22 Tikku, *A Conversation*, Persian text: 25. Simin Behbahani (b. 1927) re-worked the fixed meters and rhymes of the *ghazal* to suit her poetic needs. And she incorporated natural and everyday conversation to introduce new subject matter and expression, as the poet has said, 'I have said things . . . that were neither customary or possible to say in the traditional *ghazal*'. Simin Behbahani, *A Cup of Sin: Selected Poems*, trans. Farzaneh Milani and Kaveh Safa (Syracuse, 1999): xxiii.

23 Tikku, *A Conversation*, English text: 23.

24 'Ali-Akbar Moshir-Salimi, *Zanān-e sokhanvar* (Tehran, 1957–1959): 1: 265.

25 Tikku, *A Conversation*, Persian text: 5.

26 Tikku, *A Conversation*, English text: 23.

27 Garlick, *Tradition and the Poetics of Self*: vii.

28 Jalāli, *Bargozideh-ye ash'ār*: 6.

29 Farrokhzād, 'Ramideh', *Asir*, 19–20.

30 The difficulty of choosing between art and life and the pain of separation from her son. Jalāli, *Dar ghorubi abadi*: 19.

31 Jalāli, *Dar ghorubi abadi*: 57.

32 Farrokhzād, *Asir*: 11–14

33 Farrokhzād, *Asir*: 47–9.

34 Farrokhzād, *Asir*: 15–17.

35 Farrokhzād, 'Tanhā'i-ye Māh', *Tavallodi digar*: 76–7.

36 Farrokhzād, *Asir*: 15–17.

37 Farrokhzād, *Asir*: 151–3.

38 Farrokhzād, *Bargozideh-ye ash'ār*: 11–12.

39 Farrokhzād, *Bargozideh-ye ash'ar*, 11–12.

40 Tikku, *A Conversation*, Persian text: 70–71.

41 Farrokhzād, ''Arusak-e kuki', *Tavallodi digar*: 71–5.

42 Farrokhzād's robotic female may be playing a role in her search for a unique voice. According to Garlick (*Poetics of Self* : 27), nineteenth-century English women poets struggled against conventional femininity (in both personal and poetic matters) in their attempt to find an appropriate poetic voice.

43 Tikku, *A Conversation*, Persian text: 84.

44 Farrokhzād, *Bargozideh-ye ashʿār*: 12.

45 Farrokhzād, 'Bād mārā khvāhad bord', *Tavallodi digar*: 30–32.

46 The critic Mohammad Hoquqi, while understanding Farrokhzād's poetry as a continuum of feminine sensibility and expression of heartfelt and sincere emotion, divides her poetry into two sections. He sees the early volumes *Asir*, *Divār* and *ʿEsyān* as evidence of one side of the poet. He sees *Tavallodi digar* and *Imān biāvarim beh āghāz-e fasl-e sard* as products of another side. For Hoquqi, the first volumes are the expression of a woman struggling with conflicting womanly and maternal feelings. In the last two volumes, Farrokhzād's poetry takes on a more universal and worldly quality. Mohammad Hoquqi, *Sheʿr-e zamān-e mā, no. 4: Forugh Farrokhzād.* (Tehran, 1994): 11–12. Other critics have divided the poet's work in a similar fashion and see the last volumes as concerned with the world outside the narrow confines of the self.

47 The lines which follow are excerpted from *Imān biāvarim beh āghāz-e fasl-e sard.*

48 Farrokhzād, *Imān biāvarim*: 34.

49 Farrokhzād, *Imān biāvarim*: 29.

50 Farrokhzād, *Imān biāvarim*: 29.

51 Farrokhzād, *Imān biāvarim*: 37.

52 Farrokhzād, *Imān biāvarim*: 28.

53 Farrokhzād, *Imān biāvarim*: 30.

54 Farrokhzād, *Imān biāvarim*: 33–4.

55 Farrokhzād, *Imān biāvarim*: 27.

56 Farrokhzād, *Imān biāvarim*: 38–9.

57 Farrokhzād, *Imān biāvarim*: 39.

58 Farrokhzād, *Imān biāvarim*: 42–3.

59 Farrokhzād, *Imān biāvarim*: 39.

60 Jalāli, *Dar ghorubi abadi*: 184.

61 Jalāli, *Dar ghorubi abadi*: 120.

62 Tikku, *A Conversation*, Persian text: 67.

63 Tikku, *A Conversation*, Persian text: 68–9.

64 Tikku, *A Conversation*, Persian text: 68.

65 Tikku, *A Conversation*, Persian text: 5.

66 Garlick, *Poetics of Self* : vii.

67 Tikku, *A Conversation*, English text: 23.

68 Tikku, *A Conversation*, English text: 3.

69 Unlike Farrokhzād who turns inward to greet her muse, Shāmlu conceives of muses in the plural. His muses are external to himself. As he says: 'My first line is whatever I choose and it's my offering to the muses (khodāyān)'. Tikku, *A Conversation*, Persian text: 75.

Chapter 5

1   For gender-differentiating studies of the mirror, see Diana Tietjens Meyers, *Gender in the Mirror: Cultural Imagery and Women's Agency* (Oxford and New York, 2002) and Jenijoy La Belle, *Herself Beheld: The Literature of the Looking Glass* (Ithaca and London, 1988).

2   The stages in the developmental process of Farrokhzād's self as studied here through her use of mirror imagery easily fits Farzaneh Milan's tripartite classification of the poet's life and work into those of feminine, feminist, and female. See Farzaneh Milani, 'Forugh Farrokhzad: A Feminist Perspective' (Ph.D. dissertation, University of California at Los Angeles, 1979).

3   Farrokhzād, 'Az yād rafteh', in Behnām Bāvandpur (ed.), *Majmu'eh-ye āsār-e Forugh Farrokhzād* (Essen, Germany, 2002): 1: 70.

4   A mirror's lack of agency and its passive reflectivity were frequently drawn upon by Persian Neoplatonic philosophers, mystics and poets to promote their ethico-religious doctrines. Among others, 'Attār, 'Erāqi, Sa'di, Hāfez, and Bidel, and in the modern period, Bahār, used the idea of the mirror of the heart to convey a similar meaning. For a discussion of the mirror of the heart in classical Persian philosophy and literature, see Riccardo Zipoli, 'Semiotics and the tradition of the image', *Persica* 20(2005): 155–172 and Seyyedeh Fariba Musavi, 'Ā'ineh dar shāhkār-hā-ye adabi tā qarn-e hashtum' (unpublished MA thesis, Tarbiat Mo'allem University, Tehran, Iran, 1995): 75–86.

5   Farrokhzād, 'Ārezu', *Majmu'eh-ye āsār*: 1: 136.

6   One of the many poems by Farrokhzād that reveal her anti-transcendental views is 'Ru-ye khāk', *Majmu'eh-ye āsār*: 1: 249–50. In this poem, Farrokhzād openly declares she has never wished to change her place on the earth for that of the stars, the chosen ones, or even the angels.

7   See Musavi, 'Ā'ineh dar shāhkār-hā-ye adabi': 67–74 and 86–9.

8   Farrokhzād, 'Bandegi', *Majmu'eh-ye āsār*: 1: 185.

9   Farrokhzād, *Majmu'eh-ye āsār*: 1: 182.

10 Farrokhzād, *Majmu'eh-ye āsār*: 1: 195. *Jamāl*, the *mysterium fascinans* or the Divine Beauty, and *jalāl*, the *mysterium tremendum* or the Divine Majesty are two of God's names, usually cited together.

11 See Musavi,' Ā'ineh dar shāhkār-hā-ye adabi': 104–7.

12 Upon careful study of women's behavioral patterns in asylums, Showalter observes that schizophrenic women were obsessed with continual observation of themselves in mirrors for the confirmation of their existence. See Elaine Showalter, *The Female Malady: Women, Madness, and English Culture, 1830–1980* (New York, 1985), 211–12. In this regard a mirror is not a thing turned merely for narcissistic self-satisfaction. On the contrary, the mirror can also be associated with pain and distress.

13 La Belle, *Herself Beheld*: 22.

14 Farrokhzād, 'Sedā'i dar shab', *Majmu'eh-ye āsār*: 1: 109.

15 This technique is again employed by Farrokhzād in 'Gomshodeh' (*Majmu'eh-ye āsār*: 1: 130). Here she places it within quotation marks to emphasize its inherent otherness.

16   See Musavi,'Ā'ineh dar shāhkār-hā-ye adabi': 156–167.
17   The advent of psychoanalysis and especially Jacques Lacan's theory of a 'mirror stage' has revived the analysis of the image of the mirror in western literature. See Jacques Lacan, 'The Mirror Stage as Formative of the *I* Function: as Revealed in Psychoanalytic Experience' in *Écrits, The First Complete Edition in English*, trans. Bruce Fink (New York and London, 2006): 75–81.
18   Farrokhzād, Didār dar shab', *Majmu'eh-ye āsār*: 1: 296, 298.
19   Farrokhzād, *Majmu'eh-ye āsār*: 1: 295.
20   La Belle, *Herself Beheld*: 119.
21   Farrokhzād, *Majmu'eh-ye āsār*: 1: 296.
22   Kāmyār Shāpur and 'Omrān Sālehi, *Avvalin tapesh-hā-ye 'āsheqāneh: nāmeh-hā-ye Forugh Farrokhzād beh hamsar-ash Parviz Shāpur* (Tehran, Iran, 2002): 228–30
23   For an example see Farrokhzād's apocalyptic poem 'Āyeh-hā-ye zamini', *Majmu'eh-ye āsār*: 1: 289–93. In this poem, Farrokhzād depicts the grotesquery of the outside world with resorting to a mirror.
24   A phrase made popular by Sarah Grand (1854–1943), an Irish-born feminist writer. The New Woman (as a modern feminist ideal of the liberated woman) emerged at the end of the nineteenth century.
25   Farrokhzād, 'Imān biyāvarim beh āghāz-e fasl-e sard', *Majmu'eh-ye āsār*: 1: 337.
26   *Majmu'eh-ye āsār*: 1: 344.
27   Laura Gutiérrez Spencer, 'Mirrors and masks: Female subjectivity in Chicana poetry', *Frontiers: A Journal of Women Studies*, 15.2 (1994): 72.
28   Ibid., 70.
29   Farrokhzād, 'Panjareh', *Majmu'eh-ye āsār*: 1: 356.
30   Farrokhzād, 'Beh āftāb salāmi dobāreh khvāham dād', *Majmu'eh-ye āsār*: 1: 324.
31   La Belle, *Herself Beheld*: 160–61.
32   Farrokhzād, *Majmu'eh-ye āsār*: 2: 35–6.
33   Hélène Cixous, 'The laugh of the Medusa', in *New French Feminisms*, E. Marks and I. de Courtivron (eds) (Sussex, UK, 1981): 250.

Chapter 6

1   Mahmud Nikbakht describes Farrokhzād's first three poetry collections as imitative, clichéd, and superficial, and the last two as 'true poetry'. See Mahmud Nikbakht, *Az gomshodegi tā rahā'i* (Tehran, Iran, 1994): 8. The words *gomshodeh* ('astray') and *rahā'i* ('freedom') implied in the title are suggestive. As we will see Mohammad Hoquqi, Kāmyār 'Ābedi, Khosrowshahi, and Nāser Saffāriān share similar views of Farrokhzād's poetry.
2   See the interviews in Nāser Saffāriān, *Āyeh-hā-ye āh: Nā-gofteh-hā'i az zendegi-ye Farrokhzād* (Tehran, Iran, 2002).
3   This, as we will see, is a relatively newly constructed assumption.

4   See the discussion of the works of Ruhangiz Karāchi, Nāser Saffāriān, and others below.

5   Some memoirs about Farrokhzād mention Nāder Nāderpur and Boyuk Mostafavi.

6   See Samuel Kinser, 'Chronotopes and catastrophes: The cultural history of Mikhail Bakhtin', *The Journal of Modern History* 56.2 (June, 1984): 301–10.

7   Kāmyār Shāpur and 'Omrān Sālehi, *Avvalin tapesh-hā-ye 'āsheqāneh-ye qalb-am: Name-ha-ye Forugh Farrokhzād beh hamsar-ash Parviz Shāpur* (Tehran, Iran, 2002).

8   See her mother's interview in Saffāriān, *Āyeh-hā-ye āh*: 22.

9   Shāpur and Sālehi, *Avvalin tapesh-hā* .

10 Farrokhzād, 'Asir', *Bargozideh-ye ash'ār-e Forugh Farrokhzād* (Tehran, Iran, 1975): 19–20. The translations in this essay are my own, and I refer to the title of some of Farrokhzād's poems in English to facilitate reading.

11 Shāpur and Sālehi, *Avvalin tapesh-hā*.

12 On Farrokhzād's travelogue, see *Ferdowsi*, Nos. 313–320, Mehr-Ābān, 1336; Sirus Tāhbāz, *Zani tanhā: dar- bāreh-ye zendegi va she'r-e Forugh Farrokhzad* (Tehran, Iran,1997); or Behruz Jalāli ed., *Jāvdāneh zistan, dar owj māndan* (Tehran, Iran, 1996).

13 Farrokhzād, 'Gonāh', *Divār* (Tehran, Iran, 1956): 11–15.

14 See Farrokhzād, 'Bi-tafāvot' in *Ferdowsi* 3 (Day, 1336) or Shahnāz Morādi-Kuchi, *Shenākhtnāmeh-ye Forugh Farrokhzād* (Tehran, Iran, 2000), 363–68.

15 See Tāhbāz, *Zani Tanha*.

16 Farrokhzād, ''Esyān-e bandegi', *'Esyān* (Tehran, Iran, 1958): 13–38.

17 Farrokhzād, ''Esyān-e khodā', *'Esyān* (Tehran, Iran, 1958): 51–3.

18 *Ferdowsi* Nos. 313–320, Mehr-Ābān, 1336.

19 Tāhbāz, *Zani Tanha*. 78.

20 Farrokhzād, 'She'ri barā-ye to', *'Esyān* (Tehran, Iran, 1958): 57–60.

21 Behruz Jalāli, *She'r-e Forugh Farrokhzād az āghāz ta emruz* (Tehran, Iran, 1994): 27.

22 Farrokhzād, 'Ān ruz-hā', *Tavallodi digar* (Tehran, Iran, 1964): 9–16.

23 Farrokhzād, 'Dar ghorubi abadi', in Jalāli, *She'r-e Forugh Farrokhzād*: 350–6.

24 On committed or engagé literature see Kamran Talattof, *The Politics of Writing in Iran: A History of Modern Persian Literature* (Syracuse, NY, 2000).

25 Farrokhzād, 'Āyeh-hā-ye zamini', *Tavallodi digar*: 98–105.

26 Farrokhzād, 'Ba'd az to', *Imān biāvarim beh āghāz-e fasl-e sard* (Tehran, Iran 1974): 32–7.

27 Farrokhzād, 'Delam barā-ye bāghcheh mi-suzad', *Imān biāvarim beh āghāz-e fasl-e sard*: 51–60.

28 Farrokhzād, 'Parandeh mordani-st', *Imān biāvarim beh āghāz-e fasl-e sard*: 85–6.

29 Farrokhzād, 'Tanhā sedā-st keh mi-mānad', *Imān biāvarim beh āghāz-e fasl-e sard*: 76–81.

30 Ibid.

31 Hoquqi's work showing how certain words and figures of language appear and disappear from Farrokhzād's work confirms this analysis. See, Mohammad Hoquqi, *She'r-e zamān-e mā, no.4: Forugh Farrokhzād* (Tehran, Iran, 1994).

32   See Kāmyār 'Ābedi, *Tanhā-tar az yek barg: zendegi va she'r-e Forugh Farrokhzād* (Tehran, Iran, 1998): 25, Mehdi Akhavān-Sāles' interviews, or indeed, the majority of the sources referenced in this essay.

33   Ahmad-Rezā Ahmadi compares the relationship between Farrokhzād and Golestān to that of Rumi and Shams. See Saffāriān, *Āyeh-hā-ye āh*: 116–124. Forugh's sister, Purān Farrokhzād, and the scholar and literary critic, Sirous Shamisa, share similar views.

34   Amin Banani, 'Introduction', in *Bride of Acacias: Selected Poems of Forugh Farrokhzad*, trans. Jascha Kessler and Amin Banani (Delmar, NY, 1982): 5.

35   Gholām Heydari ed., *Forugh Farrokhzād va sinemā* (Tehran, Iran, 1998).

36   'The Black House is a cinematic poem . . . Farrokhzād's first experiment in merging cinema and poetry'. Heydari, *Forugh Farrokhzād va sinemā* : 62.

37   Farzaneh Milani, *Veils and Words: The Emerging Voices of Iranian Women Writers* (Syracuse, 1992) and Michael C. Hillmann, *A Lonely Woman: Forugh Farrokhzad and Her Poetry* (Washington D.C., 1987).

38   Haideh Moghissi also refers to the 'feminist character' of Farrokhzād's poetry in her *Populism and Feminism in Iran: Women's Struggle in a Male-Defined Revolutionary Movement* (New York, 1994): 86. Reviews of Farrokhzād's film also describe her as the 'Iranian feminist poet'. See for example, 'Being Human' http://www. combustiblecelluloid.com/classic [accessed December 2009].

39   Kamran Talattof, 'Iranian women's literature: From pre-revolutionary social discourse to post-revolutionary feminism', *International Journal of Middle East Studies* 29.4 (November, 1997): 531–58.

40   Farrokhzād, 'Ro'yā', *Asir* (Tehran, Iran, 1955): 25–8.

41   In poems such as, 'Khāterāt', 'Harjā''' , 'Buseh', 'Vedā' ', 'Afsāneh-ye talkh', 'Goriz o dard', 'Div-e shab', 'Sharāb va khun', 'Dar barābar-e khodā', and 'Anduh'.

42   'Qorbāni' and 'Pāsokh'.

43   Five times in ' 'Esyān-e bandegi', ' 'Esyān-e khodā', 'She'ri barā-ye to', and 'Az rahi dur'.

44   Farrokhzād, 'Delam barā-ye bāghcheh mi-suzad', *Divān-e ash'ār*: 451. Occasionally, the synonym *ma'siyat* is used.

45   To them, feminism was a bourgeois ideology.

46   Talattof, *The Politics of Writing in Iran*: 100–2.

47   Farrokhzād, *Divān-e ash'ār*: 305–6.

48   Ibid.

49   This could be read as a nostalgic expression of the memory of her life with her ex-husband.

50   Her husband's writings/responses do not illustrate love for her. See Shāpur and Sālehi, *Avvalin tapesh-hā* , 73.

51   Ibid., 285.

52   Morādi-Kuchi, *Shenākhtnāmeh*: 365.

53   Ibid., 366.

54   Farrokhzād, 'Anduh-e fardā', in Morādi-Kuchi, *Shenākhtnāmeh*.

55   On this topic, see Steven Cohan and Linda Shires, *Telling Stories: A Theoretical Analysis of Narrative Fiction* (New York, 1988).

56   Iraj Gorgin, *Chahār mosāhebeh bā Farrokhzād* (Tehran, Iran, 1964): 21.

57   Elaine Showalter, 'A literature of their own,' in *Feminist Literary Theory: A Reader*, (ed.) Mary Eagleton (Oxford, 1986): 11–15.

58   See Ruhangiz Karachi, *Forugh Farrokhzād* (Tehran, Iran, 2004): 23–6.

59   See Saffāriān, *Āyeh-hā-ye āh*. Contributors to this edited volume fail to notice the context in which even the male poet Rahmāni was criticized for such themes.

60   Hillmann refers to a commentator named Sirus Parhām [Doktor Mirta!] who he says criticized one of Farrokhzād's collections. This little-known critic had simply stated, 'Ms. Farrokhzād has implicitly considered the right of "sexual freedom" the most vital and essential right that a woman should seek from society. Consequently, she has endeavored to incite women against men, assuming that the "massacre" of men will do away all of women's social deprivations and thus women will be completely free!' See Hillmann, *A Lonely Woman*: 84. This would have been a perfect debut to a feminist discursive debate, but alas, no one responded. Moghissi refers to Hillmann's example as evidence for 'The resistance of attitudes of Iranian males toward Forugh Farrokhzad', Moghissi, *Populism and Feminism in Iran*: 86. Reference to such suffering is also made by Sholeh Wolpé in, *Sin: Selected Poems of Forugh Farrokhzad* (Fayetteville, NC, 2007).

61   One is the flawed and inconsequential criticism by Sādeq Sarmad in *Ferdowsi* or in *Sepid o siyāh* (which also praised the poet). Another is a 1955 piece by Nāser Khodāyār (another unknown journalist) in *Roshanfekr* (which again published Farrokhzād's poetry). His case might require further attention only because he is alleged to be the subject of Farrokhzād's poem. There are also some anecdotes related to Hamidi Shirāzi.

62   Jalāli in his otherwise valuable book reiterates the common belief that Farrokhzād was harshly criticized, similarly without providing any examples, and simply referring to Farrokhzād complaint somewhere about some sarcastic remarks made by others, see Behruz Jalāli ed., *Divān-e ash'ār-e Forugh Farrokhzād* (Tehran, Iran, 1995): 35–6.

63   For example, this was done in numerous issues of *Ferdowsi*.

64   *Arash*, 1.3 (Spring, 1962).

65   Seyyed-Hādi Hā'eri, *Ziba-tarin ash'ār-e Forugh Farrokhzād* (Tehran, n.d.) and 'Ali-Akbar Moshir-Salimi, *Zanān-e sokhanvar* (Tehran, Iran, 1956).

66   Bernardo Bertolucci (who visited Iran to make a film about Farrokhzād) took the poet's letters abroad and helped save some political prisoners. Farrokhzād also allegedly sheltered students who were being followed by police.

67   See Purān Farrokhzād (ed.), *Dar-bāreh-ye Forugh Farrokhzād* (Tehran, Iran, 2002). Contributors to Purān's Farrokhzād's volume, like those who contributed to Saffāriān's book, claim to have been close friends or disciples of Farrokhzād. This brings me to the conclusion that we should perhaps redefine the concept of Farrokhzād's 'loneliness' as well. She seems to have always been surrounded by family members, friends, and colleagues. Her loneliness had perhaps to do with being an anomaly in that male-dominated environment.

Chapter 7

1 Farrokhzād, 'Gonāh', *Divār* (Tehran, Iran, 1956): 11–15.
2 Farrokhzād, 'Joft', *Tavallodi digar* (Tehran, Iran, 1964): 123–4.
3 *Remembering the Flight: Twenty Poems by Forugh Farrokhzād: A Parallel Text in English and Persian*, trans. Ahmad Karimi-Hakkak (Vancouver, Canada, 1997): 54–5.
4 Michael Riffaterre, 'Interpretation and descriptive poetry: A reading of Wordsworth's "Yew-Tree"', *New Literary History* 4.2 (Winter, 1973): 229–56.
5 Farrokhzād, *Tavallodi digar* (Tehran, Iran, 1964): 123.
6 I have yet to see a translation which includes the asterisks.
7 As translated in *Remembering the Flight*: 81–8.
8 Ibid.: 81–2.
9 Ibid.: 83–4.
10 Ibid., 87–8.
11 Ibid., 77–8.
12 Ibid., 79–80.

Chapter 8

1 Sirous Shamisa, *Negāhi beh Forugh* (Tehran, Iran, 1993).
2 This is a reference to Farrokhzād, 'Āyeh-hā-ye zamini', *Tavallodi digar* (1964): 98–105.
3 I believe that at the time Farrokhzād was writing, women in Iran would perhaps have been more likely to hold more religious, even superstitious beliefs than their male counterparts. This was largely due to the fact that – in comparison to today – many fewer Iranian women than men completed high school or entered into university.
4 It is most difficult to locate similar examples in the poetry of Farrokhzād's contemporaries. Those examples that can be found are by no means as elaborate, nor as direct and frank in tone.
5 Farrokhzād, 'Delam barā-ye bāghcheh mi-suzad', *Imān biāvarim beh āghāz-e fasl-e sard* (Tehran, Iran, 1974): 51–60.
6 Farrokhzād, 'Panjereh', *Imān biāvarim beh āghāz-e fasl-e sard*: 61.
7 Farrokhzād, 'Ey marz-e por-gohar', *Tavallodi digar*: 135–6.
8 For the full text of the poem, see *Tavallodi digar*: 98–105.
9 This is a reference to 'Kasi keh mesl-e hich kas nist', *Imān biāvarim beh āghāz-e fasl-e sard*: 80.
10 See 'Attār, *Elāhi-nāmeh*: 215: from *Yeki binandeh-ye ma'ruf budi keh arvāh-ash hameh makshuf budi*.
11 See Shāh Ne'matollāh Vali, *Divān*, (ed.) Sa'id Nafisi (Tehran n.d.): 22: *Qodrat-e kerdegār mi-binam hālat-e ruzegār mi-binam*. This quatrain attributed to Abu Sa'id Abo'l-Kheyr is well-known:
  Az vāqe'eh-i to-ra khabar khvāham kard v-ān-ra beh do harf mokhtasar khvāham kard . . ., see Sirous Shamisa, *Seyr-e robā'i*, (Tehran, Iran, 2008): 122. Another example is

the book of Rostam Farrokhzād at the end of Ferdowsi's *Shāhnāmeh*. In the Pahlavi texts written down after the emergence of Islam (e.g. *Revāyāt-e Pahlavi*), the Arab invasion and the destruction of Iran are foretold. This trend continued until the ninth century AH. This is why in some of these narratives, even the Mongol invasion was 'prophesised'. In these visionary texts, Iran eventually reaches an era of reconstruction and revivification.

12 This is why the day on which one dies is know as 'the day of the event' (*ruz-e vāqe'eh*), e.g. Hāfez: on the day of the event, make my coffin from cypress wood (*beh ruz-e vāqe'eh tābut-e mā ze sarv konid*). In the holy Qur'ān, in the apocalyptic visions related to the Time of the End, 'the event' is synonymous with the Day of Judgement (*qiyāmat*): e.g., 'when the event happens' (*idhā waqa'at al-wāqi'a*).

13 See Farrokhzād, *Tavallodi digar*: 88.

14 *Ārash*, no.13 (Esfand, 1345). Interview conducted with Farrokhzād by Sirus Tāhbāz and Dr Sā'edi.

15 For example, the interviewers say to Farrokhzād that traditional poetic forms such as the *ghazal* and the *masnavi* are no longer of any value, and she disagrees. Elsewhere in the interview they express the desire that all poetry be political, and she does not accept their view.

16 All from Farrokhzād, 'Āyeh-hā-ye zamini', *Tavallodi digar*: 98–105.

17 See Farrokhzād, *Tavallodi digar*: 113.

18 Leftist Iranian poets often used *ham-sāyeh* ('neighbour') to refer to the Soviet Union. For examples of this usage in the poetry of Sāyeh (Hushang Ebtehāj), Mehdi Akhavān-Sāles, and Nimā, see Sirous Shamisa, *Rāhnamā-ye adabiyāt-e mo'āser* (Tehran, Iran, 2004): 193–195.

19 Farrokhzād, 'Ba'd az to', *Imān biāvarim beh āghāz-e fasl-e sard* (Tehran, Iran, 1974): 32–7.

20 The idea of progress appeared for the first time in the 17th century in the West and reached its peak in the 19th century. Those who follow this theory say that mankind is essentially on a path towards progress, and that people today have higher moral standards and are happier than people in past centuries, and that this is a process that will continue into the future. The idea of progress is contrasted with 'primitivism' in books of literary criticism, which consider people of past ages to have been happier than those living today.

21 Farrokhzād, 'Panjareh', *Imān biāvarim beh āghāz-e fasl-e sard* (Tehran, Iran, 1974): 41–7.

22 Farrokhzād, 'Ey marz-e por-gohar', *Tavallodi digar*: 135–6.

23 Same interview as referenced above.

24 Farrokhzād, 'Jom'eh', *Tavallodi digar*: 69–70.

25 Farrokhzād, 'Ān ruz-hā', *Tavallodi digar*: 9–16

26 Farrokhzād, 'Dar āb-hā-ye sabz-e tābestān'.

27 In the same interview referenced above.

28 It appears that Farrokhzād wrote just three more poems after this one: 'Kasi keh mesl-e hich kas nist', 'Tanhā sedā-st keh mi-mānad', and 'Parandeh mordani ast'.

29 A reference to Farrokhzād's, 'Kasi keh mesl-e hich kas nist', *Imān biāvarim beh āghāz-e fasl-e sard*: 64–72.

30 In Persian mystical literature, the fish often stands for the seeker, but here, the fish represents those who seek to follow the path towards freedom in limitless, open water, free from oppression.

31 *Az khāterāt-e sabz tohi mi-shavad.*

32 How do the other four great poets of modern Iran compare to Farrokhzād in this regard? In the poems of Akhavān-Sāles we hear the voice of the generation defeated with the overthrow of Mosaddeq. Akhavān is only concerned with the Shah and wants to see him toppled. Shāmlu, instead of talking about any particular tyrant or democrat, discusses tyranny and liberty per se, and that is why his poems are more universal. Shāmlu both mourns the death of liberty and praises it. Nimā is simply concerned with the struggle itself, and he is focused solely on the 'victorious king' who must, one day, become victorious, and then we are left with Sepehri who, one might say, did not care about any of these things.

Chapter 9

1 The statement as quoted by M. Ali Issari in *Cinema in Iran, 1900–1979* (Metuchen, NJ, 1989): 191 reads: 'We started the film with a [leper] woman and a mirror. The woman is the symbol of "man" who sees his life in a mirror – any mirror'.

2 Julia Kristeva defines the abject as 'the jettisoned object, [which] is radically excluded and draws me toward the place where meaning collapses'. *Powers of Horror: An Essay on Abjection* (New York, 1982): 2.

3 Kristeva, *Powers of Horror*: 4.

4 Kristeva, *Powers of Horror*: 3.

5 The term used in Persian for a leper colony translates literally as 'house of leprosy', meaning 'home for lepers'.

6 Nikki Keddie, *Roots of Revolution: An Interpretive History of Modern Iran* (New Haven, 1981): 142–182.

7 *Gharbzadegi*, a term originally coined by Ahmad Fardid, has been translated variously as 'occidentosis', 'westitis', 'westoxication' and 'plagued by the west'.

8 Jalāl Āl-e Ahmad, *Gharbzadegi (Weststruckness)*, trans. John Green and Ahmad Alizadeh, (Lexington, 1982): 11.

9 A more in-dept analysis of Āl-e Ahmad's problematic understanding and cursory treatment of the 'authentic' is beyond the scope of this essay.

10 Farzaneh Milani, *Veils and Words: The Emerging Voices of Iranian Women Writers* (Syracuse, NY, 1992): 137.

11 Hamid Dabashi, *Masters and Masterpieces of Iranian Cinema* (Washington DC, 2007): 58.

12 Dabashi, *Masters and Masterpieces*: 57.

13 Dabashi, *Masters and Masterpieces*: 58.

14 Āl-e Ahmad's statement is directed at the Iranian educational system and reads: 'How can a home whose foundations are in the process of disintegrating serve as a foundation for our schools?' *Ghabzadegi*: 148.

15 Dabashi's identification away from humanism reads: '*The House Is Black* is not about a humanist detection of beauty in the midst of misery and decrepitude. It emerges from exactly the opposite angle: It dwells in and deliberates on the dark, the repulsive, and the grotesque, to chase the grotesqueries to their utter limits. Any high-school-age teenager could go to a leprosy colony and sugarcoat the horror she saw with some sweet cotton-candy tale of their common humanity. But Iran and its cultural history had sent the single most perceptive set of eyes into that leprosarium. What they saw and showed was no juvenile humanism to amuse and entertain the good-hearted liberalism of generations to come.' *Masters and Masterpieces*: 58.

16 It is surprising that while directing his vehemence against humanism, Dabashi does not shy away from relying on 'masters' and 'masterpieces', terms which have long been tainted with the same humanist legacy Dabashi derides.

17 Issari, *Cinema in Iran*: 190.

18 Benedicte Ingstad and Susan Reynolds Whyte, *Disability and Culture*, (Berkeley, 1995): 4.

19 Ingstad and Reynolds Whyte, *Disability and Culture*: 7.

20 Narges Adibsereshki and Yeganeh Salehpour, 'Disability and Iranian Culture', from http://www.ee.umanitoba.ca/~kinsner/sds2001/proceed/pdocs/htms/28.HTM. [accessed January 2009]

21 Adibsereshki and Salehpour, 'Disability and Iranian culture'.

22 Irān Darrudi, *Dar fāseleh-ye do noqteh* (Tehran, 1998): 16–17. The English translation is my own.

23 I have relied on the English subtitles of the 2005 Facets DVD of *The House Is Black*.

24 Doug Cummings, http://filmjourney.weblogger.com/2005/02/13/the-house-is-black/#more-529. [accessed January 2009].

25 While some critics have suggested that the voice in this segment belongs to Ebrāhim Golestan, there is no consensus on this point. The film's own credits do not shed any light on the identity of the male speaker.

26 As noted earlier, some scenes in the documentary show children with their parents, indicating that sometimes entire families were moved into the leper colony. Other reminders, such as the dialogue in this sequence, demonstrate that some orphans are residents of the colony.

27 The image of a *morgh-e saqqā*, a pelican, is inscribed onto a desiccated landscape, drawing out the sense of dislocation and desolation pervading the leper colony whose inhabitants have also been plucked out of their native environment and homes.

28 Dabashi, *Masters and Masterpieces*: 67–8.

29 Michael M. J. Fischer, *Mute Dreams, Blind Owls, and Dispersed Knowledges: Persian Poesis in the Transnational Circuitry*, (Durham, NC, 2004): 257.

30 The translator's choice of the word pigeon reflects the fact that the Persian original, *kabutar*, is used to refer to both pigeon and dove.

31   Sohrāb Sepehri, *The Lover is Always Alone: Selected Poems*, trans. Karim Emāmi (Tehran, 2004): 59.

32   Sepehri, *The Lover is Always Alone*: 27.

33   Sepehri, *The Lover is Always Alone*: 49.

Chapter 10

1   John Harrington, *Film and/as Literature* (Englewood Cliffs, NJ, 1977): 176.

2   *The House is Black* has been compared to *Land without Bread* on several occasions by different film critics, such as Gholām Heydari (*Forugh Farrokhzād va sinemā* , Tehran, 1998: 287). Hushang Kavusi, in an article entitled '*Khāneh siyāh ast, yek film-e kutāh-e 'ajib*' (in Heydari, *Forugh Farrokhzād va sinemā*: 283–90), criticizes Farrokhzād's formalist treatment of the images, saying, '. . . in a film where everyone knows what it is about, and the audience has been psychologically prepared to witness an alarming subject, any additional technical shocks will no doubt damage the shock that is to be conveyed by the subject itself.' Chris Marker ('On Forugh Farrokhzad', trans., Dornā Khāzeni, *Facet Cine-Notes: Collectable Booklet* 2005), also compares *The House is Black* with *Land Without Bread* in terms of its treatment with people of a deprived region.

3   This VCD compiled by Nāser Saffāriān includes both the shorter version and the extended version of the film along with interviews with some film-makers and critics such as Bahrām Beyzā'i, Dāriush Merhju'i, Hushang Golmakāni and Kāveh Golestān.

4   Muhammad Tahāminezhād, *Sinemā-ye mostanad-e Irān* (Tehran, Iran, 1998): 42.

5   Barbara Scharres, *Ebrahim Golestan: Lion of Iranian Cinema*, Gene Siskel Film Center, 2007–2008, http://www.artic.edu/webspaces/siskelfilmcenter/2007/may/2a. html [accessed November 2008].

6   Heydari, *Forugh Farrokhzād va sinemā*: 325.

7   Heydari, *Forugh Farrokhzād va sinemā*: 56–9.

8   Heydari, *Forugh Farrokhzād va sinemā*: 58–9.

9   Heydari, *Forugh Farrokhzād va sinemā*: 32–5.

10   Heydari, *Forugh Farrokhzād va sinemā*: 64–5.

11   Heydari, *Forugh Farrokhzād va sinemā*: 32–5.

12   Tahāminezhād, *Sinemā-ye mostanad*: 42.

13   Heydari, *Forugh Farrokhzād va sinemā*: 41–4.

14   Hamid Naficy, 'Iranian Documentary', *Jump Cut: A Review of Contemporary Media*, 2005, http://www.ejumpcut.org/archive/onlinessays/JC26folder/IranDocy.html [accessed November 2008].

15   Heydari, *Forugh Farrokhzād va sinemā*: 46–7.

16   See the interviews on *The House is Black* VCD compiled by Nāser Saffāriān. In one interview, the Iranian film critic, Hushang Golmakāni, says, '. . . because she was a poet she was very sentimental, therefore she has let her heart take over her reasoning, she has put the images wherever she felt she needed to. [. . .] [The film] does not have a classical

structure; it does not fit into any of the cinematic classifications. It is an experimental piece; it is as if someone whose work is not filmmaking has made a film purely out of her sentimental feelings.' See also Heydari, *Forugh Farrokhzād va sinemā*: 294.

17 Farzaneh Milani, *Veils and Words: The Emerging Voices of Iranian Women Writers* (London and New York, 1992): 133.

18 Hamid Dabashi, *Close Up: Iranian Cinema, Past, Present and Future* (London, 2001): 222.

19 Mehrnaz Saeed-Vafa and Jonathan Rosenbaum, *Abbas Kiarostami* (Urbana, IL, 2003): 4.

20 Stella Bruzzi, *New Documentary: A Critical Introduction* (London and New York, 2000): 90, quoted from Jeremy Hicks, *Dziga Vertov: Defining Documentary Films* (London and New York, 2007).

21 V.I. Podovkin, 'Introduction to the German Edition', *Film Technique* (London, 1933).

22 Heydari, *Forugh Farrokhzād va sinemā*: 32–5.

23 V.I. Podovkin, 'Introduction to the German Edition'.

24 Heydari, *Forugh Farrokhzād va sinemā*: 59.

25 Heydari, *Forugh Farrokhzād va sinemā*: 197.

26 Hamid Naficy, 'Iranian Documentary', http://www.ejumpcut.org/archive/onlinessays/JC26folder/IranDocy.html [accessed November 2008].

27 Footage of Bernardo Bertolluci's interview with Forugh Farrokhzad in 1963 in Tehran. From the VCD entitled '*Owj-e mowj*' ('Summit of the Wave'), 2000/2004.

28 Dabashi, *Close Up*: 223.

29 Heydari, *Forugh Farrokhzād va sinemā*: 251.

30 '[M]ontage is not an idea composed of successive shots stuck together, but an idea that derives from the collision between two shots that are independent of one another.' Sergei Eisenstein, 'Montage' in Leo Braudy and Marshall Cohen (eds), *Film Theory and Criticism*, 6th ed. (New York, 2004): 26.

31 Robert Stam, *New Vocabularies in Film Semiotics* (New York, 1992): 71–3.

32 Raymond Durgnat, *Luis Buñuel, New Revised and Enlarged* (Berkeley, c1977): 58.

33 E. Rubinstein, 'Visit to a familiar planet: Buñuel among the Hurdanos', *Cinema Journal* 22.4, (Summer, 1983): 3.

34 Elisabeth H. Lyon, 'Luis Buñuel: The Process of Dissociation in Three Films', *Cinema Journal*, 13.1, (Autumn, 1973): 45–8.

35 William Rothman, *Documentary Film Classics*. (Cambridge, 1997): 27.

36 Rothman, *Documentary Film*: 28.

37 Rothman, *Documentary Film*: 28.

38 Naficy, 'Iranian Documentary', http://www.ejumpcut.org/archive/onlinessays/JC26-folder/IranDocy.html [accessed November 2008].

39 Durgnat, 'Luis Buñuel': 58.

40 Heydari, *Forugh Farrokhzād va sinemā*: 287. See Endnote 2.

41 Stam, *New* Vocabularies: 10.

42 Heydari, *Forugh Farrokhzād va sinemā*: 80.

43 Heydari, *Forugh Farrokhzād va sinemā*: 193.

44   Michael Hillmann, *A Lonely Woman: Forugh Farrokhzad and Her Poetry* (Boulder, 1987): 43–4.

45   Durgnat, 'Luis Buñuel': 59.

46   Rubinstein, 'Visit to a familiar planet': 3.

47   Heydari, *Forugh Farrokhzād va sinemā*: 76–7.

Chapter 11

1   Farrokhzād, Forugh and Amir Mas'ud trans. and eds, *Marg-e man ruzi . . . Majmu'eh'i az nemuneh-hā-ye āsār-e sho'arā-ye ālmāni dar nimeh-ye avval-e qarn-e bistom* (Tehran, 2000): 156.

2   Bāvandpur, Behnām ed., *Majmu'eh-ye āsār-e Forugh Farrokhzād* 2 vols (Essen, 2004).

3   These poets are: Hans Adler, Bruno Ammering, Ernst Blass, Franz Blei, Georg Britting, Hermann Broch, Albert Ehrenstein, Günter Eich, Georg Forestier, Alfred Grünewald (listed mistakenly as 'Adler Grünewald'), Ferdinand Hardekopf, Jakob Haringer, Georg Heym, Ossip Kalenter, Hedwig Lachmann, Else Lasker-Schüler, Hans Leifhelm, Josef Leitgeb, Horst Lange, Stefan Zweig, Arno Nadel, Rene Schickelé, Sigfried Freiberg, Wilhelm Klemm, Max Brod, Albrecht Schaeffer, and Oda Schäfer.

4   See Singer, Eric (ed.), *Spiegel des Unvergänglichen. Deutsche Lyrik seit 1910* (Munich, Germany, 1955).

5   The following poets are not included in the Persian translation: George Britting, Paul Celan, Franz Theodor Csokor, Theodor Däubler, Gerrit Engelke, Siegfried Freiberg, Richard Freidenthal, Jakob Hardinger, Walter Hasenclever, Albrecht Haushofer, Max Herrmann-Neisse, Ricada Huch, Hugo Jakobi, Erich Kästner, Wilhelm Klemm, Jakob Kneip, Theodor Kramer, Hedwig Lachmann, Horst Lange, Elisabeth Langgässer, Wilhelm Lehmann, Hans Leifhelm, Josef Leitgeb, Alfred Lichtenstein-Wilmersdorf, Oskar Loerke, Ernst Wilhelm Lotz, Walter Mehring, Arno Nadel, Otto Pick, Heinz Piontek, Eric Singer (sic!), Ernst Stadler, Ludwig Strauß, Urs Martin Strub, Georg Trakl, Berthold Viertel, Georg von der Vring, Konrad Weichberger, Konrad Weiß, Franz Werfel, Anton Wildgans, Viktor Wittner, Alfred Wolfenstein, Paul Zech, and Guido Zernatto.

6   Interestingly, a selection of Paul Celan's poetic works was translated from German into Persian by Forugh Farrokhzād's adopted son Hossein Mansouri, who moved to Munich in the mid 1970s with the help of Forugh's other late bother, Mehrdād. These translations were published in literary magazines in and outside Iran during the 1990s, i.e. long before the anthology was published in Tehran.

7   See Showkat, Hamid, *Negāhi az darun beh jonbesh-e chap-e Irān. Goftogu bā Kurosh Lāshā'i.* (Tehran, 2004): 19.

8   See Showkat, Hamid, *Negāhi az darun beh jonbesh-e chap-e Irān. Goftogu bā Mehdi Khānbābā Tehrāni* (Saarbrücken, 1987): 77, 89, 90, 313.

9   This information is based on interviews with Mehdi Khānbābā Tehrāni on 10 September 2007 and 18 September 2008. The narrator in this poem is certainly not

identical with the poet, i.e. I am not claiming Farrokhzād harbored any social-revolutionary, or even Maoist sympathies.

10   During the same period, there was a similar synchronization studio in Rome which specialized in dubbing mainly Italian Cine Citta productions and exporting them to Iran, where they were shown primarily (though not exclusively) at the Niagara movie theatre. During her visits to Rome, Farrokhzād also participated in these dubbing projects along with the opera singer, Hoseyn Sarshār, the pioneer of Iranian puppet theater, Nosrat Karimi, and Sohrāb Sepehri, who happened to be in Italy at that time.

11   During this time Khosrow Qashqā'i and several members of his clan lived in Munich. Khosrow Qashqā'i sponsored the publication of the National Front's clandestine journal *Bākhtar-e emruz* and hired the known Tudeh Party activist, Mohammad 'Āsemi for this task.

12   Singer *Spiegel des Unvergänglichen*: 141. See also Farrokhzād, *Marg-e man ruzi . . .*: 84.

13   Farrokhzād, *'Esyān* (Tehran, 1958): 127.

14   In 2002 a selection of Forugh Farrokhzād's personal letters to her husband Parviz Shāpur was edited and published by her son Kāmyār Shāpur together with the satirist 'Omrān Sālehi. In these private letters, the poet expressed great concern about the possibility that somebody other than Parviz might gain access to them. 50 years later, the publication of these letters turned Farrokhzād's premonition of, 'foreign eyes strolling across her lines' into reality. Shāpur, Kāmyār and 'Omrān Sālehi eds, *Avvalin tapesh-hā-ye 'āsheqāneh-ye qalb-am. Nāmeh-hā-ye Forugh Farrokhzād be hamsarash* (Tehran, Iran, 2002): 75–6.

15   Words and expressions like *tanāb-e rakht* ('clothes line'), *bādbādak* ('kite'), *goldān* ('vase'), *zanbil* ('basket'), *hall-e jadval* ('crossword puzzle'), *ganjeh* ('cupboard'), and *charkh-e khayyāti* ('sewing machine').

16   See Singer, *Spiegel des Unvergänglichen*: 60. In the Persian translation (Farrokhzād, *Marg-e man ruzi . . .*: 88) this text appears under the title *Pā'iz* ('Autumn').

17   'Ossip Kalenter' is the pen name of the poet and feuilleton journalist Johannes Burckhardt, who was born on 15 November 1900 into a wealthy merchant family in the city of Dresden and passed away in Zurich in 1976. In the early 1920s his name appeared for the first time in some of the most important newspapers of the Weimar Republic, such as the *Berliner Tageblatt* and the *Frankfurter Zeitung*. From 1924 he lived for a decade in Italy and then relocated to Prague after the takeover by the Nazis and the Italian fascists. During the four years he spent in Prague, he worked as an editor on the *Prager Tagblatt* together with Max Brod and Johannes Urzidil, eventually becoming a naturalized Czech citizen. In 1939 he escaped the Nazi occupation of Czechoslovakia and moved to Switzerland, never returning to Germany again until the end of his life. From 1945 onward he acted as secretary of the *Schutzverband deutscher Schriftsteller im Exil* ('The Association of German Writers in Exile') and later became president of the German exile PEN. He left behind a collection of meticulously organized documents about his efforts to aid exiled German speaking writers who were scattered across the

globe. These documents include correspondence with authors such as Oskar Maria Graf, Hermann Broch, and Alfred Kerr, as well as personal diary detailing his life and work in exile. During his high school years in Dresden, he was the only student who chose to study Russian, he subsequently chose a Russian pen name. Because his pen name also sounded Jewish, his writings were banned in Germany throughout the Nazi era.

18   The word Kalenter is etymologically related to the Persian word *qalandar* (a title given to Sufi mystics, especially in South Asia) which the poet had interpreted and translated for himself to mean 'restless soul'. The Persian connection in Kalenter's pen name was of course a coincidence, unknown to both Forugh and Amir. When Johannes Burckhardt chose the pen name Kalenter he wanted to express his own ambition to be intellectually restless, curious, and open minded. In fact he became one of the great European cosmopolites of the 20th century.

Chapter 12

1   I have discussed these issues in detail in M. R. Ghanoonparvar, *Translating the Garden* (Austin 2002).

2   The number of hits generated when I googled the names of these poets on 4 April 2008 were as follows:

Nimā Yushij, 7,680; Ahmad Shāmlu, 21,300; Mehdi Akhavān-Sāles, 6,980; Nāder Nāderpur, 2,790; Sohrāb Sepehri, 35,800; and Forugh Farrokhzād, 39,500. In contrast, when the name Simin Behbahāni was googled, despite her recent popularity and poetry-reading tours abroad in recent years, in addition to the conferences in honor of her work and the fact that she is the only major poet of her generation who is still alive, a mere 8,970 items were found.

3   These translations, respectively, are [A] Forugh Farrokhzād and Karim Emāmi, as 'Another Birth', *Kayhan International* (July 1964); [B] Girdhani Tikku, as 'Another Birth', *Studia Islamica* 26 (1967):165–6; [C] Majid Tehranian, as 'Rebirth', *Iranian Studies* (1968):68–75; [D] Ahmad Karimi-Hakkak, as 'Another Birth', *An Anthology of Modern Persian Poetry* (Boulder, 1978): 150–2; [E] Julie S. Meisami, as 'Another Birth', in Leo Hamalian and John D. Yohannan (eds), *New Writings from the Middle East* (New York, 1978): 383–5; [F] Hasan Javadi and Susan Sallee trans., as 'Another Birth', in *Another Birth: Selected Poems of Forugh Farrokhzad* (Emeryville, CA, 1981): 62–4; [G] Jascha Kessler and Amin Banani trans., as 'Born Again', in *Bride of Acacias: Selected Poems of Forugh Farrokhzad* (Delmar, NY, 1982): 90–92; [H] David Martin trans., as 'A Rebirth', in *A Rebirth: Poems by Foroogh Farrokhzaad* (Costa Mesa, CA, 1985): 97–102.

4   I have attempted to copy the translations accurately as they have been published, even in terms of their presentation on the page.

5   For my interpretation of the poem, see M. R. Ghanoonparvar, 'Another Reading of "Another Birth"', in Michael C. Hillmann (ed.), *Forugh Farrokhzad a Quarter-Century Later*, (*Literature East and West*, 1987) 24: 79–89.

6   Unfortunately, in most published versions of the Persian, the word *shekoftan-hā* is misspelled as the nonexistent *shegoftan-hā* .

7   See Ghanoonparvar, 'Another Reading of "Another Birth"'.

8   Poetic language is usually described by critics as a language that sometimes conforms to and sometimes violates conventional language. See, for example: Jonathan Culler, *Structuralist Poetics* (Ithaca, NY, 1975): 113–30.

9   Karim Emāmi reports on the translation of the poem and his conversations with Farrokhzād in 'The Poet's Reading of "Another Birth"', in Michael C. Hillmann (ed.), *Forugh Farrokhzad a Quarter-Century Later* (Literature East and West, 1987) 24:73–7. The translation and Emāmi's explanations first appeared in (*Kayhan International*, July 1964).

Chapter 13

1   Depending on which countries these writers reside in or the circumstances of their immigration or biography, the politics of their writing and of their writerly objectives differ. For those writers who are born and raised in Iran, objectives and interests are more immediately motivated by the losses associated with leaving at the time of the Revolution or shortly thereafter. For writers who are half-Iranian (Iranian-American, for example), relationships to Iran and Iranian culture might be more attenuated by the state of relations between their home country and Iran.

2   Persis Karim and Nasrin Rahimieh, 'Writing Iranian Americans into the American Literature Canon', *MELUS: Multi-Ethnic Literatures of the United States*, 33 (2008): 7.

3   Hamid Naficy, *The Making of Exile Cultures: Iranian Television in Los Angeles.* (Minneapolis, MN, 1993): 14.

4   See Ahmad Karimi-Hakkak, *Recasting Persian Poetry: Scenarios of Poetic Modernity in Iran* (Salt Lake City, UT, 1995).

5   Michael C. Hillmann, *A Lonely Woman: Forugh Farrokhzad and Her Poetry* (Washington, D.C., 1987): 21.

6   Sholeh Wolpé, *Rooftops of Tehran* (Los Angeles, 2008): xx.

7   Naficy, *The Making of Exile Cultures*: 129.

8   Naficy, *The Making of Exile Cultures*: 129–130.

9   Hamid Dabashi, *Iran: A People Interrupted* (New York, 2007): 12–13.

10   Dabashi, *Iran: A People Interrupted*: 13.

11   Dabashi, *Iran: A People Interrupted*: 13.

12   Fatemeh Keshavarz, *Jasmine and Stars:Reading More than Lolita in Tehran* (Chapel Hill, NC, 2007): 3.

13   Keshavarz, *Jasmine and Stars*: 25.

14   Azar Nafisi, *Things I've Been Silent About* (New York, 2008): 82.

15   Nafisi, *Things I've Been Silent About*: 96.

16   Nafisi, *Things I've Been Silent About*: 168–9.

17   Nafisi, *Things I've Been Silent About*: 168.

18   While most of my evidence for the role of translation is anecdotal (i.e. people in the English-speaking world have heard of Farrokhzād and know something of her importance to Iranian letters), it is interesting to note how many websites or web entries are now dedicated to Farrokhzād and her poetry. In addition, there are MySpace and Facebook pages dedicated to her life and work. These websites include photographs, biographical information, and translations of her poetry.

19   Roger Sedarat, *Dear Regime: Letters to the Islamic Republic* (Athens, OH, 2007): 63.

20   Keshavarz, *Jasmine and Stars*: 2–3.

21   Interview with Roger Sedarat via email, 12 June 2008.

22   Wolpé, *Rooftops of Tehran*: 100.

23   See Wolpé's translations in *Sin: Selected Poetry of Forugh Farrokhzad* (Fayetteville, NC, 2007).

24   Shirin Neshat, *Shirin Neshat*. (Milan, 2001): 57.

25   For both the original Persian and English translation of this poem, see Hillmann *A Lonely Woman*: 119–122. See also Wolpé's translation ('I Pity the Garden') in *Sin*: 100–103.

26   The translation of this poem is taken from Neshat, *Shirin Neshat*: 56. For more on the work of Shirin Neshat, see Farzaneh Milani's introduction, 'The Visual Poetry of Shirin Neshat' in the same volume.

27   Hillmann, *A Lonely Woman*: 119.

28   Milani, 'The Visual Poetry of Shirin Neshat': 7.

29   Milani, 'The Visual Poetry of Shirin Neshat': 7.

30   Jasmin Darznik, 'Forough Farrokhzad in the Art and Literature of the Iranian Diaspora', unpublished paper presented at the Middle East Studies Association Annual Meeting, Montreal, Canada, 24 November 2007.

31   Farzaneh Milani, *Veils and Words: The Emerging Voices of Iranian Women Writers* (Syracuse, NY, 1992): 59.

32   Maryam Habibian. 'Forugh's reflecting pool: The life and work of Forugh Farrokhzad', in *Shattering the Stereotypes: Muslim Women Speak Out*, Fawzia Afzal-'Khan ed. (New York, 2005): 254.

33   Habibian, 'Forugh's reflecting pool' 255.

34   For more by critics who explore the feminist sensibility in Farrokhzād's work see, Hillmann, *A Lonely Woman*; Milani, *Veils and Words*, and Jasmin Darznik 'The poetry, life and legacy of Forugh Farrokhzad', in *Women's Review of Books*. November/ December 2006, 17–19.

35   Désirée Aphrodite Navab, 'Tales left untold', in Persis M. Karim (ed.), *Let Me Tell You Where I've Been: New Writing by Women of the Iranian Diaspora* (Fayetteville, 2006): 282–3.

36   Although Laleh Khalili left Iran as an adolescent and studied in the USA for nearly two decades, she has lived a number of places. She currently resides in London, and teaches at SOAS. Her early poetry embodies this attention to the politics of US-Iranian relations as well as the impact of her immigration at a critical age to the USA.

37 Laleh Khalili, 'In exile' in Persis M. Karim and M. M. Khorrami (eds.), *A World Between: Poems, Short Stories and Essays by Iranian-Americans* (New York: 1999): 282–3.

38 In addition to *The House Is Black* (a film Farrokhzād made about a leper colony in Iran, now widely available in Europe and the USA), one can also purchase *The Mirror of the Soul: The Forugh Farrokhzad Trilogy*, a three-part documentary of her life and work that was originally filmed and produced in Iran by director Nāser Saffāriān. Other mainstream publications that have recently featured translations or essays about Farrokhzād include Darznik, 'Forugh Farrokhzad: Her poetry, life and legacy', and Meetra A. Sofia, 'Forugh Farrokhzad: Notes and translation from the Farsi', *The American Poetry Review*, January/February 2006. The website in English that has the most extensive biographical information, audio and visual links, and translations of her poems is http://www.forughfarrokhzad.org.

Chapter 14

1 I am grateful to Seyedeh Taebi for meticulous and thoughtful translation help with this chapter; Julie Rivkin and Margaret Homans for helping me think through an early draft; Connecticut College colleagues in English and Global Islamic Studies for valuable workshop insights; Hanna Ostby, whose vivid invocation of the phrase 'heavy baggage' survives in this piece; and Farzaneh Milani and Jasmin Darznik, whose love for Forugh's work has indelibly shaped my own.

2 Farzaneh Milani, *Veils and Words: The Emerging Voices of Iranian Women Writers* (Syracuse, 1992); Farzaneh Milani, *Words, not Swords: Iranian Women Writers and the Freedom of Movement* (Syracuse, 2011).

3 Forugh Farrokhzād, *Dar diyāri digar: khāterāt-e safar-e Orupa / 1335* , in Behrooz Jalali (ed.), *Jāvadāneh zistan, dar ofogh māndan: nāmeh-hā, mosāhebeh-hā, maghālat, va khāterāt-e Forugh* (Tehran, 1996): 68.

4 All English translations of quotations from the travelogue are by Seyedeh Taebi and me, revised and reworked from Farzaneh Milani and Bahiyyih Nakhjavani's online translation: Forugh Farrokhzād, 'Another Time, Another Place: Memories of a Trip to Europe.' *Accessing Muslim Lives*. https://accessingmuslimlives.org/uncategorized/another-time-another-place-memories-of-a-trip-to-europe/, accessed 12 November 2019.

5 Farrokhzād, *Dar diyāri digar*, 68.

6 Vita Sackville-West, *Passenger to Teheran* (New York, 2007): 26.

7 Thomas Wide, 'Around the World in Twenty-Nine Days: The Travels, Translations, and Temptations of an Afghan Dragoman,' in Roberta Micallef and Sunil Sharma (eds.), *On the Wonders of Land and Sea: Persianate Travel Writing* (Boston, 2013): 108.

8 Sunil Sharma, 'Delight and Disgust: Gendered Encounters in the Travelogues of the Fyzee Sisters,' in Roberta Micallef and Sunil Sharma (eds.), *On the Wonders of Land and Sea: Persianate Travel Writing* (Boston, 2013): 115.

9   Roberta Micallef and Sunil Sharma, 'Introduction,' in Roberta Micallef and Sunil Sharma (eds.), *On the Wonders of Land and Sea: Persianate Travel Writing* (Boston, 2013): 9.

10 Sharma, 114.

11 Naghmeh Sohrabi, *Taken for Wonder: Nineteenth-Century Travel Accounts from Iran to Europe* (Oxford, 2012: 5.

12 Ibid, 8.

13 Louise Marlow, 'Foreword,' in Roberta Micallef and Sunil Sharma (eds.), *On the Wonders of Land and Sea: Persianate Travel Writing* (Boston, 2013): vii.

14 Mana Kia, 'Limning the Land: Social Encounters and Historical Meaning in Early Nineteenth-Century Travelogues between Iran,' in Roberta Micallef and Sunil Sharma (eds.), *On the Wonders of Land and Sea: Persianate Travel Writing* (Boston, 2013): 64.

15 Wide, 'Around the World', 90.

16 Sohrabi, *Taken for Wonder*, 10.

17 Jasmin Khosravie, 'Iranian Women on the Road: The Case of Sadīqe Doulatābādī in Europe, 1923–27,' in Bekim Agai, Olcay Akyildiz, and Caspar Hillebrand (eds.), *Venturing Beyond Borders: Reflections on Genre, Function and Boundaries in Middle Eastern Travel Writing* (Würzburg, 2013): 134.

18 Ibid, 137.

19 While *zabān* literally means 'tongue' or 'language,' Khosravie translates it in this context as 'voice', 'since Doulatābādī explicitly excluded any male contributions from her publication in order to make women's voices be heard'.

20 Camron Michael Amin, *The Making of the Modern Iranian Woman: Gender, State Policy, and Popular Culture, 1865–1946* (Gainesville, 2002).

21 Khosravie, 'Iranian Women', 141.

22 Ibid, 146.

23 Farrokhzād, *Dar diyāri digar*, 67.

24 Sohrabi, *Taken for Wonder*, 11.

25 Bruce Robbins, 'Introduction Part I: Actually Existing Cosmopolitanism,' in Pheng Cheah and Bruce Robbins (eds.), *Cosmopolitics: Thinking and Feeling Beyond the Nation* (Minneapolis, 1998): 4 (emphasis mine).

26 Michael C. Hillman, *A Lonely Woman: Forugh Farrokzhad and Her Poetry* (Washington, 1987).

27 Farrokhzād, 'Another Time, Another Place,' 66.

28 All English translations of quotations from Farrokzhād's poems are by Seyedeh Taebi and me, revised and reworked from: Forugh Farrokhzād, Hasan Javadi and Susan Sallée (trans.), *Another Birth and Other Poems* (Washington, 2010). These lines are from the poem 'Bāzgasht' ('return'), 18–23.

29 Farrokhzād, *Dar diyāri digar*, 67.

30 Ibid, 67.

31 Ibid, 72.

32 Ibid, 73.

33   Ibid, 67.
34   Ibid, 71 (here, Farrokhzād's original specifies *dasthā-ye mādarān beh* ('mothers' hands on') a *gāhavāreh-ye kudakān*' ('babies' cradle').
35   Micallef and Sharma, 'Introduction', 3.
36   Wide, 'Around the World', 105.
37   Farrokhzād, *Dar diyāri digar*, 76.
38   Ibid, 77.
39   Ibid, 78.
40   Ibid, 80–81.
41   Ibid, 73, 107, 99, 105, 105. Khosravie details how Dowlatābādi was 'detained … harassed, arrested, and separated from her doctor despite her visibly bad condition' ('Iranian Women', 142) at the Iraqi border. The arbitrary and mocking tone of the military officers she encounters echoes Farrokhzād's distaste for policemen in Italy.
42   Farrokhzād, *Dar diyāri digar*, 99.
43   Persian idiom for suddenly changing the subject.
44   Farrokhzād, *Dar diyāri digar*, 102.
45   Sohrabi, *Taken for Wonder*, 109.
46   Farrokhzād, *Dar diyāri digar*, 67.
47   Ibid, 102 (emphasis mine in both Persian and English quotations).
48   Rosi Braidotti, *Nomadic Subjects: Embodiment and Sexual Difference in Contemporary Feminist Theory* (New York, 1994): 25.
49   Nasrin Rahimieh, *Missing Persians: Discovering Voices in Iranian Cultural History* (Syracuse, 2001): 10.
50   Farrokhzād, *Dar diyāri digar*, 86.
51   Ibid, 86.
52   Ibid, 104.
53   Sohrabi, *Taken for Wonder*, 117.
54   Farrokhzād, *Dar diyāri digar*, 104.
55   Khosravie, 143. Khosravie argues that Dowlatābādi 'was mainly preoccupied with "othering" fellow Iranians abroad as this was the intended focus of her narrative,' using the travelogue to document the harassment she experienced and critique the misrepresentations of Iranians in Europe. Faced with a group of Englishwomen who assumed Iranian women were uneducated and oppressed, at one point, she 'elaborated in full on Iranian women's progress, modern schools, and other reforms which had a positive impact on the conditions of female life in Iran' with statements such as '"The history of Iran shows that women are capable and powerful"' (147–148).
56   Farrokhzād, *Dar diyāri digar*, 112.
57   Ibid, 100–101.
58   Khosravie, 'Iranian Women', 151.
59   Farrokhzād, *Dar diyāri digar*, 110-111.
60   Rahimieh, *Missing Persians*, 17.

61   Hans-Georg Gadamer, *Truth and Method* (London, 2004): 302–3.

62   Ibid, 306.

63   Sohrabi, *Taken for Wonder*, 114.

64   Jan Assmann, 'Form as Mnemonic Device: Cultural Texts and Cultural Memory,' in Richard A. Horsley, Jonathan A. Draper, John Miles Foley (eds.), *Performing the Gospel. Orality, Memory, and Mark. Essays dedicated to Werner Kelber* (Minneapolis, 2006): 69 (emphasis mine).

65   Farrokhzād, *Dar diyāri digar*, 113.

66   Ibid, 113.

67   Fawzia Fuad's daughter Shahnaz, however, stayed in Iran and was very much part of the Shah's family. This may be another point on which Farrokhzad felt solidarity with Fuad, since obtaining a divorce recognized by first Egyptian, then Iranian authorities meant leaving her four-year-old daughter behind in Iran. Princess Shahnaz of Iran paid tribute to her estranged mother by naming her only daughter Fawzia.

68   Farrokhzād, *Dar diyāri digar*, 114.

69   Farrokhzād, 'Ba'd-hā' ('afterwards'), in Farrokhzād, Javadi and Sallée (trans.): 25–28.

Chapter 15

1   Zuzanna Olszewska, 'A Hidden Discourse: Afghanistan's Women Poets' in Jennifer Heath and Ashraf Zahedi, eds. *Land of the Unconquerable: The Lives of Contemporary Afghan Women* (Berkeley, 2011), 342.

2   Maga Rahmani, in her pioneering work on women poets, *Pardeneshinān-e sokhan-guy* (Kabul, 1949), mentions how women poets were 'hidden [covered] to the extent that their names and writings were not permitted to be uncovered. A look at their poetic pseudonyms show how they referred to this fact: Hejabi, Makhfi, Mastureh, Mahjub, Nehani, etc. These pseudonyms indicate how those who used them were isolated from [active] social life. Throughout history, women have been oppressed by men and deprived of all their individual and social rights . . . The dominant culture would look upon women's education as both a frivolous and a dangerous matter and insisted that the sole occupation of a women should be to serve her husband and raise children.' Quoted in *She'r-e zanān-e Afghanistan*, selected by Mas'ud Mirshahi (Paris, 2000), 11–12.

3   In her erudite study of the poetry of Afghan refugees in Iran, the anthropologist Zuzanna Olszewska, deals thoroughly with the poetry of Afghan women. Zuzanna Olszewska, *The Pearl of Dari: Poetry and Personhood among Young Afghans in Iran* (Bloomington, 2015).

4   In addition to Laila Sarahat Rowshani, whose poetry is the subject of the present essay, some other notable women poets in Afghanistan who were influenced by Forugh Farrokhzad are: Homaira Neghat Dastgirzadah (*Āftāb-e āvāreh,* Herat, 2011), Khaleda Forugh (*Sarnevesht-e dast-hā-ye fasl-e fānus,* Peshawar, 2000), Zahra Hossainzadah (*Nāmeh'i az lāleh-ye kuhi,* Tehran, 2003), Mahbubah Ebrahimi (*Bād-hā khvāharān-e man-and,* Tehran, 2007), Fariba Haidary (*Va āvāz-hā-ye banafsh-e bi-qānun,* Herat,

2007), Somaya Ramesh (*Yek fasl-e khvāb-e anār*, 2013), and Elaha Sahel (*Khoshbakhti rang-e zardi dārad*, 2010), among others. For a collection of recent poetry, specifically by women of Herat (Afghanistan), see *Load Poems Like Guns*, trans. and intro. Farzana Marie (Duluth, 2015).

5   Laila Sarahat Rowshani was born in 1958 in Charikar, in Parwan province, but was raised in Kabul. After graduating from Malalai High School, she enrolled in the Faculty of Letters, Kabul University, from which she graduated in 1980. After teaching Persian at a Kabul high school for a number of years, she assumed the editorship of a women's magazine. In 1996, with the Taliban take-over of Kabul, Laila left Afghanistan and, after spending a few years in Pakistan as a refugee, she migrated to the Netherlands, where she published the periodical *Havvā dar tab'id* ('Eve in exile'). She passed away in Leiden in July 2004. Her collections of poetry include *Tolu'-e sabz* (Kabul, 1986), *Tadāvom-e faryād* (Kabul, 1991), *Az sang-hā va āyineh-hā* (Peshawar, 1997), and *Ru-ye taqvim-e tamām-e sāl* (Kabul, 2004).

6   For Nima Yushij's reception in the New Poetry movement in Afghanistan, see Wasef Bakhtari, 'Diruz, emruz, va fardā-ye she'r-e Afghanistan,' *Majalleh-e She'r* 14:2 (1994), 70-82. See also Wasef Bakhtari, 'Chand sokhan dar bāreh-ye seresht-e she'r va farāz u forud-e she'r-e mo'āser,' *Hāshiyeh-hā-ye sargardān*, ed. Naser Hotaki (Kabul, 2016), 251–272.

7   Dominic Parviz Brookshaw has offered a reading of one of Forugh Farrokhzad's posthumously published poems ('Delam barā-ye bāghcheh mi-suzad') that effectively shows how political, yet not strictly ideological, her poetry was. See 'Places of Confinement, Liberation, and Decay: The Home and the Garden in the Poetry of Forugh Farrokhzad,' in Dominic Parviz Brookshaw and Nasrin Rahimieh, eds. *Forugh Farrkhzad, Poet of Modern Iran: Iconic Woman and Feminine Pioneer of New Persian Poetry* (London, 2010), 48-51. See also 'Abd al-Ali Dastgheyb, *Pari-ye kuchak-e daryā: naqd va tahlil-e she'r-e Forugh Farrokhzad* (Tehran, 2006).

8   For an overview of various aspects of Afghanistan's recent tumultuous history, see M. Nazif Shahrani, ed., *Modern Afghanistan: The Impact of 40 Years of War* (Bloomington, 2018). See also Amin Saikal, *Modern Afghanistan: A History of Struggle and Survival* (London, 2004).

9   Quoted from Laila Sarahat Rowshani, 'Va shab, do-bāreh shab,' *Kabulnath*, Vol. 9, No. 198 (2013). All translations from the original Persian mine (W.A.).

10   Laila Sarahat Rowshani, 'Yegāneh-ye yegāneh,' *Az sang-hā va āyineh-hā* (Peshawar, 1997), 11.

11   Laila Sarahat Rowshani, 'Barā-ye dast-hā-ye to,' *Tolu'-e sabz* (Kabul, 1986), 57–58.

12   'Āyati barā-ye Jāvedānegi,' *Az sang-hā*, 28.

13   'Ramz-e pā'iz,' *Tolu'-e sabz*, 26–27.

14   'Chelcheleh,' *Simfuni-i bād-hā* (Kabul, 2012), 19.

15   'Nowheh,' *Az sang-hā*, 68.

16   '"Azā-ye sarv," *Az sang-hā*, 72.

17   See, for instance, the following poem where Laila mourns the deaths of her loved ones – Angela, Farid, and Baran: 'Gom-kardeh-hā,' *Az sang-hā*, 41–42.

18   'Sabr-e shekast-khordeh,' *Az sang-hā*, 56–57.
19   'Āyineh-hā-ye Kabul,' *Ru-ye taqvim-e tamām-e sāl*, 34.
20   'Khorshid rā biyāvar,' *Ru-ye taqvim*, 8.
21   'Basit-e bi-sedā'i,' *Ru-ye taqvim*, 5–6.
22   'Mordāb,' *Ru-ye taqvim*, 37.

Selected Bibliography

Forugh Farrokhzād

Poetry: (there are numerous editions of Forugh Farrokhzād's poetry. These are some of the most commonly used):

Asir [Captive] (Tehran, 1955).
Divār [The Wall] (Tehran, 1956).
'Esyān [Rebellion] (Tehran, 1958).
Tavallodi digar [Another Birth] (Tehran, 1964).
Imān biāvarim beh āghāz-e fasl-e sard [Let Us Believe in the Start of the Cold Season] (Tehran, 1974).
Bargozideh-ye ash'ār-e Forugh Farrokhzād (Tehran, 1975).
Divan-e ash'ār-e Forugh Farrokhzād, Behruz Jalāli ed. (Tehran, 1995).
Majmu'eh-ye āsār-e Forugh Farrokhzād, Behnām Bāvandpur ed., 2 vols. (Essen, 2002).

Film:

Khāneh siyāh ast: noskheh-ye asli. (2002). VCD, compiled by Nāser Saffāriān, Tehran.

Short stories/prose works:

Behruz Jalāli. (ed.) (1996). *Jāvdāneh zistan, dar owj māndan*, Tehran.
Behruz Jalāli. (ed.) (1997). *Dar ghorubi abadi: majmu'eh-ye āsār-e mansur-e Forugh Farrokhzād*, Tehran.

Letters:

Shāpur, Kāmyār and Sālehi, 'Omrān. (eds). (2003). *Avvalin tapesh-hā-ye 'āsheqāneh-ye qalb-am: nāmeh-hā-ye Forugh Farrokhzād beh hamsar-ash Parviz Shāpur*, Tehran.

Interviews:

Gorgin, Iraj. (1964). *Chahār mosāhebeh bā Farrokhzād*, Tehran.
Tikku, Girdhari with Alireza Anushirvani. (2004). *A Conversation with Modern Persian Poets*, Costa Mesa, CA.
Bernardo Bertolluci's interview with Farrokhzād in Tehran in 1963. (2004). In *Owj-e mowj* ('Summit of the Wave'), VCD, compiled by Nāser Saffāriān, Tehran.
Nāser Saffāriān (director). *The Mirror of the Soul: The Forugh Farrokhzad Trilogy* (2007). DVD. Facets.

Literary biographies:

Ja'fari, Maryam. (2006). *Shahr-āshub: bar asās-e zendegi-ye Forugh Farrokhzād*. Tehran.
Milani, Farzaneh. (2016). *Forugh Farrokhzād: zendegi-nāmeh-ye adabi*. Toronto.

Translations of Farrokhzād's Poetry:

Emāmi, Karim and Farrokhzād, Forugh. (trans.) (July 1964). 'Another Birth,' in *Kayhan International*.
Gray, Elizabeth T. (trans.) (2022). *Let Us Believe in the Beginning of the Cold Season: selected poems*. New York, NY.
Javadi, Hasan and Sallee, Susan. (trans.) (1981). *Another Birth: Selected Poems of Forugh Farrokhzad*, Emeryville, CA.
Karimi-Hakkak, Ahmad. (trans.) (1997). *Remembering the Flight: Twenty Poems by Forugh Farrokhzād: A Parallel Text in English and Persian*, Vancouver.
Kessler, Jascha with Banani, Amin. (trans.) (1985) *Bride of Acacias, Selected Poems of Forugh Farrokhzad*, Delmar, CA.
Martin, David. (trans.) (1985). *A Rebirth: Poems by Foroogh Farrokhzaad*. Costa Mesa, CA.
Wolpé, Sholeh. (trans.) (2007). *Sin: Selected Poems of Forugh Farrokhzad*. Fayetteville, NC.

Secondary literature:

'Ābedi, Kāmyār. (1998). *Tanhā-tar az yek barg: zendegi va she'r-e Forugh Farrokhzād*, Tehran.
Adibsereshki, Narges and Salehpour, Yeganeh. 'Disability and Iranian culture', http://www.ee.umanitoba.ca/□kinsner/sds2001/proceed/pdocs/htms/28.HTM. [accessed January 2009].

Āl-e Ahmad, Jalāl. (1982). *Gharbzadegi (Weststruckness)*, trans. John Green and Ahmad Alizdeh, Lexington, KY.

Alishan, Leonardo P. (1987). 'Forugh Farrokhzād and the forsaken earth', in *Forugh Farrokhzād: A Quarter Century Later*, (ed.) Michael C. Hillmann, Austin, TX.

Amin, Camron Michael. (2002). *The Making of the Modern Iranian Woman: Gender, State Policy, and Popular Culture, 1865–1946*. Gainesville, FL.

Assmann, Jan. (2006). 'Form as Mnemonic Device: Cultural Texts and Cultural Memory,' in Richard A. Horsley, Jonathan A. Draper, John Miles Foley (eds.), *Performing the Gospel. Orality, Memory, and Mark. Essays dedicated to Werner Kelber*. Minneapolis, MN.

Āzād, M. (ed.). (1998). *Zendegi va she'r-e Forugh Farrokhzād*, Tehran.

Bakhtari, Wasef. (1994). 'Diruz, emruz, va fardā-ye she'r-e Afghanistan,' *Majalleh-e She'r* 14, 2: 70–82.

Bakhtari, Wasef. (2016). 'Chand sokhan dar bāreh-ye seresht-e she'r va farāz u forud-e she'r-e mo'āser,' in Naser Hotaki (ed.), *Hāshiyeh-hā-ye sargardān*. Kabul.

Banani, Amin. (1982). 'Introduction', in *Bride of Acacias: Selected Poems of Forugh Farrokhzād*, trans. Jascha Kessler with Amin Banani, Delmar, CA.

Behbahani, Simin. (1999). *A Cup of Sin: Selected Poems*, trans. Farzaneh Milani and Kaveh Safa, Syracuse, NY.

Braidotti, Rosi. (1994). *Nomadic Subjects: Embodiment and Sexual Difference in Contemporary Feminist Theory*. New York, NY.

Braudy, Leo and Cohen, Marshall. (eds). (2004). *Film Theory and Criticism*, 6th edition, New York.

Brookshaw, Dominic Parviz. (2003). 'Palaces, pavilions, and pleasure-gardens: The context and setting of the medieval *Majlis*', *Middle Eastern Literatures*, 6.2.

Bruzzi, Stella. (2000). *New Documentary: A Critical Introduction*, London and New York.

Chehabi, H.E. (2003). 'The banning of the veil and its consequences', in Stephanie Cronin (ed.), *The Making of Modern Iran: State and Society under Riza Shah, 1921–1941,* London.

Cixous, Hélène. (1981). 'The laugh of the Medusa', in *New French Feminisms: An Anthology*, Elaine Marks and Isabelle de Courtivron (eds), Sussex.

Cixous, Hélène and Clément, Catherine. (1991). *The Newly Born Woman*, trans. Betsy Wing, Minneapolis.

Clinton, Jerome W. (1972). *The Divan of Manūchihrī Dāmghānī: A Critical Study*, Minneapolis.

Cohan, Steven and Shires, Linda. (1988). *Telling Stories: A Theoretical Analysis of Narrative Fiction*, New York.

Culler, Jonathan. (1975). *Structuralist Poetics*, Ithaca, NY.

Cummings, Doug. http://filmjourney.weblogger.com/2005/02/13/the-house-is-black/#more-529. [accessed January 2009]

Dabashi, Hamid. (1987). 'Forugh Farrokhzād and formative forces in Iranian culture', in *Forugh Farrokhzād: A Quarter Centuiry Later*, (ed.) Michael C. Hillmann, Austin, TX.

Dabashi, Hamid. (2001). *Close Up: Iranian Cinema, Past, Present and Future*, London.

Dabashi, Hamid. (2007). *Masters and Masterpieces of Iranian Cinema*, Washington DC.

Dabashi, Hamid. (2007). *Iran: A People Interrupted*, New York.

Darrudi, Irān. (1998). *Dar fāseleh-ye do noqteh*, Tehran.

Darznik, Jasmin. (November/December 2006). 'The Poetry, life and legacy of Forugh Farrokhzad', *Women's Review of Books*.

Dastgheyb, 'Abd al-Ali (2006). *Pari-ye kuchak-e daryā: Naqd va tahlil-e she'r-e Forugh Farrokhzad*. Tehran.

Dastgirzadah, Homaira Neghat. (2011). *Āftāb-e āvāreh*. Herat.

Davaran, Ardavan. (1981). '"The Conquest of the Garden": A significant instance of the poetic development of Forugh Farrokhzad,' in *Another Birth: Selected Poems of Forugh Farrokhzad*, trans. Hasan Javadi and Susan Sallee, Emeryville, CA.

Durgnat, Raymond. (ed.). (c 1977). *Luis Buñuel: New Revised and Enlarged*, Berkeley, CA.

Ebrahimi, Mahbuba. (2007) *Bād-hā khvāharān-e man-and*. Tehran.

Eisenstein, Sergei. (2004). 'From film form', in *Film Theory and Criticism*, 6th edition, Leo Braudy and Marshall Cohen (eds.), New York.

Emami, Karim. (1987). 'The poet's reading of "Another Birth"', in Michael C. Hillmann (ed.), *Forugh Farrokhzad: A Quarter-Century Later, Literature East and West* 24.

Esmā'ili, Amir and Sedārat, Abo'l-qāsem. (1968). *Jāvdāneh Forugh*, Tehran.

Farrokhzād, Forugh and Farrokhzād, Amir Mas'ud. (trans. and eds.). (2000). *Marg-e man ruzi: majmu'eh'i az nemuneh-hā-ye āsār-e sho'arā-ye ālmāni dar nimeh-ye avval-e qarn-e bistom*, Tehran.

Farrokhzād, Purān. (ed.). (2002). *Dar-bāreh-ye Forugh Farrokhzād*, Tehran.

Fischer, Michael M. J. (2004). *Mute Dreams, Blind Owls, and Dispersed Knowledges: Persian Poesis in the Transnational Circuitry*, Durham, NC.

Forugh, Khaleda. (2000). *Sarnevesht-e dast-hā-ye fasl-e fānus*. Peshawar.

Gadamer, Hans-Georg. (2004). *Truth and Method*. London.

Garlick, Barbara. (ed.). (2002). *Tradition and the Poetics of Self in Nineteenth-Century Women's Poetry*, Amsterdam and New York.

Ghanoonparvar, M. R. (1984). *Prophets of Doom: Literature as a Socio-Political Phenomenon in Modern Iran*, Lanham, MD.

Ghanoonparvar, M. R. (2002). *Translating the Garden*, Austin, TX.

Habibian, Maryam. (2005). 'Forugh's reflecting pool: The life and work of Forugh. Farrokhzad', in *Shattering the Stereotypes: Muslim Women Speak Out* (ed.) Fawzia Afzal-Khan, New York.

Hā'eri, Seyyed-Hādi. (n.d.). *Zibā-tarin ash'ār-e Forugh Farrokhzād*, Tehran.

Hāfez, (1999). *Divān*, Qāsem Ghani and Mohammad Qazvini eds, Tehran.

Hajibashi, Zjaleh. (1987). 'Redefining "Sin"', in Michael C. Hillmann (ed.), *Forugh Farrokhzad, A Quarter Century Later, Literature East and West* 24.

Haidary, Fariba. (2007). *Va āvāz-hā-ye banafsh-e bi-qānun*. Herat.

Hamalian, Leo and Yohannan, John D. (eds). (1978). *New Writings from the Middle East*, New York.

Harrington, John. (1977). *Film and/as Literature*, Englewood Cliffs, San Francisco, NJ: Prentice Hall.

Heller, Eric. (1974). *Kafka*, London.

Heydari, Gholām. (ed.). (1998). *Forugh Farrokhzād va Sinemā*, Tehran.

Hicks, Jeremy. (2007). *Dziga Vertov: Defining Documentary Films*, London and New York.

Hillmann, Michael C. (1979). 'Sexuality in the verse of Forugh Farrokhzad and the structuralist view', *Edebiyat* 3.ii.

Hillmann, Michael C. (1987). (ed.), *Forugh Farrokhzad, A Quarter Century later*, *Literature East and West* 24.

Hillmann, Michael C. (1987). 'Forugh Farrokhzad: A chronology', in *Forugh Farrokhzad: A Quarter Century Later* (ed.) Michael C. Hillmann, Austin, TX.

Hillmann, Michael C. (1987). *A Lonely Woman: Forugh Farrokhzad and Her Poetry*, Washington D.C.

Hillman, Michael. (1990). 'An autobiographical voice: Forugh Farrokhzad', in Afsaneh Najmabadi (ed.), *Women's Autobiographies in Contemporary Iran*, Cambridge, MA.

Hoquqi, Mohammad. (1994). *She'r-e zamān-e mā, 4: Forugh Farrokhzād*, Tehran.

Hossainzadah, Zahra. (2003). *Nāmeh'i az lāleh-ye kuhi*. Tehran.

Ingstad, Benedicte and Whyte, Susan Reynolds. (eds). (1995). *Disability and Culture*, Berkeley, CA.

Issari, M. Ali. (1989). *Cinema in Iran, 1900-1979*, Metuchen, NJ.

Jalāli, Behruz. (1994). *She'r-e Forugh Farrokhzād az āghāz tā emruz*, Tehran.

Javadi, Hasan and Sallée, Susan. (trans.) (1981). *Another Birth, Selected Poems of Forugh Farrokhzad*, Emeryville, CA.

Karāchi, Ruhangiz. (2004). *Forugh Farrokhzād*, Tehran.

Karim, M. Persis and Khorrami, Mohammad Mehdi. (eds). (1999). *A World Between: Poems, Short Stories and Essays by Iranian-Americans*, New York.

Karim, Persis M. (ed.). (2006). *Let Me Tell You Where I've Been: New Writing by Women of the Iranian Diaspora*, Fayetteville, NC.

Karim, Persis and Rahimieh, Nasrin. (2008). 'Writing Iranian Americans into the American literature canon', *MELUS: Multi-Ethnic Literatures of the United States*, 33.

Karimi-Hakkak, Ahmad. (1978). *An Anthology of Modern Persian Poetry*, Boulder, CO.

Karimi-Hakkak, Ahmad. (1995). *Recasting Persian Poetry: Scenarios of Poetic Modernity in Iran*, Salt Lake City, UT.

Katouzian, Homa. (2002). *Sadeq Hedayat: The Life and Legend of an Iranian Writer*, London and New York.

Katouzian, Homa. (2006). *Hasht maqāleh dar tārikh o adab-e mo'āser*, Tehran.

Katouzian, Homa (ed.). (2008). *Sadeq Hedayat: His Work and His Wondrous World*, London and New York.

Kāvusi, Hushang. (1998). 'Khāneh siyāh ast, yek film-e kutāh-e 'ajib,' in *Forugh Farrukhzād va sinemā*, Gholām Heydari (ed.), Tehran.

Keddie, Nikki. (1981). *Roots of Revolution: An Interpretive History of Modern Iran*, New Haven, CT.

Keshavarz, Fatemeh. (2007). *Jasmine and Stars: Reading More Than Lolita in Tehran*, Chapel Hill, NC.

Kessler, Jascha and Banani, Amin. (trans.). (1982). *Bride of Acacias, Selected Poems of Forugh Farrokhzad*, Delamar, NY.

Khosravie, Jasmin. (2013). 'Iranian Women on the Road: The Case of Sadīqe Doulatābādī in Europe, 1923–27,' in Bekim Agai, Olcay Akyildiz, and Caspar Hillebrand (eds.), *Venturing Beyond Borders: Reflections on Genre, Function and Boundaries in Middle Eastern Travel Writing*. Würzburg.

Kia, Mana. (2013). 'Limning the Land: Social Encounters and Historical Meaning in Early Nineteenth-Century Travelogues between Iran,' in Roberta Micallef and Sunil Sharma (eds.), *On the Wonders of Land and Sea: Persianate Travel Writing*. Boston, MA.

Kinser, Samuel. (June 1984). 'Chronotopes and catastrophes: The cultural history of Mikhail Bakhtin', *The Journal of Modern History*, 56.2.

Kristeva, Julia. (1982). *Powers of Horror: An Essay on Abjection*, New York.

La Belle, Jenijoy. (1988). *Herself Beheld: The Literature of the Looking Glass*, Ithaca, NY.

Lacan, Jacques. (2006). *Écrits: The First Complete Edition in English*, trans. Bruce Fink, New York and London.

Lyon, Elisabeth H. (Autumn, 1973). 'Luis Buñuel: The process of dissociation in three films', *Cinema Journal*, 13.1.

Malakān, Ebrāhim. (1996) 'Forughi digar dar *Tavallodi digar* ', in *Forugh Farrokhzād: Jāvdāneh zistan dar owj māndan* (ed.) Behruz Jalāli, 2nd edition, Tehran.

Marie, Farzana. (trans.) (2015). *Load Poems Like Guns: women's poetry from Herat, Afghanistan*. Duluth, MN.

Meyers, Diana Tietjens. (2002). *Gender in the Mirror: Cultural Imagery and Women's Agency*, Oxford and New York.

Milani, Farzaneh. (1979). 'Forugh Farrokhzād: A feminist perspective', PhD dissertation, University of California at Los Angeles.

Milani, Farzaneh. (1982). 'Forugh Farrokhzād: A feminist perspective', in *Bride of Acacias: Selected Poems of Forugh Farrokhzād*, trans. Jascha Kessler with Amin Banani, Delmar, CA.

Milani, Farzaneh. (1982). 'Love and sexuality in the poetry of Forough Farrokhzad: A reconsideration', *Iranian Studies* 15.

Milani, Farzaneh. (1987). 'Nakedness regained: Farrokhzad's Garden of Eden', in Hillmann, Michael C. (ed.), *Forugh Farrokhzad, A Quarter Century Later Literature East and West* 24.

Milani, Farzaneh. (1988). 'Forugh Farrokhzād', in Ehsan Yarshater (ed.), *Persian Literature*, Albany, NY.

Milani, Farzaneh. (1992). *Veils and Words: The Emerging Voices of Iranian Women Writers*, Syracuse, NY.

Milani, Farzaneh. (Spring 1999). 'Voyeurs, nannies, winds, and gypsies in Persian literature', *Critique: Critical Middle Eastern Studies* 8:14.

Milani, Farzaneh. (1999). 'Farrokzād, Forūg-Zamān', in Ehsan Yarshater (ed.), *Encyclopaedia Iranica*, IX, New York.

Milani, Farzaneh. (2011). *Words, not Swords: Iranian Women Writers and the Freedom of Movement*. Syracuse, NY.

Mirshahi, Mas'ud. (ed.) (2000). *She'r-e Zanān-e Afghanistan*. Paris.

Moghissi, Haideh. (1994). *Populism and Feminism in Iran: Women's Struggle in a Male-Defined Revolutionary Movement*, New York.

Morādi-Kuchi, Shahnāz. (2000). *Shenākhtnāmeh Forugh Farrokhzād,* Tehran.

Moshir-Salimi. (1957–1959). 'Ali-Akbar, *Zanān-e sokhanvar*, 3 Vols., Tehran.

Movahhed, Ziā. (1998). 'Farrokhzād dar raftār bā tasvir', in *Forugh Farrukhzād va sinemā,* Gholām Hòeydari (ed.), Tehran.

Musavi, Seyyedeh Fariba. (1995). 'Ā'ineh dar shāhkār-hā-ye adabi tā qarn-e hashtum', unpublished MA thesis, Tarbiat Mo'allem University, Tehran.

Naficy, Hamid. (December 1981). 'Iranian documentary', *Jump Cut: A Review of Contemporary Media* 26.

Naficy, Hamid. (1993). *The Making of Exile Cultures: Iranian Television in Los Angeles,* Minneapolis.

Nafisi, Azar. (2008). *Things I've Been Silent About*, New York.

Neshat, Shirin. (2001). *Shirin Neshat*, Milan.

Nikbakht, Mahmud. (1994). *Az gomshodegi tā rahā'i*, Tehran.

Olszewska, Zuzanna. (2011). 'A Hidden Discourse: Afghanistan's Women Poets' in Jennifer Heath and Ashraf Zahedi, eds. *Land of the Unconquerable: The Lives of Contemporary Afghan Women*. Berkeley, CA.

Olszewska, Zuzanna. (2015). *The Pearl of Dari: poetry and personhood among young Afghans in Iran*. Bloomington, IN.

Pawel, Ernst. (1988). *The Nightmare of Reason: A life of Franz Kafka*, London.

Podovkin, V.I. (1933). 'Introduction to the German edition', *Film Technique*, London.

Rahimieh, Nasrin. (1992). 'Beneath the veil: The revolution in Iranian women's writing', in Anthony Purdy (ed.), *Literature and the Body*, Atlanta, GA.

Rahimieh, Nasrin. (2001). *Missing Persians: discovering voices in Iranian cultural history*. Syracuse, NY.

Rahmani, Maga. (1949). *Pardeneshinān-e sokhan-guy*. Kabul.

Riffaterre, Michael. (1973). 'Interpretation and descriptive poetry: A reading of Wordsworth's "Yew-Tree"', *New Literary History* 4:2.

Robbins, Bruce. (1998). 'Introduction Part I: Actually Existing Cosmopolitanism,' in Pheng Cheah and Bruce Robbins (eds.), *Cosmopolitics: Thinking and Feeling Beyond the Nation*. Minneapolis, MN.

Rothman, William. (1997). *Documentary Film Classics*, Cambridge, UK.

Rowshani, Laila Sarahat. (1986) *Tolu'-e sabz*. Kabul.

Rowshani, Laila Sarahat. (1991). *Tadāvom-e faryād*. Kabul.

Rowshani, Laila Sarahat. (1997). *Az sang-hā va āyineh-hā*. Peshawar.

Rowshani, Laila Sarahat. (2004). *Ru-ye taqvim-e tamām-e sāl*. Kabul.

Rowshani, Laila Sarahat. (2012). *Simfuni-i bād-hā*. Kabul.

Rowshani, Laila Sarahat. (2013). 'Va shab, do-bāreh shab,' *Kabulnath* 9:198.

Rubinstein, E. (Summer, 1983). 'Visit to a familiar planet: Buñuel among the Hurdanos', *Cinema Journal* 22.4.

Sackville-West, Vita. (2007). *Passenger to Teheran*. New York, NY.

Saeed-Vafa, Mehrnaz and Rosenbaum, Jonathan. (2003). *Abbas Kiarostami*, Urbana, IL.

Saffāriān, Nāser. (2002). *Āyeh-hā-ye āh: nāgofteh-hā'i az zendegi-ye Farrokhzād*, Tehran.

Saikal, Amin. (2004). *Modern Afghanistan: a history of struggle and survival*. London.

Sandler, Rivanne. (1988). 'Change up to a point: Iranian women's poetry to the 1950s', in *Forugh Farrokhzād: A Quarter Century Later*, (ed.) Michael C. Hillmann, Austin, TX.

Scharres, Barbara. (2007–2008). 'Ebrahim Golestan: Lion of Iranian cinema', Gene Siskel Film Center, http://www.artic.edu/webspaces/siskelfilmcenter/2007/may/2a.html [accessed November 2008].

Sedarat, Roger. (2008). *Dear Regime: Letters to the Islamic Republic*, Athens, OH.

Sepehri, Sohrab. (2004). *The Lover is Always Alone: Selected Poems*, trans. Karim Emami, Tehran.

Shāh Ne'matollāh Vali. (n.d.). *Divān*, (ed.) Sa'id Nafisi, Tehran.

Shahrani, M. Nazif. (ed.) (2018). *Modern Afghanistan: the impact of 40 years of war*. Bloomington, IN.

Shamisa, Sirous. (1993). *Negāhi beh Forugh*, Tehran.

Shamisa, Sirous. (2004). *Rāhnamā-ye adabiyāt-e mo'āser*, Tehran.

Shamisa, Sirous. (2008). *Seyr-e robā'i*, Tehran.

Shāpur, Kāmyār and Sālehi, 'Omrān (2002). *Avvalin tapesh-hā-ye 'āsheqāneh: nāmeh-hā-ye Farrokhzād be hamsar-ash Shāpur*, Tehran.

Sharma, Sunil. (2013). 'Delight and Disgust: Gendered Encounters in the Travelogues of the Fyzee Sisters,' in Roberta Micallef and Sunil Sharma (eds.), *On the Wonders of Land and Sea: Persianate Travel Writing*. Boston, MA.

Showalter, Elaine. (1985). *The Female Malady: Women, Madness, and English Culture, 1830–1980*, New York.

Showalter, Elaine. (1986). 'A literature of their own', in Mary Eagleton (ed.) *Feminist Literary Theory: A Reader*, Oxford.

Showkat, Hamid. (1987). *Negāhi az darun be jonbesh-e chap-e Irān: goftogu bā Mehdi Khānbābā Tehrāni*, Saarbrücken, Germany.

Showkat, Hamid. (2004). *Negāhi az darun beh jonbesh-e chap-e Irān: goftogu bā Kurosh Lāshā'i*, Tehran.

Singer, Eric. (ed.). (1955). *Spiegel des Unvergänglichen: Deutsche Lyrik seit 1910*, Munich.

Siyāhpush, Hamid. (ed.) (1997). *Zani tanhā: Yādnāmeh-ye Forugh Farrokhzād*, Tehran.

Sofia, Meetra A. (January/February 2006). 'Forugh Farrokhzad: Notes and translation from the Farsi', *The American Poetry Review*, 35.

Sohrabi, Naghmeh. (2012). *Taken for Wonder: Nineteenth-Century Travel Accounts from Iran to Europe*. Oxford.

Spencer, Laura Gutiérrez. (1994). 'Mirrors and masks: Female subjectivity in Chicana poetry', *Frontiers: A Journal of Women Studies*, 15:2.

Stam, Robert, Burgoyne, Robert and Flitterman-Lewis, Sandy. (1992). *New Vocabularies in Film Semiotics: Structuralism, Post-structuralism, and Beyond*, London and New York.

Stern, J. P. (ed.). (1980). *The World of Franz Kafka*, London.

Tāhbāz, Sirus. (1997). *Zani tanhā: dar-bāreh-ye zendegi va she'r-e Forugh Farrokhzād*, Tehran.

Tahāminezhād, Muhammad. (1998). *Sinemā-ye mostanad-e Irān*, Tehran.

Talattof, Kamran. (November 1997). 'Iranian women's literature: From pre-revolutionary social discourse to post-revolutionary feminism', *International Journal of Middle East Studies*, 29.

Talattof, Kamran. (2000). *The Politics of Writing in Iran: A History of Modern Persian Literature*, Syracuse, NY.

Tikku, Girdhari. (1967). 'Furūgh-i Farrukhzād: A new direction in Persian poetry', *Studia Islamica* 26.

Wide, Thomas Wide. (2013). 'Around the World in Twenty-Nine Days: The Travels, Translations, and Temptations of an Afghan Dragoman,' in Roberta Micallef and Sunil Sharma (eds.), *On the Wonders of Land and Sea: Persianate Travel Writing*. Boston, MA.

Wolpé, Sholeh. (2008). *Rooftops of Tehran*, Los Angeles.

Zand-Akash: Iranian or Greater Bundahishn, Ch. 4, 'As regards the Adversary's approach to the Creation', http://www.avesta.org/mp/grb1.htm#chap4 [accessed December 2008].

Zarrinkub, Hamid. (1996). 'Darun-māyeh-hā-ye she'r-e Forugh', in *Forugh Farrokhzād: Jāvdāneh zistan dar owj māndan* (ed.) Behruz Jalāli, Tehran.

Zipoli, Riccardo. (2005). 'Semiotics and the tradition of the image,' *Persica* 20.

Zubizarreta, John. (Summer, 1992). 'The woman who sings no, no, no: Love, freedom, and rebellion in the poetry of Forugh Farrokhzad', *World Literature Today* 66.3.

Index